*Student
Unrest
in India*

AILEEN D. ROSS

Student

Unrest

in India

A COMPARATIVE
APPROACH

McGill–Queen's University Press
MONTREAL LONDON 1969

© McGill–Queen's University Press 1969
Standard Book Number 7735-0041-3
Library of Congress Catalog Card No. 68-55076
Designed by Robert R. Reid
Printed in Canada

This book has been published with the help
of a grant from the Social Science Research
Council of Canada, using funds provided
by the Canada Council.

*To
Shanta
and
Surya*

Preface

My interest in Indian students began in 1954 when I was in India studying the changes which were occurring in the structure of family relationships as families moved from rural areas to cities. At that time, it seemed to me that it was the student generation that was suffering from the sharpest impact of social change. I returned to India in 1961 for a year, and again in the summer of 1965. During that time I studied a sample of Indian students in Bangalore, a South Indian city. I also interviewed many lecturers and visited numerous colleges. A full account of the sample and methodology is given in Appendix I.

No one who has been long in India can fail to be interested in the so-called student indiscipline which is occurring in many of the colleges. "Indiscipline" is the term commonly used in India to describe the student restlessness, which may occur on a formal or on an informal level. It will be used in this study to describe any student behaviour that is contrary to that expected of a student. As used by the layman, it implies disapproval or condemnation. In India the phenomenon of indiscipline is particularly perplexing, as the students have shown comparatively little rebellion against the traditional rigid requirements of the Hindu family. Why do obedient, respectful young men and women often indulge in such different behaviour in an environment other than the home? Do the colleges give provocation for this revolt, or are they merely the objects of a release of tensions deriving from much deeper, hidden causes?

India is one of the countries that has had a long history of student revolt; at times these revolts have been so well organized and so violent that the educational and government authorities have been forced to give in to the students' demands. The present wave of student indiscipline began in the north of India after Independence and spread gradually to all parts of the country; and now, outbreaks of defiance occur in the mofussil or up-country colleges as readily as they do in the larger cities. Also, there has been a growing participation in indiscipline on the part of women students.

Indiscipline of an informal nature is also increasing in Indian colleges.

It takes the form of rudeness, disturbances, incessant chattering in class, and the ridiculing of lecturers. The amount of informal indiscipline in women's colleges varies, but even in the Roman Catholic colleges, which have always had strict discipline, it is said that the students are becoming more and more restless and are often difficult to keep in order. The rate at which indiscipline has spread among women students in India has varied according to the region, the size of the city, and the location of the college within the city. In Bangalore several of the colleges that women attend are situated far from the centre of the city and have very little formal indiscipline to cope with. However, the largest women's college is located in the heart of the city, on the pathway between the three men's colleges which furnish leaders for most of the public demonstrations. The staff of this women's college has had to cope with a great deal of turmoil, and with the girls' frequent desires to join in protests staged by the men students.

Control of the students has become a critical problem. When the students' protest action first began, it was modelled on the demonstrations that had occurred during the fight for independence. At that time such eminent leaders as Gandhi and Nehru gave the students their blessing, and it was a matter of prestige to take part in agitations. This same attitude was carried over into the first demonstrations after Independence and contributed to the problem of student control. Another reason which adds to this problem is that, since students hold a somewhat privileged position in society, and since some of them come from families who have the power to protect them from severe punishment, the authorities cannot deal with them in the way they would normally discipline disturbers of the peace.

As this study progressed, it became evident from the increasing number of student demonstrations around the world that in order to understand the problems faced by Indian students in their efforts to achieve a satisfactory adjustment to adult life, the total world picture must be taken into account. The Introduction of this study describes the worldwide nature of the recent increase in adolescent and student restlessness so that the particular case of Indian students can be seen in the perspective of a general movement occurring in all parts of the world.

Chapter 1 contains a detailed account of a series of student strikes that took place in Mysore State. These strikes were not politically motivated or controlled, and for this reason they are instructive in showing

viii

how student leaders have been able to channel the growing restlessness of their fellow students into well-organized, disciplined action.

In Chapter 2 the college setting is described, for it is the stage on which the drama of student unrest is carried out. The rapid expansion of college and university facilities, the great increase in the number of students, and the difficulty of providing adequately trained lecturers have all had a disturbing effect upon Indian students. It is evident, however, that these are not the only factors which have caused student agitations, for many of the demonstrations have not been directed against the colleges to which the student belonged.

One universal phenomenon affecting all countries is rapid social change. In India structural changes in the traditional caste, family, religious, and economic systems have greatly influenced the lives of many students. New opportunities to use leisure time have arisen, and deeply set mores surrounding the relationship between the sexes are being challenged by new conceptions of friendship, dating, and individual choice in marriage. The effects of these variables on the extent to which this sample of students took part in undisciplined behaviour are analyzed in Chapters 3, 4, and 5. However, not all the students in this sample were found to be undisciplined and discontented.

To try to obtain a deeper understanding of the reasons some students were in an almost perpetual state of defiance, and why others never participated in organized demonstrations, a comparison was made between two groups of students. One group consisted of a small number of "model" students who studied hard, enjoyed college life, and resented the indiscipline of other students. The second group contained students who were not interested in their studies, and who had taken part in demonstrations. The study of these two contrasting groups helps us realize some of the factors that tend to release student frustration. The results appear in Chapter 6.

Sometimes the collective action of the students appears to be merely a release from boredom, and in this sense it could be compared to the "high jinks" that have always been part of student life. But an increasing number of these demonstrations are concerned with such basic interests as educational policy, civil rights, and war, and this protest activity is gradually coming to be regarded by sociologists as a new and important element of social structure. In the final chapter of this book, an attempt is made to organize our present knowledge, as well as the knowledge gleaned from this study, so that it will be useful to future scholars. It is suggested that this new type of collective behaviour has a positive function in our society in that it acts as an agent through which adjustments can be made to the disorganizing effects of social change.

Acknowledgements

The ideas for this study have come gradually and from a great variety of sources. My own students at McGill University have helped me think through many of the implications of the New Youth Culture. As is often the case, their interest has been stimulating and constructive.

In India I was met everywhere with courtesy and with eagerness to be of assistance. In view of the subject of this study, it is obvious that the many devoted and capable teachers whom I met in the Indian colleges were especially helpful. My particular thanks are due to those who spent many hours advising and assisting me in various ways; namely, Father Lawrence Colaca, Miss Gnanadickam, Professor M. S. Gore, Professor K. M. Kapadia, Dr. Sushela Lingiah, Sister Yvonne Marie, Professor and Mrs. D. Narain, Dr. C. R. Paulus, and Mr. R. A. Phani Shayi.

To gain some insight into the point of view of Indian parents I could not possibly have had better guides than my many friends in the Child Study Association of South India.

My research assistants, all recent graduates, were an invaluable source of information. To Mrs. Mary Isaac, Mrs. R. M. Varma. A. Manjunath, E. Jaychandra Raj, and B. S. Suryanarayan go my deepest thanks for initiating me into many of the mysteries of student life. I would also like to thank the student leaders who so willingly gave up time to assist me.

The study, however, could not have progressed in the way it did without the devoted attention of the two people who have guided me both geographically and intellectually through much of India. N. S. Shanta, M.A., Lecturer in Psychology, and C. S. Suryanarayana Rao, M.A., Reader in Psychology, have been my companions and assistants on my three visits to India.

I am also grateful for the financial assistance given me by the Centre for Developing-Area Studies at McGill University, and by the Social Science Research Council of Canada.

My special thanks go to Mrs. Lloyd Paul, who made sense out of much of the script on her typewriter, and who was an indefatigable and cheerful co-worker.

A. D. R.

Contents

Introduction

"It is quite frightening that force, intimidation and deliberate violation of rules all occurred on the campus of one of this country's most distinguished educational institutions." (Dick Erickson, Editorial on the student revolt at Berkeley in *California Monthly*, February, 1965.) The editorial spoke of the "tragic events" which had occurred, and declared that the situation had developed into a "virtual civil war without arms." It also told of the bitterness that had developed between staff and students since the Berkeley "affair," and of the thousands of letters which had been sent to the Chancellor's office from the Alumni, whose reaction to the situation had been "immediate, continuous, and vociferous."[1]

The morning after reading the above editorial I received a letter from a lecturer at a college in one of the towns of Madras State, where the students had led the anti-Hindi language riots in January, 1965. He wrote:

> Over nine hundred of our students went on strike today, and plan to continue indefinitely. This morning's march was fairly peaceful, though a couple of students were beaten with lathis, and several were arrested. The college has just been closed for four days, and I doubt that the attempt to re-open on the 16th [August] will be a success, as that is the day the Language bill passes through the States legislature. And goodness knows what will happen on August 15 [Independence Day] when the flag is hoisted and the national anthem sung (or not sung).

On that same morning the *Deccan Herald* described the situation in Hyderabad, where the students were on strike, demanding the abolition of the detention rule for the first years of the three-year course:

> Police fired tear-gas shells thrice and lathi-charged on two occasions in the Osmania University campus resulting in injuries to forty-five persons, including fifteen policemen. . . . Trouble started when a thousand students

1. For other descriptions of the protests of the students at the University of California at Berkeley, see: Nathan Glazer and Philip Selznick, "What Happened at Berkeley," and A. L. P., "A Season of Discontent."

attempted to force their entry into the university hall. A clash ensued as the students surged forward, the police beat them with lathis and then fired tear-gas shells when stones were hurled. The campus hostel was also the scene of stone-pelting. . . . Several students jumped out of the windows [to escape the tear gas] and were beaten by the police. Two students fractured their limbs when landing. . . . The Student Union spokesman said that the strike would continue until their demands were met. (August 13, 1965.)

Descriptions of student demonstrations are an almost daily occurrence in the Indian newspapers, and those who have been close observers of the agitation and unrest in that country over many years might be inclined to smile at the sense of panic underlying the editorial on the Berkeley demonstrations of 1964, and implied in many of the articles that have appeared since that event. However, what is disturbing to a social scientist is that only a very few of the journalists and scholars who have been writing about unrest in the United States have viewed it in a world-wide perspective.

Hardly a day goes by without some reference to an outbreak of unusually violent student agitation in one part of the world or another. The causes have obviously varied a great deal from area to area, but one factor does seem to be present in all cases—the need to adapt to rapid economic and social change.[2] In the West this has frequently taken the form of adjusting to conditions brought about by the "new affluence" in such countries as the United States and many nations in Western Europe. The new and unexpected reaction to the affluent society has been given little attention by social scientists. In the developing countries, on the other hand, conditions are the reverse of affluent; yet the student in Madras, Bangalore, or Hyderabad, as well as in Accra, Tokyo, Saigon, or Panama, is also facing changes which are dynamic when compared with the traditional way of life of his parents. A number of recent studies has indicated that there has been a world-wide trend toward increasing restlessness and crime among young people since the end of the Second World War, and that there is no sign that this trend is likely to decrease in the near future.

2. T. C. N. Gibbens, "Teenage Riots Round the World." Gibbens says that writers who claimed that youthful crime was caused by broken homes, working mothers, poverty, slum conditions, or movies, have been rudely awakened by the new trends which show that the backgrounds of the offenders do not fit in with these theories. In the German youth riots, for example, among six hundred young people who were arrested, it was found that their backgrounds (family) were not different from the general expectation. "The large majority were regularly employed, and had good reports from employers."

On the North American continent, the "bobbysoxers" of the 1930's constituted perhaps the first clear sign of the new Youth Culture which was beginning to appear.[3] After the Second World War, however, there arose in many countries a number of new youth groups who were no longer characterized merely by deviant patterns of dress and relatively harmless behaviour, but by something more violent and alarming. In the West the "teddy boys" appeared in England, the "bloussons noirs" in France, the "bodgies" in Australia, the "halbstarken" in Austria and Germany, and the "nozen" in the Netherlands. Even behind the Iron Curtain this new phenomenon was seen in the "holligans" in Poland, the "stiliagyi" in the U.S.S.R., and the "tapkaroschi" in Yugoslavia. In the East there were the "mambo boys" of Japan and the "tai-pau" of Taiwan.[4]

One of the universal similarities of these groups is that they appeared in each country as it recovered from the War and became affluent; that is, after a commercial culture had arisen, bringing with it mass advertising and entertainment, cars, a proliferation of gadgets, and a teenage market.[5] Other similarities are that the participants usually seem to be in their teens, that they tend to form gangs (which may be loosely or tightly organized), that they often wear a particular type of dress or hair-cut, and that violence is often the *raison d'être* of their activity, or is the end result of it. The number of young girls taking part in these activities has increased, but boys still predominate. An increasing number comes from towns and suburbs, and from the middle classes.[6] The term "bloussons dorés," for example, is now used in France to refer to gangs from the wealthier families, in contrast to the original "bloussons noirs," who formerly came from the lower-income families.[7] Their behaviour

3. Two studies that describe the new Youth Culture are: S. N. Eisenstadt, "Archetypal Patterns of Youth," and David Gottlieb and Charles E. Ramsey, *The American Adolescent*.

4. T. R. Fyvel, *The Insecure Offenders*, p. 20. See also: William C. Kvaraceus, *Juvenile Delinquency a Problem for the Modern World*, p. 11.

5. Fyvel, pp. 22-30. This new phenomenon has broken down many of the former values and beliefs, and has thus left young people discontented and aimless. "It provides entertainment but no guidance." It constantly presents the young people with visions of unattainable good things which they are unable to get, and thus makes them "permanently discontented and deprived."

6. *Ibid.*, p. 20.

7. William C. Kvaraceus, *Juvenile Delinquency a Problem for the Modern World*, pp. 18, 49. Kvaraceus speaks of the wealthier gang members as "hidden delinquents," for their families can often protect them from the law, and so the transgressions of the young people do not always appear in crime statistics. He believes that the age and social class of those involved indicate that there are many new factors, as yet scarcely explored, that are causing the present world-wide unrest.

3

ranges from "stealing, vandalism and property offences, petty extortion, and gambling, to violent behaviour, rowdiness, truancy, immoral or indecent conduct, drinking, and drug addiction."[8] It varies from country to country, according to the cultural norms and the channels open for the release of the young people's energies.

New kinds of violence have also appeared within student groups in many countries, both affluent and developing. Some of their demonstrations may arise when a country is going through a political crisis. The leading part Hungarian students played in the 1956 rebellion is an extreme example of this tendency,[9] but many countries such as Japan, Korea, Vietnam, France, Pakistan, and Peru have had students in the forefront of their recent political upheavals. Normally, students return to their academic roles with the coming of political stability, and their open rebellion becomes confined to a rather harmless and accepted version of "wine, women, and song."

On the other hand, many student demonstrations are now occurring in relatively peaceful parts of the world in highly industrialized, affluent countries, as well as in those countries that are going through the initial stages of industrialization. Growing numbers of students are now taking part in this protest activity, and as their demonstrations have tended to become both more violent and better organized, the impact of student activity on the politics and the educational system of many countries has become more important than ever before.[10]

For what apparent reasons do students rebel? Demonstrations can be attributed to a variety of causes and issues, but some sort of preliminary classification seems necessary as a step toward understanding the different ways in which indiscipline is carried out, and the main reasons be-

8. *Ibid.*, pp. 15, 16. Kvaraceus gives examples of this behaviour: In Poland, teenage gangs damaged a railway train and molested the passengers, all for no apparent reason. In Canada groups of boys have entered houses and mutilated or painted the furniture and walls without stealing anything. In Thailand bands of young men terrorize or injure people without robbing them. These examples show that the behaviour of such gangs often seems to have no real purpose, but is malicious.

9. James A. Michener, *The Bridge at Andau*, p. 79. One of the most familiar examples of students defending their countries occurred in Hungary at the time of the Russian invasion in 1956. The revolution of the Hungarians was initiated by students; they destroyed buildings, burned propaganda- and newspaper offices, commanded teams of young boys and girls, and along with them, tackled Russian tanks with handmade bombs.

10. Humayun Kabir, *Education in New India*, p. 151. Kabir says of the Indian demonstrations, "There have recently been some instances of grave indiscipline among students. ....In some cases things have gone so far that teachers in schools or invigilators in examinations have been attacked. In others, there have been clashes with the police or sections of the public. Apart from such extreme examples of indiscipline, there has been a spirit of general turbulence and rebellion among large sections of the younger generation."

hind it as stated by students and/or the public. The problem of classification is not altogether easy, and the difficulties are augmented by the fact that student protest movements are subject to rapid changes in goal and orientation, due to the constant turnover of students in college, and to the equally rapid changes in conditions that impinge on a country, both from without and from within. Moreover, in a large country, students may be attracted by many issues. In the United States, for example, some student activity has, in recent years, been oriented toward the civil rights movement, some toward educational reform, and some toward the war in Vietnam. Diversification is seen also in a developing country.

[The Nigerian students] engaged in five major protests between January 1959 and June 1960: against Prime Minister Harold Macmillan for the United Kingdom's passive attitude toward apartheid and African nationalism, against the South Africans for the Sharpeville shootings, against the French for testing atomic weapons in the Sahara, against the Eastern Regional Government for a pension bill, and against the Western Regional Government for a housing bill.[11]

An analysis of the various types of demonstrations published in newspapers, magazines, and journals seemed to suggest five situations that tend to release collective action: political crises, economic insecurity, "causes," the desire for educational reform, and the need for emotional release, or fun.[12]

POLITICAL PROTESTS

Rioting for political reasons has already been mentioned, and we have seen that in Hungary, Pakistan, Japan, Korea, and in many other countries, student unrest has been closely connected either with political instability inside the country, or with the threat of an external enemy. As college students form a captive audience, and have arrived at the age when they are supposed to take over the major share in the fight for survival, they can be easily mobilized for political action and can become extremely influential.[13] Speaking of Japanese and Korean students,

11. E. Wight Bakke, "Roots and Soil of Student Activism," p. 164. Bakke gives an interesting view of the similarities and differences of the student demonstrations in different countries.
12. George Z. F. Bereday, "Student Unrest on Four Continents: Montreal, Ibadan, Warsaw, and Rangoon," pp. 188-204. Bereday uses the classifications of vertical tensions between groups as compared to horizontal tensions between generations. His categories comprise ethnic, racial, social, and educational cleavages. He, too, is careful to state that broader dissatisfactions lie beneath the surface of these vertical cleavages.
13. For detailed studies of students and politics, see the various articles in the *Comparative Education Review*, Vol. 10, June 1966. See also: Enrique Tierno Galvan, "Unrest in Spain's Universities," pp. 96, 97.

who had been both active and successful in resisting the attempts of their politicians to improve relations between their two countries, the *London Observer* of 31 August 1964 described the students as "a dominant political force affecting major national policy decisions."

The United States has appeared to be the main political villain for students in a number of countries in recent years, and anti-American demonstrations often have followed the new pattern of attacking an embassy, or some property or symbol of the country, such as a United States information centre. It also has become the pattern for students to launch attacks on, or demonstrate in front of, the property or embassies of potential foreign "enemies," whoever they may be.

Students in different countries vary in their degree of political interest. Indonesia, Japan, India, and many of the Latin American countries can be cited as examples of countries where student political action has been forceful, and often effective. In Europe students have tried to influence government policy or action, and even in South Africa, where the political situation makes student protest against apartheid difficult, students from the four English-language universities have held many demonstrations. Within the Communist countries there have been recently strong student demonstrations against their respective governments. Beginning in 1956 in a rather covert way, such as tearing down official posters and writing slogans on walls, the students have gradually grown more daring.[14] In the past few years Poland, Czechoslovakia, and East Germany in particular have had to face serious public student demonstrations.

In Great Britain, North America, and other areas populated by people of Anglo-Saxon origin, students in the past have not usually taken an active interest in politics.[15] But recently a New Left movement has swept through the universities of most of these countries. It began in the early 1960's, and its first overt manifestation on the North American continent was probably at Berkeley in the autumn of 1964. The ensuing demonstrations prompted by this movement on many North American campuses might have been classified, in this Introduction, under "the desire for educational reform," or "causes," for members of the New Left actively supported and were motivated by such issues as the civil

14. Richard Cornell, "Students and Politics in Communist Eastern Europe," p. 176.
15. Seymour Martin Lipset and Philip G. Altbach, "Student Politics and Higher Education in the United States," p. 343. The authors point out that the American students' approach to politics is pragmatic rather than ideological, whereas in the developing countries, political ideologies are often the basis of student movements.

rights movement. But, as the New Left is trying to develop a revolutionary movement, it was thought better to place the demonstrations that they have been instrumental in leading under the heading of "political protests."

The birth of the New Left in the United States is said to have been due to the civil rights movement, the antipathy of students to the "multiversity," and the lack of a strong left wing political party through which the students could express their views.[16] Its programme is not yet clearly formulated, but it includes, "the rejection of many prevailing American institutions, a vaguely democratic-socialist political ideology, a faith in participatory democracy, and a commitment to direct social action . . . its ultimate goal is radical reform of American society and the characteristic nature of human roles and relationships on which it rests."[17] Its militancy is disturbing to many Americans, for they are not accustomed to having students either plan revolutionary political action, or aim to destroy the structure of the society.[18]

Not nearly as much is heard of the right wing activists, even though they are often an energetic group, for their activities are less newsworthy, and are centred around maintaining the *status quo* and defying the radical activists of the New Left.

As the New Left has gathered strength and support from activists on

16. A. H. Halsey and Stephen Marks, "British Student Politics," pp. 123, 124. The authors say that, in contrast, the New Left student movement in Britain was born in the political upheavals of that country in 1956. Its main orientation has been theoretical rather than practical because of the strong position of the Labour party.

17. Richard E. Peterson, "The Student Left in American Higher Education," p. 293. See also Carl Davidson, "The New Radicals and the Multiversity," p. 60. Mr. Davidson is inter-organizational secretary for the Students for a Democratic Society, the organization that is one of the strongest supporters of the New Left. In discussing the programme of the New Left he says: "The student movement has come under criticism from both the right and the left for its lack of coherent ideology and strategy for social change . . . political analysis and strategy is something that grows slowly out of years of political experience and struggle. . . . Too often we are bogged down in theoretical disputes, when the only way we can answer those questions is in *practice*, in political experimentation, in action. This is why we must remain open on many political questions."

18. Robert E. Scott, "Student Political Activism in Latin America," *Daedalus*, pp. 96, 97. What has been said about student power in Latin America could well apply to many of the leaders of the New Left: "Without any real base in numbers or influence, these radical activists seek to increase their chances for success by resorting to spectacular demonstrations of power through organized violence and other indications that they reject and hold in contempt the operating political decision-making system.

"Whether or not they act with this end consciously in mind, such actions place student radicals beyond the pale of legitimacy. In the eyes of national political leaders, liberal or otherwise, these extreme manifestations of student political values represent a subsidiary system that is attempting to destroy the more general system from which it draws its nourishment."

many of the North American campuses, two threatening terms have become identified with their actions; namely, "student power" and "confrontation." These terms are used in the main to refer to their struggle to gain power from their respective university administrations. In their confrontations the administration has been defined more and more as a separate and, by implication, hostile element, as compared to the staff and the students. The goal of the New Left is to achieve enough student power to share equally in all decision-making so that the university will become a really democratic institution. This ideal may be the motivation behind a good deal of the action of the "fringe" students who become members of the group, or who are persuaded to join in demonstrations that others have planned; but the central core of leaders seems to be motivated by the desire for power and the joy of defying the university authorities, rather than by educational reform.

Their enthusiastic belief that they can change the world will probably enlist more students in the future than will the hippies' desire to escape present-day society. But whether the movement will broaden so as to retain the allegiance of the students as they move into the wider world is still unknown. There are signs that even some of the most ardent Leftists are beginning to gradually draw back into the "fold," as they assume the responsibilities of adult society, and as they become influenced by its rewards.[19]

Student disturbances triggered by political situations are not always as useful for gaining an insight into the reasons underlying student unrest as are many other kinds of demonstrations. Students seldom act alone when it is a matter of physical or political survival; more often, large sections of the population will be involved in the action, and students may be forced to take part willy-nilly, as, for example, in time of war. In such cases their participation would not necessarily be due to the frustrations of social change, and so would not be within the scope of this particular study.

19. Barbara Haber and Al Haber, "Getting By With a Little Help From Our Friends," pp. 99, 100. The authors wrote these lines after attending a conference of members of the New Left who had entered professional occupations: "The most pervasive problem expressed [at the Conference] was the feeling of isolation from the mainstream of the movement. Many people described difficulty in finding emotional sustenance for political activism. They felt they were going dry, losing perspective. Political argument was becoming formalistic; conviction was floating away. Taking risks and being a marginal man was losing its reason. Signs of middle age stodginess were overcoming them. . . . Professionals have access to many rewards. Under the best of circumstances, these may lead to abandoning the tough requirements of the political role."

ECONOMIC PROTESTS

Demonstrations may result from a change in a country's internal conditions—a change which may alter the occupational structure so that although new opportunities open up, entrance to them appears to be blocked to certain groups. This seems to be the main underlying cause of two recent student movements on the North American continent: that of the Negroes in the Southern United States, and that of the French-speaking Canadians in the Province of Quebec.

Hughes has spoken of conditions that led to protest demonstrations among these two groups. In the first place, both have become rapidly urbanized at a time when the occupational structures of their countries have been undergoing considerable change. Both the Negroes and the French-speaking Canadians have moved to the cities in great numbers at a time when their countries are facing a decided decline in the need for unskilled workers. Thus, many are unemployed, or have not had the education or training that enables them to enter the skilled, semi-skilled, professional, or higher business positions.[20] This problem has arisen at a time when the new city life and the mass media of communication have given them higher standards of aspiration. Moreover, as the educational systems of both groups have lagged behind present-day requirements, even those individuals with college degrees find themselves insufficiently prepared to compete with the white American students on the one hand, or with the English-speaking Canadian students on the other.

The present unrest of the French-speaking Canadians is the first movement of its kind to arise and gain strength during a period of peace and national prosperity. The Negro protest in the United States has also occurred at a time when Negroes are better off financially, are more educated, and have more and higher occupational positions than at any other period of their history. The movements are alike, too, in that the

20. Everett C. Hughes, "Race Relations and the Sociological Imagination," p. 883. "At the last census, French Canadians had become more urban than other Canadians; Negroes, more urban than other Americans. With the precipitous drop in the agricultural labor force in both countries, these minorities have undergone changes of occupational structure probably greater than those of the rest of the population. Both minorities, in the industrial and urban order in which their fate now lies, are concentrated at lower points of the socio-economic scale than are the dominant groups. . . . The two minorities are alike in that they have gone from a rural condition to an urban, and see themselves as thereby put into a position of increased disadvantage; and at precisely that time in history when such disadvantage is no longer a purely domestic matter."

For a description of the way in which the Negroes now fit into the socio-economic scale, see: Leonard Broom and Norval D. Glenn, *Transformation of the Negro American*, New York: Harper & Row, 1965.

9

students are not protesting alone, as in India, but are struggling side by side with a large cross-section of their own populations. College students from these two groups are therefore only part of a protest movement. Sometimes the students agitate separately, but more often they are part of a planned nation-wide movement (as in the case of the Negroes) or of a provincial movement (as in the case of the French-speaking Canadians).

The demonstrations of the French-speaking Canadian students have not, in themselves, initiated much violence. Several extreme separatist groups, to which some students belonged, took part in numerous cases of bombings during the winter and spring of 1963 in Montreal and Quebec City. Students have also indulged in much informal indiscipline, such as heckling professors, attempting to have certain educational authorities removed, and expressing unusually outspoken anti-staff, anti-university sentiments in the student press and other publications.

The protest of the Negro students has grown into a remarkably strong, well-organized movement in a relatively few years, and has recently led to some violence. SNCC (Student Non-Violent Coordinating Committee) was for a while one of the most militant forces in the civil rights movement. Negro students have also helped to organize such associations as the NSM (Northern Student Movement), CORE (Congress for Racial Equality), and the committee on Appeal for Human Rights.[21] These organizations have conducted many sit-ins, lie-ins, swim-ins, and other types of protest action.

MORAL PROTESTS OR "CAUSES"

When aroused by a moral issue, university students often behave in a way that is deviant to their usual activity. The issue may have nothing to do with their own security. Indeed, it may be occurring in a distant country of which they know little; or it may be a phenomenon which has some remote but indirect bearing on their lives, such as the ban-the-bomb movement. It may, on the other hand, be concerned with conditions in their own countries. Movements of this nature tend to arise in countries which are undergoing rapid change—change that may have been brought about by such new inventions as the atomic bomb. Elsewhere, the structure of a society may have changed so that the discriminatory treatment of people of another class or colour is seen in a new

21. Lipset and Altbach, "Student Politics and Higher Education in the United States," p. 337.

light. Students, already stirred by the impingement of change on their own lives, may become more emotionally aware of the problems of other people, and their general feelings of anxiety or frustration may be channelled into collective action to "do something about it."

Some writers argue along these lines, but put it a little differently. They think that when rapidly changing conditions prevent a society's ideologies from keeping up with practical events students often become disillusioned, and the only solution they can arrive at is to destroy as much of the existing system as possible.[22]

There is no doubt that agitators receive great satisfaction from the sense of unity with others who are fighting for a "worthwhile" purpose. For most students, however, a good deal of propaganda will normally be required to rouse them to action for a cause that does not impinge immediately on their own interests.

Students often find distant causes more attractive than local ones, as they appear more romantic, and the issues seem simpler. At least part of the motivation to join the Peace Corps undoubtedly stemmed from this attitude. Student leaders found it more difficult to recruit tutors among white students in the Northern American universities to work for Negro rights in their own big city slums, for example, than to recruit student volunteers for the Southern civil rights movement. The apparent reason was that there was greater glamour in facing danger in faraway Mississippi. The numerous ban-the-bomb demonstrations of students in various countries would come under this classification.

Although the Univerity of California at Berkeley has been called the "fountainhead of to-day's new student militancy in America," students across the continent have been challenging not only the administrations of their universities, but almost every form of existing order. "There is a raucous sound on American campuses. It is the sound of protest. Get out of Vietnam! Liberate the Negro! Wipe out proverty!"[23] Even five years ago most American students fitted more into the stereotype of the "bland generation," and their chief aim seemed to be to secure a respectable degree that would help them become successful in

22. Frank A. Pinner, "Student Trade-Unionism in France, Belgium and Holland," p. 197. "The individual feels an acute need for an explanation of his discomfort or uneasiness. One of his possible responses may be the espousal of an ideology which presumes to demonstrate the moral or historical wrongness of existing conditions. He does not envisage playing a social role at all unless society is totally transformed in accordance with principles of justice or historical necessity."

23. "The Sound of Protest." (An A.P. Special Report, *Daily American*, Rome, June 8, 1965.)

the business or professional world. A loss of faith in some of the traditional values seems to account, at least in part, for the change in their attitudes and for their new enthusiasm.[24] However, not all those who have taken part have necessarily been deeply interested in the "cause." Rather, they have participated for fun or for excitement. It could hardly be expected that nearly six million students, coming from a wide cross-section of the continent, would be affected by the same conditions, or respond to the same appeals. Even in Berkeley "only a small percentage of students . . . was involved in violations of the law of the university regulations."[25] Moreover, the United States is an affluent country, and many of the students simply are not affected by the problems of change. What tensions and frustrations they do have they are able to release through the many kinds of entertainment and sport which are available to them.[26]

Some of the students have received jail sentences for sitting-in, or for leading demonstrations.[27] However, this form of punishment has become so common for young people in America since the civil rights movement began that it is seldom looked on as a hardship, and indeed, probably confers a good deal of prestige on the students involved. Even the most strait-laced American citizen would hardly look on this type of protest activity as a "crime."

The main problem for students who want to organize a protest movement over some moral or social issue is to hold the allegiance and interest of their fellow students long enough to make their demonstrations effective. Since the Berkeley protest of 1964, the rifts among American student activists have widened. These leaders no longer agree on tactics, or on which issues to take up. On the whole the civil rights movement has had more support than any other issue, but fashions in protest change. In the early sixties student interest was centred on peace and nuclear testing. In 1963 the test ban was achieved, and the students

24. Richard Abrams, "The Student Rebellion at Berkeley—an Interpretation," pp. 387, 388. The author says: "Even the smallest schoolboy today . . . knows that those principles are blatantly violated every day in the week, and he knows, too, that if there is any meaning to morality at all, such violations are immoral. . . . Why should we be astonished if many college students today are contemptuous and cynical . . . about their cautious elders, and about those who can be moved by fear but not by principle?"

25. Clark Kerr, "A Message to Alumnae," p. 96.

26. "The Sound of Protest."

27. *Time* (Asia Edition), August 6, 1965. "The leader of the free speech movement was put in jail for one hundred and twenty days. Many students thought that this sentence was too severe, and six hundred agitators marched through Berkeley in protest singing 'We Shall Overcome.' "

turned to civil rights. After that they "rediscovered" poverty and turned to the needs of the poor in general.[28] At the same time interest in the Southern struggle declined.

However, the civil rights movement in the United States was important for several reasons. It taught students a whole series of new tactics of resistance, and familiarized the public with these tactics. It also showed that the new generation of faculty members still retained their student feelings of frustration, as many of them assisted the students in their protests.[29] It is probable that, although new generations of students will be continuously moving into the college and universities, tactics and techniques of organization are by now so well known that future students will be able to demonstrate more rapidly and more effectively. Also, as the concept of the New Left has seeped down to high school pupils, more and more students will arrive at college with at least some experience in demonstrations and protest movements.

EDUCATIONAL PROTESTS

The aim of many recent protest movements has been to protect the interests of students *as* students. This type of student indiscipline can lead to "positive" social change, even though the underlying cause of it may be to release tensions. This is the kind of collective action that is most likely to enlist the support of the largest number of students, for educational problems may impinge on them all.

In India, the great majority of student demonstrations in 1963 were stated to be for some sort of educational reform, or to protect the interests of students. Newspapers cannot be relied on to report all disturbances for, as student demonstrations have become an almost normal pattern of behaviour in India, they are no longer news, and may escape the notice of the journalist. They do, however, at least give some idea of the amount of restlessness that is worth recording, but it would probably be nearer the truth to double, or perhaps even treble, the following figures. They were taken from the reports of two leading newspapers, the *Times of India*, and *The Hindu*, which give fairly adequate coverage to events in the north and south of India. The two newspapers covered many of the same incidents from February 1, 1963, to January 31, 1964, but some were reported in only one newspaper. In all, ninety-

28. "Campus '65," p. 54.
29. Nathan Glazer, "What Happened at Berkeley," p. 290.

six demonstrations were recorded.[30] Forty-three of these took place south of Bombay, and fifty-two to the north. The location of one is not known. They occurred in all states except Orissa and Gujarat. In twenty-one of these cases students manhandled someone or threw stones. In seventeen they went on strikes—nine of these included hunger strikes. In sixteen they "protested," in sixteen they abstained from class, and in fifteen they "demonstrated." In addition there were six "clashes" and five incidents of severe heckling.

Ten of these incidents lasted from one to five days; four from six to ten days; two from sixteen to twenty days; and one, thirty-four days. Three universities closed indefinitely, locking the students out. In seven of these disturbances, the police interfered without violence; in eleven, there were arrests; in three, the police used tear gas; and in seven, they carried out lathi charges.

In ten incidents, 100 to 250 students took part; in eighteen, 250 to 600 students; in four, 600 to 1,000 students; and in five, 1,000 to 2,000 students. In three cases, over 2,000 students participated. In one of these, 3,600 students, and in the other, 10,000 students were involved.

The number of incidents varied for each month. Five took place in February, two in April, four in June, eighteen in July, sixteen in August, eight in September, eighteen in October, five in November, nine in December, and eleven in January 1964.

The above figures give only a rough idea of the size of the demonstrations, the action that took place, and the number of students participating. But they suggest that indisicipline is widespread in India, and that it engages much of the time and energy of many students.

The newspaper descriptions also mentioned the causes of the demonstrations, as stated by the students. Of the ninety-six incidents, twenty-five could be classified as having no set purpose. These seemed to have occurred as a release of tensions, or for enjoyment. The remaining seventy-one were carried out to protest against some phase of the educational system, or to protect students.[31]

30. Various estimates have been made in regard to the number of annual student demonstrations in India. See: Philip G. Altbach, "Student Politics and Higher Education in India," Daedalus, p. 267. Altbach estimates that there were 700 demonstrations as well as 113 violent outbursts in 1964. By 1966 this figure had risen to 2,206 demonstrations, of which 480 were violent.

31. Ibid., p. 267. Altbach says that in 1964 3 per cent of the agitations were due to other than academic issues. In 1965 this figure rose to 5 per cent and in 1966 to 17.4 per cent. This means that the great majority of the demonstrations were stated to be over academic matters.

Issues included dissatisfaction with a college administration, the dismissal of a principal, the inefficiency of lecturers, bad conditions in a hostel, and discontentment with the language in which the students were instructed. These descriptions seem to suggest that Indian students find it easiest to promote collective action around issues which are nearest to the students' interests. Political interests were probably involved in a number of these demonstrations, but the description of the main strikes in the colleges in Mysore State (Chapter 1) shows that students carried out protest demonstrations without any assistance or backing from politicians.

Educational protests are not new to students in Latin America, where they have probably had more influence on university administration than in any other part of the world. In Argentina, for example, the University Reform movement had great influence on the reform of different aspects of the system of higher education, and was active in the defence of academic freedom against state power.[32]

In Europe, students from several countries have been particularly active since the Second World War in pressing for educational reforms.

> The current conditions in European universities—overcrowding and obsolescence of facilities which take near-disaster proportions—together with changes in the social composition of the student body, account for unrest among the students. . . . In the last week of November 1963, nearly all the French universities were closed by a strike and demonstrations by students and professors demanding larger appropriations for higher education.[33]

National associations of students, such as the National Association of Labour Student Organization in England, give students more control over their educational destinies and better bargaining power. In Belgium students belong to two unions, the Vereniging der Vlaamse Studenten for Flemish students, and the Mouvement des Étudiants Universitaires for the French students. These two organizations join forces over certain educational matters.[34]

The academic years of 1967-68 was the first year that students on most of the campuses across Canada went into direct action against their university administrators. There had been demonstrations before

32. Kenneth N. Walker, "A Comparison of University Reform Movements in Argentina and Colombia," pp. 257-72.
33. Pinner, p. 192.
34. *Ibid.*, pp. 185, 186.

that time, and through these student leaders had learned gradually the tactics of confrontation. News of successful exploits spread like wild-fire from campus to campus, and even those who did not join in the open demonstrations were excited by the success of the activists in gaining many minor and some major concessions from their administrations. Certain provincial associations were strengthened by amalgamation, such as the formation of BCAS, the British Columbia Assembly of Students. The most important gains of the students were in obtaining the right to have representatives on many university committees.[35]

The increasing interest in academic matters shown by students in the United States is also a recent phenomenon. The Berkeley agitation in 1964 perhaps began the fashion of confrontation. It focussed attention on the administration of the university, and on such issues as freedom of speech on the campus.[36] The reaction of the public, of the alumni, and of the academic world to this incident was immediate and troubled. This was probably due to three major factors. First, very little disturbance of this sort had ever occurred in the United States. Secondly, the media of mass communication are always ready to give wide and often dramatic publicity to an unusual event, and the Berkeley demonstrations were certainly "news." (It has been said that today's generation is the most discussed and publicized generation in history.) Thirdly, the United States has proportionately more social scientists to analyze topical events than any other country, and in this case they began immediately to analyze the developments at Berkeley.[37]

The growing number of demonstrations about education shows that many of today's students are not content to allow their educational

35. The potential strength of some of the student organizations is seen in that l'Union Générale des Etudiants du Québec (UGEQ) has some 70,000 members. It represents all the students of the Province of Quebec, and was formed in 1964 through the amalgamation of three former student associations of the three French-speaking universities.

36. Seymour Martin Lipset, *The Berkeley Student Revolt*, pp. xi, xii of Introduction.

37. Philip Selznick, "Berkeley," p. 83. Selznick says that although the 1964 incidents at Berkeley have been referred to as constituting "the most dangerous crisis in the history of the University of California," as a "civil war," and a "tragic event," in reality they consisted of a series of rather minor violations of university regulations, supported by sit-ins and demonstrations.

Clark Kerr, "The Exaggerated Generation," pp. 28-36. Kerr tells how the mass media exaggerates many of the student demonstrations. At Berkeley, in December 1966, for example, reporters said that 8,000 to 10,000 students voted to strike, whereas the actual number was 2,000 (this number included wives, onlookers, and non-students). On another occasion 2,400 students were actually counted at a demonstration, but the number was reported by different journalists as being 6,000 to 7,000. " 'Crowdsmanship' is a game in which all have an interest in raising the score . . . a sit-in becomes a riot, then a rebellion, finally the 'revolution.' "

politics in the student disturbances may prevent a more profound analysis of the causes underlying the unrest.

In India student unrest had its beginnings in the political protest demonstrations, which were organized during the fight for independence; now, over twenty years after political freedom and the establishment of a relatively stable government, the student protest processions, strikes, and riots are often, and perhaps usually, for non-political reasons. Many Indians are deeply concerned with this problem; it is discussed constantly in speeches, newspapers, journals, and books. Student unrest has become a phenomenon very difficult to control, possibly because in its initial phases the educational authorities had little idea that they were facing the beginning of a mass movement. Entirely new patterns of protest have developed among Indian students, and their organizations are becoming a new and important element, both in the determination of educational policy and in other areas of Indian society.

The following account of three Indian student riots examines in detail the development of new methods for organizing and directing student protest movements, and shows how closely the effectiveness of the demonstrations can be related to the degree of efficiency with which they were organized.

1

The Organization of
Student Action:
A Case Study

What determines whether a group of students from one college rather than another moves into collective action? Why do only some students become involved? Why are some incidents well organized and relatively harmless, whereas others end in violence?

The chaotic nature of much of the early action of students in the colleges of the state of Mysore eventually became so formalized that by 1963 student leaders were able to organize a strike of thousands of students and maintain complete discipline for thirty-seven days. In comparison to the wild and unorganized behaviour of the students in the Youth Festival strike in 1959, the 1963-64 strike could be described as the stage of formal organization of a social movement.[1]

Smelser's analysis of social movements is one of the most comprehensive in recent sociological literature. He contends that a society must be structurally conducive to the development of the type of elementary collective behaviour that will lead to a social movement before one can arise. That is, the condition of the society must be such that new types of behaviour are possible, or are likely to appear. If, for example, a society is divided into competing groups on an ethnic, religious, or socio-economic basis, it will "form a set of structurally conducive conditions for the flow of hostility."[2] If there is no opportunity for people to

1. I. C. A. Dawson and W. E. Gettys, *An Introduction to Sociology*, pp. 689-709.
2. Neil J. Smelser, *Theory of Collective Behavior*, pp. 228-13. On page 8 Smelser defines collective behavior as "mobilization on the basis of a belief which redefines social action, but is formed or forged to meet undefined or unstructured situations."

express their hostility so that grievances will be given adequate attention, they are more likely to take the law into their own hands.[3]

All modern societies have conditions that are conducive to hostile outbursts, but outbursts do not always occur. According to Smelser, the factor that must be present is the structural strain which is found in most modern societies and which is accompanied by feelings of anxiety and frustration. The strain is institutionalized, however, in economic, political, religious, and other social relationships, and before it can lead to more than individual deviant behaviour, the idea of action must spread through the group. In other words, the situation must have a common meaning for those who share the strain, so that they are willing to act together.[4] Then a dramatic event must occur to precipitate action. And even after it has begun, collective action will not continue unless leaders arise who are able to sustain it until it becomes formally organized.

These, then, according to Smelser, are the conditions that will determine whether collective action will arise, and whether it will continue until it gradually turns into an organized social movement integrated into the structure of society. At every point in this development of action, the instruments of social control, such as the government, the police, or public opinion, may play decisive roles in lessening or increasing the activity. They may also be important in determining its length and severity.[5]

In what way can this theoretical framework help in analyzing the indiscipline of Indian students? Is the present educational system structurally conducive to arousing the hostility or anxiety of the students? It is clear that these questions cannot be answered by looking at the educational system alone, for it is only part of a highly complex, interrelated set of relationships. The major groupings which have some bearing on what happens to students at the college level must also be explored. The main groups, besides the educational system, are the government, the caste system, and the family. The radical changes that are occurring in these areas as India seeks to change from a traditional to a highly in-

3. *Ibid.*, p. 237. "The interaction between dissatisfaction (strain) and closing off avenues of protest (structural conduciveness) produces a situation which easily gives way to violence."

4. *Ibid.*, p. 16. Smelser refers to this as the growth and spread of a generalized belief. "This meaning is supplied in a generalized belief, which identifies the source of strain, attributes certain characteristics to this source, and specifies certain responses to the strain as possible or appropriate."

5. *Ibid.*, pp. 17, 18.

dustrialized society are indeed causing conditions which are structurally conducive to frustration, insecurity, and unrest.

The strains of change have borne particularly heavily on college students because theirs is one of the groups most exposed to the new trends and on whom there is the greatest pressure to "get ahead," or at least to get jobs remunerative enough to bridge the gap between the rising standard of aspirations and the lowering of real money income among the middle classes.[6]

Another structurally conducive condition influencing Indian students to move into collective action is that mass demonstrations, of one sort or another, often of a violent nature, are so widespread throughout the country they remind students, day in and day out, that there are ways of taking the law into their own hands.[7] The rituals of demonstrations are also well known. Processions, slogans, black flags, the burning of effigies, hunger strikes, and self-immolation are all fashions of protest that have spread, sometimes from other countries, to Indian student demonstrations. The protests of all these different types of people show that the basic conditions for collective action impinge on many people in India.

If there are no channels through which grievances can be brought to the attention of those who might alleviate them, then the situation will be structurally conducive to producing collective action. The authoritarian nature of the Indian educational system, and the fact that students find it difficult to have personal contacts with their lecturers or with people in the higher administrative positions, make them believe that their problems are not understood or do not receive enough sympathy. Student unions or associations are often the only media through which

6. Indra Sen, "Education of the Youth," p. 115. "The modern youth in India is really working under a number of conflicting and . . . confused stresses and strains, national and international . . . and therefore his behaviour is naturally many times impulsive, aggressive, and violent, and shows much contradiction."

7. Random examples of these follow: *The Hindu*, October 13, 1961: "About fifty people were arrested following demonstrations by passengers and local people who held up the Ranchi express for about six hours. It started as a protest against the late arrival of a train. The people prevented it moving by continually pulling alarm chains. Many squatted on the tracks."

The Hindu, January 17, 1962: "[At a cricket match] the mobs tried to get near the players when they were leaving the field. Some individuals threw stones and chappals; a few officers and policemen, as well as some of the public, were injured."

Times of India, August 24, 1965: A cartoon shows a man marching in a procession to protest against a food shortage. His placard bears the inscription: "We want food, Goa, steel plant, refinery, release of detenue, removal of stateless, etc." He is saying to his companion, "I have listed all the demands because I find it tiresome to demonstrate every day!"

23

they can air their grievances. The unions were first organized in India on the same lines as those of the universities of Oxford and Cambridge. They were intended to foster debates and dramatics, to maintain libraries, and to promote the general social life of the university. Before 1941 every student who joined a college in India had to belong to a students' union, and fees were compulsory. All those who held office were students. Later, when fees were made voluntary, the membership decreased. During the struggle for independence, the unions became forums for student political activities. This did not always meet with the approval of the university authorities, and occasionally a union would be suspended.

After Independence the unions continued to serve as a focus for political action on the campus. This led to further suspensions, and student associations were sometimes set up to take their place. The main difference between the two was that, whereas the unions had been run by the students themselves, a professor was usually in charge of the organization and administration of the associations. The abolishment of some unions and the leadership of professors prevented students from gaining experience in running organizations. This is said to be one reason why there has been so little influential student leadership in Indian colleges, for students are not trained to take responsibility or learn the skills of organization, either in the family or at school. Another reason is that students who have been leaders in the student unions or in student associations sometimes stay on at college under some academic pretext or other after they graduate, and so continue to lead and control the student activities. These leaders tend to be either "professional students," that is, individuals who are afraid to face the realities of the world outside the university, or students who have strong political inclinations and want to gain power.[8]

The leadership of most student organizations in Mysore State resembles that of all formal associations in that it is composed of a few very active students who control its activities, and a large number of relatively passive members. The central core is made up of enthusiastic, politically-minded students, who sometimes use the organization as a

8. *Report on the Problem of Student Indiscipline.* "In India, students have come to regard the Student Union merely as a bargaining counter, or as a forum for voicing grievances. In fact, the unions have become a peculiar type of trade union. Like the trade unions, the office bearers negotiate with the university authorities on behalf of the students. . . . In certain universities, there are some union leaders who have stayed on in the university for eight or nine years, or even much longer. Such 'professors' of student leaders are often responsible for misguiding the fresh entrants into our universities."

378.1981   R733s

c. 1

platform to demonstrate their potential leadership qualities. This helps to prepare the way for a political career when they graduate.

A great deal of propagandizing and soliciting of votes goes on before elections for the student unions, and communal influence is often seen in the voting pattern. Some students are so eager to be elected that they go to great expense to publicize themselves. In one recent election in a Mysore college, a student published and distributed a double-sheet newspaper to advertise his nomination for election. It included advertisements and several photographs of the student posing with important people at college gatherings.

The main student organization, the student union, has therefore not been used as a liason between student and staff, nor as a sounding-board from which the authorities could learn of student needs, and there is no other formal way in which information can flow between the two groups. This lack of communication, combined with little personal contact between student and lecturer, leaves the students with a deep sense of frustration when they feel that they have problems needing attention. It is certainly one important factor, along with many others, that has led to student indiscipline.

The students feel strongly that through their demonstrations, whether their goals be short-term ones, such as changing an examination paper, or long-term ones, such as reducing fees, they gain the power to change some aspects of their lives.[9] In view of the strong traditional controls of family, caste, and religion over their behaviour, this was indeed a heady discovery. Thus, their beliefs in their own right to demonstrate and in their ability to alter their fate through collective action are important factors in initiating their demonstrations.

Their long experience in challenging the educational authorities and the police has gradually convinced them that they can get away even with violence to achieve their ends, and violent action, such as the destruction of property, is a satisfactory and often pleasing way of releasing frustrations.

Since 1950 the pattern of organized revolt has spread to many parts of India in spite of the fact that there has been no central organizing agency, nor even a national student association to support or promote it. However, student strikes have gained much notoriety through the newspapers, so that by the time Indian students arrive at college they have read of student agitations in the press and have heard of them

9. Smelser, pp. 79-84.

25

from parents, brothers, or fellow students. They may even have taken part in demonstrations while at high school. Thus, they are quite prepared to entertain the idea of demonstrating when they arrive, and may even know of the pattern of procedure through experience.

There are opportunities for students from different regions to get together on such occasions as the annual Youth Festival at New Delhi. There are also various student conferences, such as those held by Roman Catholic colleges, and these meetings are sometimes attended by several thousand students of both sexes. At such conferences news of what is going on in other colleges and regions inevitably spreads.

The three final factors that are structurally conducive to outbreaks of student indiscipline, according to Smelser's theory, are communication, accessability of objects of attack, and ecology. In India communication is facilitated among the students because they are in close proximity to each other, day after day, month after month, for four years. Undergraduate students normally have a good deal of time to gossip, as few study until examination time, and there are not many extra-curricular activities to attract their attenion. Ideas and rumours thus circulate rapidly. News of the shortcomings of the educational system, and of student demonstrations have been features of the daily press for many years. Thus, students are familiar with other student protests.

The objects of the students' grievances are also close at hand. Whether the issue is the educational authorities or the system itself, there is always college equipment that can be stoned, or staff that can be harrassed. If the ire of the students falls on the government, there are innumerable symbols to attack. Post offices, municipal offices, railway stations, street lights, statues, and corporation buses have all received a great deal of student attention in past years. If a cinema is uncooperative, or if a commercial house does not close in support of a student demonstration it is to be taught a lesson. The police, the special enemy of the students, are usually well in evidence if there is any likelihood of trouble. Thus, there is an infinite variety of tangible objects or people against whom the students can direct their collective action. Usually it is a matter of chance that decides their target.

Another factor that helps the communication of ideas from student to student is the ecology of Bangalore, where many colleges are in close proximity to each other. Three of the colleges whose students usually lead demonstrations are only a few blocks apart.

Ecologically, the composition of the population of the city where demonstrations take place will also help to account for the rapidity with which different students move into action, and for the reactions of students once they begin to agitate. The violence of the riots that have accompanied student strikes in Aligarh University has been very largely due to the large proportion of Muslims in that city, and to the underlying tensions that still exist between Muslims and Hindus in the north.

Given these structurally conducive conditions and their accompanying anxieties and tensions, it can be seen that any spark may set off an explosion. Any critical event such as a raise in tuition fees, or the feeling that an examination paper is unfair, or the belief that there has been some infringement of student "rights," may cause the students to rebel.[10]

Three of the most important student strikes in Mysore will be described to show the way in which students of that state have organized their demonstrations so that in 1963 they were able to carry out a prolonged strike without any violence and eventually attain their aim—the reduction of tuition fees; or in other words, how their first unregulated outbursts have gradually turned into a social movement.

THE YOUTH FESTIVAL STRIKE

The Youth Festival strike began on December 8, 1959, and lasted for three days. It arose rather spontaneously, erupted into violence, and petered out without obtaining its aim. It was the first major student strike in the state, and was confined to the students of Bangalore and Mysore cities. It caused a great deal of public concern.

The second strike of note occurred on July 25, 1962, and lasted until August 1. It was called to fight a raise in tuition fees. Students from many of the colleges in the state took part. It was peaceful except for one incident that occurred when students from a mofussil college in-

---

10. In some cases the students seem to be so ready to demonstrate that they use the slightest pretext to go on strike, as in the following incident. One of the clerks at College A was rude to the secretary of the students' union. The latter demanded an apology and the students went on strike until the Principal brought them together and the clerk apologized. But the strike continued because the secretary wanted a public apology. This strike erupted into such violent behaviour that the Principal and staff were horrified by it. A few months later, the same students thought that the students of a medical college across the road had insulted their Principal. They began throwing rocks from behind their compound wall across the road into the compound of the other college. They could not even see the other students, but kept pelting stones and rocks over the walls in an aimless but violent fashion. This went on for hours. The underlying reason in this case seems to have been that the students of College A felt that the medical students looked down on them, and some felt frustrated at not being admitted into medicine.

dulged in stone-throwing. It ended without achieving its aim, but with promises from the government that serious consideration would be given to their requests.

The third strike began on December 11, 1963, and lasted for thirty-seven days. In a sense it was a resumption of the 1962 strike, as its main concern was again to prevent a raise in tuition fees. It was peaceful throughout. Characterized by brilliant tactics, and supported by public opinion, it was finally successful in forcing the government to reverse its position on fees.

The Precipitating Factors

No single reason can explain why students demonstrate. It is evident that students join protest movements for a variety of reasons, and some would never voluntarily leave their classrooms or take part in unruly behaviour unless forced to by other students. Some events, however, can be seen as particularly important in moving students to action. The decision to hold the colourful sixth annual All India Youth Festival in the city of Mysore was the stated reason for the first of the three strikes, but the students of Bangalore were already in the mood to respond to the idea of demonstration. Several recent incidents had built up their desire for excitement. A few months before the Youth Festival was to take place the students had participated in a very exciting model United Nations Assembly conducted by the Youth Association of Asia. Student leaders and orators from the different colleges of Mysore took part in the sessions, and in this way became acquainted. The Assembly was given a good deal of newspaper publicity and was carried out with effective showmanship. The second event, which caused unusual excitement, was the occupation of Indian territory by Communist China in the third week of November. This led to emotional demonstrations against China in all parts of India. Student leaders met in Bangalore and decided to organize a day of protest. Pamphlets were printed; and on the day, students marched in a procession from their respective colleges to their central meeting place, Mysore Bank Square, shouting slogans against China. About three thousand university students left their classrooms to join in the demonstrations, and at the square they pledged "to fight to the last drop of our blood to save India."[11]

11. *Deccan Herald*, December 1, 1959. The information for the description of the three strikes comes from the *Deccan Herald*, *The Hindu*, principals, lecturers, student leaders, and students.

Twenty-seven student representatives harangued the students at this meeting, and effigies of Chinese leaders were burned. Again the local newspapers gave these demonstrations a lot of publicity. It is important to note that not one woman student took part in these protests. The day went by peacefully except for one unpleasant incident which took place when men students surrounded a bus that was carrying some of the Maharani College students home. The girls managed to escape into a nearby ladies' club.

When the public is asked the reason for the Youth Festival strike, they will say that it occurred because the students wanted holidays and made the Youth Festival an excuse to go on strike. However, the students' memories of the fun they had had at the Assembly and at the Chinese demonstrations were still fresh and they wanted more excitement. The Youth Festival became a good excuse for releasing their energies.

The holding of the Youth Festival at Mysore was a great honour for that city, for it was the first time it had been held outside of Delhi. About one thousand men and five hundred women students from thirty-four different universities were to compete in the various dramatic events. The Festival was given much publicity; it was painted in glowing colours in the local press for days before it occurred. Bangalore is only about ninety miles from Mysore, and some of the Bangalore students dreamed of the freedom they would have when they got away to Mysore and escaped the vigilant eyes of family and relatives. They had visions, too, of being able to move among girls more freely. Thus, the students were emotionally aroused about the coming event and gradually began to feel that this was *their* festival. Then, just a short time before the Festival began, they were told that they would not be given holidays from college to attend it. A great many students were deeply disappointed at being denied this treat, particularly in view of the few opportunities they had for other kinds of excitement. One informant said that "sex and disappointment" caused the riots.

One of the mistakes made in planning the Festival was to hold it while the colleges were still in session, instead of waiting a few weeks for the Christmas holidays when the students would be free to attend. If the later date had been chosen, the limitation on the number of students who were permitted to enter the administrative building to see the performances would never have had to be made. It was thought that not many of the Bangalore students would have actually bothered attending it, because of the cost of travelling to Mysore, and because they were really not interested in amateur dramas and dancing. As for the Mysore students, the great majority would probably have gone home for the holidays and so not have been able to attend. This would have cut down the number of students wanting free entertainment, and so would have prevented the anger of those who were not admitted, which was one of the factors that precipitated violence. The administrative building where the Festival was to take place held only 2,500 people, and 1,500 of these were the competitors themselves.[12]

The main reason that the strike got out of hand was lack of trained leadership. The "real" student leaders in Bangalore had been approached by a group of students ten days before the Festival began, and asked to organize a strike if holidays were not granted. But they believed that the desire for a holiday was not a sufficient reason for a strike. Nor did they think that many of the students really wanted to go to Mysore to see the Festival. Thus, they refused to have anything to do with it. They argued that the students who did want to see the Festival could easily take leave to go to Mysore to see it. It was, therefore, a group of students who had had little, if any, leadership training who began the demonstrations. This accounts for the fact that the strike did not mobilize all the students, was not properly planned, got out of control, and ended in violence.

Mobilization for Action

The way in which potential participants are mobilized into action varies greatly from one situation to another. Smelser says that collective behaviour may be initiated by a person who merely "gets people going," with no idea of carrying out any prolonged activity. This could be the trouble-maker type, or someone who merely craves excitement; or it might be a momentary release of aggression. On the other hand, collective behaviour may be initiated by a "leader," that is, a person who has some definite, even though temporary, aim and who is able to enlist others in his project. Collective behaviour may be "rigged" in the sense that some subversive organization may want to capitalize on the state of unrest.[13] It is quite probable that all these types of leadership or

12. The Festival was held in this auditorium because it was not intended to be a public performance by a group of professional artists, but rather a cultural fête for the benefit of competing teams. So it took the form of competitions between university students rather than polished, sophisticated presentations for the public. But the public, and especially some of the students, wanted and expected to see it.

13. Smelser, p. 11. One type of leader may be able to enlist support over a long period of time, whereas another may not be able to plan and organize beyond the initial stage of rousing people to action.

potential leadership have been present during the many outbreaks of student indiscipline in India.

The major problem in organizing student movements is that they do not have enduring leadership. Students remain at college for such short periods of time that their associations are seldom stable. The student associations are organized or maintained by each new crop of students, and those that gradually learn leadership skills as they move through college are soon replaced by a new group of untrained leaders. Thus, leadership is passed on in a very haphazard way. One student may be deeply concerned with some project or type of student activity and able to keep the students united behind him, only to be followed by a weak leader who may not have the interest or ability to carry on. The would-be leader in India usually has to learn by experience after he gets to college. Few arrive fully capable of initiating projects or of carrying them out, for they have had little opportunity to assert their independence, to take on responsibility, or to lead others. Indian high schools do not have as many extracurricular activities as do those in Western countries, so that the students do not have even this slight opportunity to learn some of the skills of leadership, although it is likely that a growing number of them have gained some experience by leading high school demonstrations.

Lecturers and principals often complained that their students had little ability for organization. But though invitations and details of procedure were often left to the last minute, most events attended by this observer seemed to run relatively well. The great number of strikes and demonstrations undertaken by students in recent years seems to demonstrate that many Indian students have in fact been able to stir others to action —action which sometimes lasts over a long period of time, as during the negotiating of fees.

At the time of the Youth Festival student activity began in Bangalore about 12:00 noon on Tuesday, December 8. St. Joseph's College students seem to have begun the agitation. About two hundred of them formed a bicycle procession to the Central College shouting, "We want holidays to attend the Youth Festival!" They entered the college, banged on the classroom doors and tried to get the students to join them. A number of students did so, and they all moved on to other colleges—the Maharani, the Government Intermediate, the Commercial, and Mount Carmel. Students from the two men's colleges joined them. At each college they visited the students were talking in excited groups, and their

31

own excitement increased as they moved from college to college. Thus, the "milling" process began.[14] They finally ended their procession at the traditional meeting place for agitators, Mysore Bank Square. Generations of students have gathered there whenever rumours have spread that some activity is being contemplated. It is there that leaders harangue the students and initiate action. It is the Bangalorians' "Trafalgar Square."

In the beginning they were out mainly for a good time, marching and shouting. But gradually, as the excitement mounted, the students became unruly. They proceeded to the Vidhana Soudha (the House of Assembly) to try to talk to members of the Legislative Assembly. On the way, some convenient piles of stones, ready for road-mending, were used to break street lights. The students also obstructed traffic, used stones to pelt buses and cars (including the car of the Inspector General of Police), and pulled up trees. Weak leadership was the main reason for the rapidity with which the students became a disorganized mass, behaving violently and destructively.[15] When the students finally arrived at the Vidhana Soudha, they were about 1,000 strong. They began to clamour for holidays. The timidity of the members of the Legislative Assembly in not confronting them further enraged the students. After demonstrating for some time, they paraded through the city, again stoning policemen, buses, passing vehicles, and electric domes. The police retaliated by firing tear-gas shells and arresting a number of the demonstrators. Several students and policemen were injured. After the first day, policemen were posted inside all the college compounds. The students were insulted by this action, and before they would return to college, they insisted that the policemen be removed.

The next day the rioting grew even more violent. Fighting between the students and the police began early in the morning at the Central

14. Herbert Blumer, "Collective Behaviour," p. 174. "The primary effect of milling is to make the individuals more sensitive and responsive to one another, so that they become increasingly preoccupied with one another and decreasingly responsive to ordinary objects of stimulation. . . . Their attention becomes increasingly focused on one another and less on objects and events which would ordinarily concern them. Being preoccupied with each other they are inclined to respond to one another quickly, directly, and unwittingly. . . . People in this state are much more disposed to act together, under the influence of a common impulse or mood, than they are to act separately . . . under [the] influence (or collective excitement) people become more emotionally aroused and more likely to be carried away by impulses and feelings; hence rendered more unstable and irresponsible."

15. City buses always seem to be a target for student demonstrations. This is perhaps due to the fact that they are enticing moving objects to aim at, that students have suffered from long waits for transportation or overcrowded conditions when on them, and because they represent some sort of authority that seems to make no effort to cater to their needs.

College hostel, where the crowd was pelting passing vehicles with stones. Several policemen were injured, one seriously. Then the police chased the students into the hostel and used their lathis so freely that it was later described as "hammering" the students. Tear gas was thrown into each room, and when some people resisted, the doors of their rooms were broken down. Witnesses described the corruptness of several policemen who stole watches and money. Police entered some of the college classrooms, and in an ensuing scuffle a professor was hurt. About fifty students were injured, some seriously. One student who was ill and had had nothing to do with the strike was so badly beaten by the police that he died on the way to the hospital. This incident proved to be one of the main sustaining factors of the strike, for word of it passed rapidly among the students and so infuriated them that many more joined in the demonstrations. Many other incidents of police brutality were told by interviewers who had witnessed the scenes.

The students moved on to the Kurabara Sangha hostel, where they were attacked by the police using tear gas and lathis. About thirty more students were injured. The students then broke up into groups and pelted the police with stones; the police retaliated with more tear gas. By this time the goondas had joined in and, by the evening, they outnumbered the students. The goondas continued to break electric domes and neon lights around the city. At the end of the day, about forty students had been taken up by the police.

When the students who had started the agitation found that it was completely beyond their control, they went to the "real leaders," who had refused to organize the strike, and begged them to help. These leaders consented and organized a peace committee, composed of student representatives from the different colleges, to try to stop the rioting and restore order.

Word got around that the older leaders had taken over, and on the following day, although rioting and destruction continued, it was carried on very largely by goondas and urchins who continued to pelt stones at the remaining electric domes and at the city buses. It was later estimated that damage to the buses on the two days came to Rs.40,000, and it took Rs.12,000 to replace the electric domes. The police gradually restored order with more tear gas and mild lathi charges, arresting fifteen people. All the cinemas in the centre of the city were closed for the day.

On Friday the city was quiet on the whole, and only a few stray incidents occurred, such as the stoning of buses.

33

The women students did not become involved in the strike until the second day. The position of the main women's college in Bangalore makes it extremely vulnerable to agitation, as it lies on the pathway between two of the colleges which have supplied most of the leaders for the different student demonstrations. The girls could actually hear the whacks of the lathis and the screams of the students when they were attacked by the police. Some of them said that this was the reason they "went wild" and broke college property.

When the boys paraded to the gates of the college compound and demanded that the girls should come out and join them, many of the girls were in such a state of agitation that they were ready to go into action. As they were prevented from leaving the compound they vented their feelings on the college.

They first rushed around the corridors shouting for a holiday. They did not understand enough of what was going on to know what slogans to shout and some, who were caught up by the excitement, did not even know what they were shouting about. They made so much noise that many lecturers finally had to stop lecturing. In one case, however, when the lecturer did continue, the girls rushed into the class and tried to pull out the attending students. In another case they dragged an older male lecturer out of his class. The Principal's description of the affair shows that the behaviour of the girls was as hysterical and uncontrolled as that of the men students. Because it was completely unprecedented behaviour for women students in Bangalore, the college authorities had no idea of how to deal with it.

The Principal: I had no idea that the girls were going to behave as they did. It all came on very suddenly. The boys came and called over our compound fence: "Come out, sisters, you must support us!" The ringleaders of the girls were the student president and a girl from the Punjab.

The girls had a meeting in the quad just outside my office. There had been a few orderly strikes in the past, when the girls had met outside the building and made resolutions, but this took place right inside our building. Nothing else had ever happened like this in the college before. The girls got more and more excited. Finally they became violent, and began breaking windows and other college property. They kept on shouting and yelling. I never could have imagined they could have behaved like that! The Punjab girl tried to pull the bus driver out of the bus that had come to collect them. You have no idea how terrible it was to see the expressions on their faces—absolute fury! I couldn't ever have imagined they could look like that—it was terrible!

Finally I sent for the police, and they sealed off both gates, so that the girls could not get out. I had forbidden them to join the boys. The parents kept phoning: "Is my girl safe? Is she in the compound?" Government officials kept phoning: "Is everything under control?"

The police and boys were fighting just outside the gates. There was firing and finally tear gas. I had four buildings to look after—the college, the nursery school, the Home Science building, and the hostel. Only two young teachers were with the children in the nursery, and I couldn't possibly leave them there. But the police would not let me go for them as there was firing. Finally they took me, and we brought them back to the college. The children were terrified, their eyes were sore with tear gas, and we had a bad time getting them to leave the building.

Gradually, as the day wore on, the girls got tired of shouting. They were very hungry, too, and in the evening we collected all the vehicles we could get and sent them home. Only a handful did the damage; the others just stood around laughing at them and encouraging them. Still others were quite against it all. I was afraid of their going home alone, as the boys might molest them, so we got the police and had them send special buses to take them home. By this time the police had routed out the boys who were milling around the compound. But some of the girls refused to go home in the buses; instead they went out into the streets and thumbed their way home.

It is not clear just how much communication there was between the students of Mysore and Bangalore before the Youth Festival began, or at the time of the rioting. Newspaper reports and other accounts suggest that student demonstrations began in both places at almost the same time. The ensuing actions of the festival authorities, the police, and the government kept the news alive through newspapers and by word of mouth, thus adding to the general emotional state of the students, and keeping them at fever pitch.

In Mysore City about 2,000 students gathered at the administrative building in which the Festival was being held on December 8, and demanded free admission to all the shows, as well as holidays for the city colleges for the period of the Festival. The situation was not helped by the fact that the director of the Festival was an unpopular politician. He became the butt of student aggression, and he tried to keep out of their way, for when they became violent, they declared they would kill him if they caught him.

When the students were told that it was physically impossible to admit all of them to the administrative building because of its size, and that there was, therefore, no purpose in their getting holidays, they became unruly and began to throw stones at neon signs and street lights,

35

and to damage windows and flower beds. When they failed in their attempt to enter the building forcibly, some turned their attention to the participants of the Festival and tried to set fire to the tents and thatched huts of the Youth Festival camp. Others set fire to the furniture in the Indian guest quarters. The damage was estimated at Rs.5,000.

The mob of students roamed around until nine that evening, attacking passing cars, and stoning street lights until the city was in darkness. Thirty-four policemen were injured by stones. When the police tried to disperse the students, a journalist told them to squat down in order to prevent the police from charging them and beating them with lathis. The police then began to provoke them by throwing stones at them. Finally the boys could not resist rising to retaliate, and at that point the firing began. The police fired four rounds of ammunition and killed one student. Although the firing dispersed the students, it added to their excitement and to their antagonism toward the police so that trouble flared up again the next day, Wednesday, when the students again collected. They were soon engaged in even more violent behaviour than the day before, such as uprooting trees and smashing the remaining electric street lights. Then they marched to the hostel of a women's college, demanding that the girls should come out and demonstrate with them. This incident might have had unfortunate results had it not been for a courageous young warden who stood in front of the main door and defied them.

One of the students who had been in the hostel told this story.

> The second day the boys beseiged the girls in their hostel, for the girls had not joined them and the boys were mad with them. The boys threw bottles and stones into the compound and through the windows. Finally they went to a gas station where the men did not dare deny them large buckets of gasoline, and came back with them and burnt down the hostel gate. The girls were terrified. "My God, were we scared! Our young warden saved us by going out and telling the boys that they could do what they liked to her, but they must leave the girls alone. This fortunately intimidated them, and they finally went away. Later they wrote all sorts of bad things about the girls on the streets."

The police finally resorted once more to tear gas, and when this was not effective, they shot four rounds of ammunition. Three civilians were hurt by the shots.

Early Thursday morning the police cordoned off the university grounds in the hope that this would prevent the students from collecting again in large groups. That day the students were relatively quiet; they shouted slogans, and waved black flags and the blood-stained shirt of a wounded student. A few threw stones. The police then turned their attention to the crowd of goondas and citizens and chased them with lathi charges for some hours to disperse them. Observers said that the state of panic was so great that the police beat people indiscriminately. Many were injured, including three women.

Two efforts were made on Friday to try and calm the situation. All the schools and colleges were given holidays until December 20, and a group of prominent lawyers tried to negotiate with the students. The mischief continued, but few students took part, and destruction was mainly carried out by goondas. All shops remained closed for the day. As far as the student body was concerned, the strike was officially over.

Social Controls

Collective outbursts do not occur in a void, but in a situation where many kinds of social controls, from informal norms to the formally organized institutions of law, are already established. As students are not normally expected to demonstrate, particularly violently, their behaviour will be looked on as deviant, and various attempts will be made to control it. Parents and fellow students will be among those who try to exert informal controls. On the formal side attempts to control will come from the educational authorities, the government, the police, and organized public groups. These are formidable opponents for students in a country in which family controls are still very strong, and in which the police are so accustomed to handling violence of different sorts that they are prepared for any outburst.

The government, as the supreme authority of law and order, is supposed to be ready for any emergency, but the members of the government of Mysore State seem to have been startled and intimidated by the Festival strike. Student violence of this nature had never occurred in the state, and they were not prepared for it. Nor did they have much warning before the agitation began. The Minister of Education had seen two student vice-presidents and the president of a college union on Monday, December 7 and Tuesday, December 8. He had agreed that five hundred students could go to the Festival, but this did not satisfy the leaders. When the students finally had talks with other ministers at the Vidhana Soudha, they refused to declare holidays, as they said this would be interfering with the educational authorities. It is not clear why the educational authorities did not then make a decision about the matter.

On Wednesday, December 9, with the violence at its height, student hostility became intense. About fifty members of the Mysore Legislative Assembly locked themselves in the Parliamentary hostel, and dared go from there to the Legislative Assembly only in groups, in police vans, escorted by armed police. Observers believed that had they come out, faced the students, and talked reasonably with them, the trouble would have ended. Several members of the goverment did have the courage to go out later and face the mob, but their speeches were not strong enough to stop the student violence.

The situation was so serious on Thursday that the State Assembly held a six-hour debate. At this meeting profuse expressions of sympathy were made by the members to the injured students, and the Chief Minister assured them that an enquiry would be made into the police actions. However, he also said that the police had acted with restraint. The general themes of the speeches of opposition members during the debate were the imperative need for a sympathetic and rational approach to student problems, and blame for the over-zealous action of the police.

The police have long been thought of as the main enemy of the students. This antagonism is due partly to the historical role they played during the fight for independence. At that time Indians looked on them as traitors because they worked with the British, and stories are told of the way they beat the crowds with their lathis, and of their physical cruelty to the Indians who were jailed. Since then they have been held in contempt by the public in general, and by students in particular. This attitude has not been modified by their violence to students during the many years of student demonstrations. Finally, they are not highly educated—many are said to be illiterate—and they are poorly paid. There are rumours that they are often rude, drunk, and corrupt. Students have little respect for them and resent being ordered about by illiterate policemen "who cannot even read road signs."

A description by Rao in one of his novels shows how the very appearance of the police may stir the students to action.

The Principal sent a telegram to the Vice-Chancellor saying "College attacked," and hastily called for police protection. Half an hour later, four underfed, underpaid, skinny policemen in their limp khakis and pale faces arrived on the scene. Each carried a lathi in his hand. With the arrival of the guardians of order and peace, a new wave of agitation began.[16]

One of the principals in Bangalore is so well aware of this fact that, although he is supposed to report to the police immediately students begin to agitate at his college, he never does so, but manages the situation himself and then sends in a report.

The effect of the police on the students should be seen in relation to the problem of keeping order in a vast country that is going through a period of chaotic social change. Also, the prestige of the "student" is so much higher than that of other young people in all countries that the public feels he should not be handled like an ordinary criminal.

Another factor that adds to the problem is that goondas, urchins, and the rougher elements of the cities are only too ready to join any violent student behaviour. Thus, the police must handle two types of violence at the same time, with public encouragement of rough handling of criminals, but not of students.

At the time of the Youth Festival strike the police, as well as the government, were quite unprepared to cope with the student violence in such a way as to calm the participants, rather than to enrage them. They, too, had never faced such student violence and destruction, and they did not appear to have received adequate guidance from their officers. They antagonized the students on the first day of the strike, when they tried to disperse them with tear-gas shells. On Wednesday such police actions as entering the hostel of the Central College and beating the students, increased, rather than controlled, the agitation. Their behaviour on that day may have been partly due to the stoning they had received from the students on the previous day, but there seems no doubt that they acted in a brutal manner, especially toward the student who later died on the way to the hospital. His death triggered further violence. It was also one of the main reasons for the change in public opinion in favour of the students.

When goondas joined in the fighting the police had another problem on their hands. However, on Thursday, when the students dropped out and only the goondas continued to riot, the police were able to handle these familiar agitators more effectively. They gradually restored order with tear gas and "mild" lathi charges. Fifteen people were arrested.

16. Bhaskara Rao, *Candle Against the Wind*, p. 49.

Later, in the House of Assembly, members of the government said that the police had "acted with restraint." However, this was hardly the impression of the students, the lecturers, or many of the civilians.

In Mysore City the police had the same problem, but it was accentuated by the fact that they had to protect the 1,500 Youth Festival participants as well. The students engaged in even greater violence in that city, burning the gates of a women's hostel, and setting fire to the Youth Festival tents.

There is no doubt that the way in which demonstrations are handled has at least some effect, either on preventing student indiscipline from getting out of hand, or on stopping it altogether. The principals of the Mysore colleges appear to have played a rather insignificant role in the agitations. The men students seem to have by-passed their authority almost at once, and to have gone to the top state officials with their requests. A few of the women principals were able to hold their students within the college compounds, but they could not prevent destruction of college property. Many Indians have felt that if the educational authorities had taken stern measures, or been able to control the students in the early demonstrations after Independence, the students might never have gained the strength and determination to continue their agitations. Nor might their pattern of protest have spread so rapidly to all parts of India.

Public support of student rebellion, even in such subtle forms as the indirect approval parents may give it at home, makes the task of the educational authorities much more difficult. If they are certain that they are justified in stopping the indiscipline, and have the public and the government behind them, then they tend to act with more assurance. This is seen in many Roman Catholic colleges, in which discipline is strict, and the staff is at least partly composed of priests and nuns who have undergone highly disciplined training themselves. Several of these colleges have gradually learned to cope with student demonstrations through firmness and threats. A women's college in Bangalore continued to work "normally" throughout the thirty-seven days of the 1963-64 strike. This does not mean that any college could succeed in following this example, unless the basic discipline had been in existence for some time. Another Christian college, whose students played a leading role in the Youth Festival strike, had very few students in the 1963-64 strike. The reason seems to be that the Principal has become very strict in handling unrest. It is said that any of the students from this college who join strikes, or agitate in any way, are expelled. Moreover, as the college authorities insist that their students work very hard, loss of time in agitation means that students will not keep up with the class. Both of these colleges are private and so more individual initiative is left to the staff than in the government colleges.

Each principal is necessarily concerned with handling his own students. But he can do little once a student agitation has begun, as it generally proceeds along well-laid patterns. It is seldom possible to prevent the leading agitators from invading the colleges and persuading the students to leave class. There are always some students who are ready for excitement, even though they may have no interest in, or knowledge of the issue. (For example, the attempted Goa strike in 1965.) The contagion of the excitement spreads, and the more stable students may also be drawn into the demonstrations. At first it is all great fun. Released from boring lecturers, the students shout slogans, parade, and plaster posters on passing cars, tongas, scooters, or bullock-carts. It may end in the even greater release of throwing stones and damaging property. There is also the excitement of the publicity, of the crowds, and of being photographed by dozens of press photographers.

The attitude of parents to these demonstrations varies according to the aim of the strike, and to the extent to which it appears to affect their own sons and daughters. Few are actually aware of how their children behave at college. Many of them are upset by the physical conditions of the college and by the lower standards that now prevail. Also, they are often deeply concerned with the problem of getting seats for their children in the professional colleges, or with the possibility that their children may be among the large percentage of failures. But, as in other countries, their main worries are related more to the fate of their *own* children than to the educational system as such. They often support certain issues over which the students demonstrate, and may even encourage them, as in the 1963-64 Mysore strike. On the other hand, many parents forbade or tried to prevent their sons and daughters from taking part in the Youth Festival strike. There is still strong parental disapproval of much of the student indiscipline. Parents are afraid of the physical harm that their children may suffer, of the stigma of a jail sentence, of the loss of reputation for daughters who take part in behaviour which is completely unseemly in view of the traditional norms, of the loss of educational benefits if their children are penalized, and of the loss of time in preparing for the examinations.

Many of the students said that it was fear of parental disapproval that kept them out of the Youth Festival strike. Others said that their feeling of responsibility for the sacrifices their families had made to send them to college was so deep that it kept them from wasting their time in rebellious behaviour. Parental attitudes could thus be said to play a very definite role in controlling indiscipline, although parents made no move to organize formally to express their views until the 1963-64 strike.

Still another source of control over student behaviour is the sometimes vague, sometimes organized entity known as public opinion. Public opinion was completely against the students at the beginning of the Youth Festival strike. People were horrified at the student violence. The press, too, was at first against them. An early editorial in the *Deccan Herald* reads: "Student unrest has for some time been taking a dangerous form. . . . The public will strongly condemn the students for taking the law into their hands. . . . The damage to property, and injuring innocent decent people has brought disgrace to the state." (December 10, 1959.) This attitude, however, began to change, particularly after the police opened fire and killed an innocent student.

However, on the Saturday after the strike was over, the editorial of the *Deccan Herald* again spoke out against the students:

> By their outrageous behaviour, they turned themselves into a menace to public peace and created a grave situation . . . it was a disgraceful exhibition of student hooliganism. This malady of student rowdyism, which has exhibited itself during the last few weeks in many important university centres, has taken shocking form, showing scant regard for public decency and the ordinary citizens' rights. In Delhi, students have been forcibly stopping trains: they want a change in the timetable. There has been atrocious misbehaviour in Allahabad, forcing the Vice-Chancellor's resignation. And from Lucknow come reports of violent demonstrations, attacks on professors and generally "an orgy of hooliganism."
>
> The vast majority of the students are well behaved, conscientious and interested in their studies. . . . [The agitations are due to] the pernicious influence of a few "roughs."

No formally organized association sided publicly with or against the students in this strike. Voluntary organizations had little time to meet and pass resolutions, for the whole incident occurred so suddenly, and was over in such a short period of time, that public opinion had not enough time to crystallize.

It was, therefore, only the groups that were prepared to deal with crises—the government, the police, and the press—that attempted in any way to sway public opinion or to handle the situation. However, it was the "real" student leaders, who had refused to have anything to do with the strike in the first place, who did more than anyone else to control the students and restore order.

The rapid loss of influence by the students who had first instigated and led the demonstrations soon became obvious. When the crowd arrived at the Vidhana Soudha, and some members of the Legislative Assembly wanted to speak with the student leaders, no one knew who they were. When the demonstrations got completely out of hand, some of the students appealed again to the "real" leaders and begged them to take over. They did so because of the police action, and because no leadership was being shown either by the educational authorities or by the government. The chief leader lived at the Y.M.C.A., and his room became the meeting place of this group of students. It was here that they planned how to "clean up the mess."

The first thing they did was to call a mass meeting of students in Cubbon Park, a large park in close proximity to some of the leading colleges. They did so in spite of the fact that by that time all meetings had been prohibited. The students were told to go there in twos and threes and to stand somewhat apart so that they would not constitute a "meeting." Over one hundred students assembled in this way, and many more stood on the outskirts. Policemen encircled the crowd and stood among the students; and even though the students could have been arrested at any moment, they were so enraged by the killing of the student and at police brutality that their courage was high. Technically, the police could not interfere with a crowd of scattered individuals. The students later used this procedure in a procession of loosely scattered twos and threes.

At the Cubbon Park meeting a representative from each college was chosen to form a committee. The main task of this group was to negotiate with the Chief Minister, and with other important people. Even at that stage of the crisis they found it difficult to get access to government officials, but they finally managed to speak to the Chief Minister long enough to say, "You fought for freedom, and now will not see that we get it!" On hearing this, the Chief Minister immediately called them into his office for a discussion.

Later the new leaders had five thousand pamphlets printed telling their side of the story. These were distributed by students and were, to some degree, instrumental in helping to change public opinion in their favour.

Conclusions

The violence of the Youth Festival strike had two important effects on the small group of leaders who continued to be the mainstay of student organization in Bangalore. It gave them a horror of violence as an instrument for achieving their ends, and it convinced them that this was not a technique that would bring about positive results. Settling the issues gave them experience in controlling the students, negotiating with the government, and "handling" the police.

THE 1962 STRIKE

Precipitating Factor

The 1962 student strike was an important advance in organization and leadership over the Youth Festival strike. It was carried out by a newly formed Student Action Committee, was peaceful except for one incident at Shimoga, and gave the leaders a good deal more experience in directing and controlling the students. It also gave them training, both in the use of tactics for dealing with the authorities, and in methods for enlisting public opinion on their side.

The precipitating factor was the decision of the government to raise college tuition fees and reduce the number of freeships and scholarships. Rumours to this effect had been circulating for some time, so that the students were prepared for action. The Student Action Committee, which had been formed by some of the "real" leaders of the Youth Festival strike, had held a number of meetings of students before they announced, on July 23, that if the government did not abolish the scheme, they would go on strike for seven days, beginning on July 26.[17] The government made no response to this threat, so on Wednesday, July 25, the strike began.

Mobilization for Action

By Thursday the strike had spread to so many colleges that 10,000 students in Bangalore marched in a mass procession. Students from the

17. The college year begins around July 1 in most Mysore colleges.

professional colleges of law, medicine, and engineering, who were not threatened by the rise in fees, joined the procession in sympathy. Slogans shouted were "Down with the Minister of Education!" and "Vidya Mantrige Haro Hara!" The procession ended with a mass meeting at which the students resolved to continue their peaceful strike. The leaders were firm: "Any resort to violence will force us to call off the strike." The only incident in that city occurred when students entered colleges in which the students were still in class, and tried to persuade them to join the strike. Otherwise they kept their vow that the strike would remain peaceful. The girls from several co-educational colleges and from the Women's Polytechnic gave passive support to the strike. The Maharani College students picketed the college entrance, standing behind the closed gates shouting, "We want justice!" Later they went over to the Central Institute of Home Science close by and asked their sister students to join them. On Thursday, July 26, it was estimated that 1,800 of the 2,300 women students in Bangalore were abstaining from classes. The students of Mount Carmel College, however, did not respond to the appeal to strike.

By Friday it was estimated that 14,000 students were out of class. About 2,000 women students continued to picket Maharani College and the Central Institute of Home Science. A cycle squad of men students demonstrated in front of St. Joseph's College, where the students were still in class, and the authorities immediately closed the college for the day. The squad went on to Mount Carmel College, shouting slogans, but the women students again did not respond. Then they made a virtual siege on National College for about an hour, and although they made a terrible clamour by ringing their bells, and in spite of their boos and jeers, the students remained "glued to their seats." They were called names such as "blacklegs," "cowards," "bookworms," etc. When the situation finally appeared threatening, the staff allowed the students to leave class.

On Saturday still more students stayed out of class, and the Agricultural and Veterinary college students went on a three-day sympathetic strike. Girls from Maharani College and the Central Institute of Home Science picketed Pre-University College girls who tried to enter their classes, but were successful in preventing only 50 per cent of them from doing so. A group of some 2,000 students picketed some senior students who were in class and persuaded them to come out. At Vijaya College students refused to leave their classrooms, even after being addressed by student leaders, and at National and Central Colleges P.U.C. students remained in class even when booed and called "kudimis" (bookworms and weaklings). They had been warned by the authorities that they would be dismissed if they went on strike. The students of Mount Carmel and St. Joseph's College again remained in class.

On Sunday evening about 3,000 students attended a protest meeting near the Mysore Bank Square in a heavy downpour of rain. They were addressed by twenty student leaders. One of the speeches dealt with the proposed gain of Rs.4 lakhs that would be made out of the raise in fees, and which the government had said would go in part toward increasing the pay-scales of the lecturers. The speaker maintained, however, that as the government had recently demoted one hundred and eleven lecturers to the position of tutor, it looked as though the government regarded them with disfavour. Thus, the students were willing to support the hunger strike that the lecturers were planning. Another leader demanded that morning classes, which had been suspended, should be restored at one of the colleges.

On the same day, violence broke out when the Chief Minister was laying a foundation stone at the new market building in Shimoga. The function was staged by the Samyukta Yuvajana Nagarika Samiti, a local youth organization, and students. At the function the Chief Minister had advised the students to keep calm and had said that their demands would be given sympathetic consideration, but the students continued to shout slogans and demand definite assurances. Some dashed to the dais waving black flags. Others, enraged at seeing the posse of policemen with fixed bayonets outside the hall, hurled stones at the dais. They were dispersed by the police.

A second spate of stone-throwing occurred later, when the Chief Minister was on his way to Hubli. Stones were thrown at his car, and some students squatted in front of it. The police took eight students into custody. The third incident occurred when the demonstrators went to the police station to demand the release of the eight students. Police had to use their lathis to prevent the crowd from breaking into the station. Three students and three policemen were injured.

In Mysore City, where over 6,000 students abstained from classes on the first day of the strike, processions and meetings were held, and students from the Medical and Law Colleges went on sympathetic strike. Over five hundred students in Kolar, all the students from the First Grade College in Hassan, and many from the colleges in Tumkur,

Manasagangothri, and Chitradurga also went on strike on July 25. In all these places there were processions of students shouting slogans.

On Monday, July 30, the student leaders in Bangalore decided to suspend the strike for the remaining two days to enable the government to make proposals which would redress the fee situation. They also held a mass protest meeting at which the committee disowned any responsibility for the incidents of violence at Shimoga. The leaders had been deeply shocked by the violence, for they had been very proud of their peaceful record. They made a press statement to this effect.[18]

On Wednesday, August 1, after the strike had ended, the leaders announced that they had obtained their objective, namely to mobilize an awareness of the real problems of the students: "The Mysore Ad-hoc Committee rededicates itself to the pledge given to the students that it will strive with every endeavour by constitutional means to safe-guard the interests of the students. It does consider itself answerable to the student population, expecting at the same time fullest co-operation." (*Deccan Herald*, August 2, 1962.)

The students returned to class as soon as the strike was over, and all colleges were said to have normal attendance.

During the strike student leaders from Mysore and the other towns went to Bangalore several times to meet with the Central Committee. In this way they kept in very close touch and acted in unison. It was the first time that a skeleton, state-wide student organization had been formed.

The leaders later admitted that the strike was a failure, for it did not obtain its objective. They called it off because they had trusted the Chief Minister when he said that the fee structure would be reconsidered if they went back to class; because President Radnakrishnan was to visit Bangalore at that time, and a strike would not have given him a good impression of the city; and because the leaders felt that the stone-throwing at Shimoga would have repercussions throughout the state, and they might not be able to maintain the peaceful nature of the agitation. Finally, they said, "We knew that we were beaten."

18. They expressed their deep regret in a press statement. They said that the students at Shimoga had been disturbed by serious local conditions, such as the demand for an investigation into a murder, and a probe into the alleged suicide of an assistant engineer. Moreover, their student leaders had been attending a meeting in Bangalore at the time, so presumably there was no one to control them. On August 5, members of the Central Action Committee went to Shimoga at the request of the local students to study the incident.

Social Controls

The formal controls that finally broke the strike were the same as those which operated at the time of the Youth Festival strike. The government, which had been instrumental in raising the issues that led to the abstention from classes, was of course against it. Government tactics were effective in that the promise to reconsider the fee structure was the main reason that led the students to end the strike.

As the proposed raise in fees had been discussed for some time, members of the Opposition had already decided their stand on the issue when the strike began. On July 27, some of them left the Legislature in protest. That day the Minister of Education announced that the increase in fees would only affect fourteen arts, science, and commerce colleges in the old Mysore area. The professional and technical colleges would not be affected. The increase would bring in Rs.4 lakhs to the State Exchequer. Furthermore, he defended the recent fee increase because of the "compelling large expenditure" on all aspects of education.[19] He gave statistics to prove that the scale of fees in the old Mysore area had not undergone revision recently, and that the rise in fees compared favourably with the scales prevailing in Madras and Andhra States. The other object of the rise was to bring uniformity in fees to all the colleges in the state. He reiterated several times during the strike his statement that the government "would not budge an inch" in its decision with regard to fees.

There is little doubt that most members of the government were greatly relieved that the strike was carried out peacefully. They remembered the unpleasant incidents of the Youth Festival strike, and pleaded with the government to be tactful and sympathetic with the students. Perhaps the man who suffered the greatest anxiety during the

19. *Deccan Herald*, July 27, 1962. "Fees had remained unchanged for over a decade. With the government's increased commitments to compulsory primary education and more free educational concessions at the secondary level, it could not bear the high cost of college education."

Other points made were: the government now spends over Rs.175 lakhs on higher education. It would have to spend another Rs.50 lakhs if tuition fees in the old Mysore area were restored to the old level. In Madras State the per capita expenditure on college education was 40 nP, but in Mysore it was 75 nP. The government would continue to give freeships and half-freeships to the poor students in government colleges. These, together with the scholarships, would provide about 50 per cent of the students with free concessions. Thus, only 50 per cent of the students would pay the increased fees at college. Only 6,361 students out of 11,559 in fourteen government colleges were affected by the rise in fees. The other 5,198 enjoyed freeships or scholarships.

48

strike was the Mayor. On July 30, the *Deccan Herald* announced that "the most worried citizen" had spent five sleepless nights, harried by the thoughts of the anti-social elements that might creep into the agitation and endanger public property. He told a parents' meeting that electric street lamps worth Rs.2 lakhs had just been installed in the city, and he had been afraid that they might be the target of any violence that arose.

An incident that increased the student distrust of the government occurred on Saturday, July 28, when two girl students from Maharani College led a group of students to the Vidhana Soudha to see the Minister of Education. The procession was turned back by the police, but the two leaders were taken to see the Minister. He made them a "sporting" offer: the government would give girl students special concessions and would allot some of the Rs.4 lakhs raised by the increase in fees to increase the amenities for girl students, if they stopped the strike. They refused his offer.

The Chief of Police was also, undoubtedly, a "most worried man," but as there was no direct provocation in the form of violence by the students except in Shimoga, the police were not forced to play a major role in the strike. No mention was made of them in the press, but they were occasionally seen in press photographs, always on guard, and with van-loads of extra police in the offing. As the *Deccan Herald* wrote on July 29: "Thus continues the agitation—the police waiting in the shade of the trees with the wireless-equipped vans plying the streets." Perhaps they had learned a lot from the experience of the Youth Festival strike, and were wiser in keeping more in the background.

It is quite possible that all the parents whose children were affected by the proposed increase in fees, or would be in the near future, were in favour of the student demonstration, and it is quite likely that many of the students were encouraged by their parents at home. However, on the whole the public utterances of the parents were moderate and emphasized that *they* were the ones who should be dealing with the problem, not the students. So they were partly encouraging, partly discouraging.

The first public action of the parents occurred on Monday, July 30, when the Mahila Vibhag of the Mysore Pradesh Congress Committee called a meeting of parents. The Mayor, women legislators, and corporation councillors attended the meeting. Mothers attended in larger numbers than fathers. After commending the peaceful way in which

49

the students had conducted their demonstrations, the parents appealed to them to call off the strike immediately. They passed a four-part resolution: (*a*) As the responsibility for solving this problem fell on the parents and not on the students, the parents would attend to the matter. (*b*) A committee would be set up to meet with the Chief Minister and Minister of Education. (*c*) A permanent fund should be established to help poor students. (*d*) A standing committee of parents should be organized to act as a liason between teachers and students, and to look after the well-being of the students at all stages of their education.

The next parental action mentioned in the press occurred on July 31, when a delegation went to ask the Student Action Committee to call off the strike unconditionally.

After the strike, on August 11, a representative group of forty parents met with the Minister of Education. They told him that this meeting would never have taken place had the students not stirred them by their demonstrations. They said that the proposed fee increase was too high and too sudden, particularly in view of rising prices. Compensation should be given to all students whose parents' income was under Rs.3,600 per annum. They also said that the rise would have a particularly adverse effect on girls' education, as there would not be enough money to cover it, as well as that of their sons. If the fees were raised, the Rs.4 lakhs gained should be distributed in freeships and scholarships to poor students.

The Minister of Education replied that the rise was aimed mainly at bringing about a uniformity in fees throughout the state. He stressed the point that the government would make sure all students with merit went to college. However, he reiterated his statement that the government would not go back to the former fee level.

On the same day the Ad Hoc Committee of the Bangalore Students' Association called a convention of parents and guardians to back their demands. They also planned to launch a state-wide signature campaign in support of their cause, and copies of the mass memoranda were to be sent to the state government, the President of India, and the Union Home Ministry. Spokesmen refuted the suggestion that the issue was one to be thrashed out by the government and parents, instead of by the students, although they appreciated the fact that parents were wholly in sympathy with their demands.

When the Parents' and Guardians' Convention met, it passed a resolution rejecting the rise in fees. It said that in a welfare state, fees, instead of being raised, should be reduced gradually to the point where all education is free, and the aim should be free higher education for all whose incomes are below Rs.3,600 per annum. It also decided to form a state-wide parents' organization to look after the interests of the students. Urging the students to discontinue their agitation and leave the matter to them, the parents offered to represent them before the Chief Minister and the Minister of Education.

This second strike, then, roused a feeling of responsibility in a wider number of people. Opposition members of parliament, parents, and some organized groups publicly expressed their concern and suggested remedies.

The opposition parties were able not only to make their support of the students' position clear in the Legislative Assembly, but also to make public statements. The President of the Jan Sangh party and the Karnataka Communist party publicly supported the students' peaceful protest. On July 28, a non-political organization, the Akhil Bharat Sarva Seva Sangh, offered its services to bring about a settlement.

The press, too, gave advice. In an editorial in the *Deccan Herald* on July 27, the students were asked to act with restraint. They were told that they were mistaken in thinking that picketing and other "objectionable agitational tactics" would make an impression on the authorities. They would only harm themselves by organizing abstention from classes. Instead they should tackle the problem by constitutional means and let their parents, public organizations, and the people's representatives settle it.

On July 29, the same paper praised the students for their conduct during the strike: "Whether the striking students achieve their objective or not they have gained a big victory—unanimous is the reaction of the public, the Government and the parents that their conduct has been praiseworthy." On July 31, the *Deccan Herald* came out strongly against the "shocking" incidents at Shimoga. It deplored the fact that some of the students had resorted to violence in spite of their assurances that their demonstrations would be peaceful. It said that picketing, mass processions, and public demonstrations constitute an open invitation to the enemies of law and order to exploit the situation for their own purposes, and no government with any sense of responsibility could allow itself to be cowed by violence.

It is quite possible that the forceful way in which the press voiced its opinion was influential in strengthening the resolution of the student leaders that peaceful methods of protesting were much more influential than violent ones.

Conclusions

In comparison with the Youth Festival strike, the 1962 strike was more carefully planned and carried out. The group of leaders who formed the Student Action Committee had had a good deal of experience; the issue touched many of the students directly, and it also touched the interests of parents who might also hold formal positions in organizations.

Meetings were held before the strike was declared, so that most of the students would be ready to act. Meetings were also held in different parts of Bangalore every day, during which the morale of the students was upheld and the latest information circulated. At each one of these the students were warned of the necessity of keeping the demonstrations peaceful.

There was co-ordination of action between the colleges of the various cities and towns in the state, and the students managed to get public opinion on their side, as well as the sympathy of the press. They co-operated with the government in suspending the strike early, in order to enable the government to make new proposals to redress the situation. Immediately the strike was over the students returned to their classes.

THE 1963-64 STRIKE

Precipitating Factors

The third important student strike in Mysore State began on December 12, 1963, and lasted until January 17, 1964. This was the longest, the best organized, the most peaceful strike that the students had ever carried out; it was completely successful in that the students finally achieved their aim. The leaders had spent the previous four months preparing for it and had laid their plans carefully. The support of students from the mofussil colleges was co-ordinated through a Central Student Action Commitee. The strike was so successful that it did much to convince both the students and the public that students were capable of handling their own affairs.

The revised fee scale, which raised tuition fees by about Rs.54, was put into effect at the beginning of the college year in July 1963.[20] The number of freeships and half freeships was also reduced, in spite of the assurance given the students in 1962 that they would be increased, and that the fee scale would be reconsidered. This failure of the government to live up to its promises was one of the main reasons that the strike continued until the government had publicly announced a reinstatement of the old fee scale on January 17. This failure also accounted for the fact that the leaders would not trust the government's assurances early in January that their requests would be given most sympathetic consideration if the strike were called off.

The precipitating factors of this strike, then, were the rise in tuition fees, the reduction in concessions to students, and the leaders' lack of faith in the government. The students demanded the reduction of tuition fees to the level existing in 1960-61, and stipulated that the percentage of freeships and scholarships should remain the same—30 per cent for men students, 50 per cent for women students. They also wanted adequate canteen facilities for the National Cadet Corps students, and the abolition of Part IV in the degree classes.

Tensions over these issues had been rising for some years, and the student body was thus prepared for action.

Mobilization for Action

The 1963-64 strike lasted long enough to emphasize some of the problems faced by the leaders in keeping the demonstrations peaceful, and

20. A press note in the *Deccan Herald* (January 17, 1964) gives this account of the government's determination to raise fees: "The Resources and Economy Committee appointed by the Government had recommended that the low scale of tuition fees in Government educational institutions in Mysore be raised to those prevailing in the State of Madras. One reason for this was that the Government Colleges in Coorg, South Kanara and Bellary, although affiliated with the University of Mysore, were charging higher fees in comparison to the other colleges. So a revised scale of fees was put into effect in the academic year of 1962-63."

Representations of students protested against these raises. The Educational Minister then announced some concessions, one being that students whose parents' income was Rs.3,600 per annum or below should be given a concession to the extent of fifty per cent of the fee increase, but only for the period 1962-63. After that the revised tuition fee would be collected from all students, from the period 1963-64 on.

Fee Scale		1960-61	1963-64
P. U. C. Students	*Arts*	Rs 90	Rs 144
	Science	90 (+ 27 lab fee)	144 + 10
	Commerce	90	144
Degree Courses	*B.A.*	126	184 + 12
	B.Sc.	126 (+ 36 lab fee)	184
	B.Com.	126	184
	M.A.	144	256
	M.Sc.	144 + 45	256 + 15

the morale of the students high. Maintaining an orderly strike is particularly difficult when the participants are young, impulsive, and inexperienced, and when the group membership changes rather rapidly. The type of leader who will be most effective in such a situation is one who has charismatic qualities, for student organizations do not usually retain the same membership over a long enough period of time for strong leadership personalities to evolve.

The student leadership in the 1963 strike was very different from that of the Youth Festival strike. The leaders were better trained for the job. A few of them had been the "real" leaders who had brought the Youth Festival strike under control and had also led the 1962 strike.

Seven of the fifteen-member Central Student Action Committee that was formed on December 11 were law students. They knew each other well, and had worked together on other projects. It was not difficult for them to recruit the remaining eight members from among the leading students of the Bangalore colleges, but they had to be very sure of the integrity of these recruits, as several of them were offered bribes to stop the strike. All the members of the committee were graduate students. All had gained experience in leadership through their participation in student or other organizations. One of the leaders had been Secretary of the Law College Union, the most powerful student position in Bangalore. They were all good debaters who could effectively arouse enthusiasm among the students. Some felt that their studies of mob psychology at college had helped them to understand how to handle these large groups of students.

The issues of the strike did not affect them personally as they were all well enough off to be unconcerned about a rise in fees.[21] In any case the raise in tuition fees did not affect the professional colleges. None of the leaders received freeships or scholarships, so a reduction in these benefits would not affect them. Thus, their interest in the strike did not arise from any thought of personal gain. Instead, it seemed to stem

21. The Law College in Bangalore is a private college, so it can have higher fees than it would if it were a government college. This means that it tends to attract students who are well off. Only a very small percentage of the students (one estimate is 1 per cent) takes up law as a career after graduating. Most go into the civil service, for a law graduate starts at a higher level there, and so many of the examinations and steps to promotion are eliminated. This means that students who study law are not necessarily dedicated to the profession. They usually have their afternoons free, and want diversion. Organizing students not only fills this need but also gives them the benefit of publicity. Thus, they are often found in the forefront of student activities.

On the other hand, graduate students at Central College in Bangalore seldom lead demonstrations, for, as they will pursue careers in the fields they are studying, they do not want to waste their time. Moreover, leadership in strikes would only threaten their careers, not help them.

54

from two sources. In the first place some of them were concerned about the hardships that a rise in fees would cause many of the students. But it is not likely that even the socially conscious leaders would have given up so much of their time and energy if they, like the rest of the Central Action Committee, did not enjoy the excitement and satisfactions of leadership. Most of them hoped that the publicity they would receive would at least help them to get elected to an executive position in a student's union, or bring them to the attention of one of the political parties.[22] For the latter have their eyes on student leaders, as college is an excellent training place for future politicians. The interest of most of the leaders in this strike was thus only partly related to their interest in student problems.

The leaders had gone around to the different mofussil colleges, when the strike appeared imminent, and had discussed it with those on whom they thought they could rely. Then they selected one student from each district to be on the Mysore State Student Action Committee.

Mr. X, the student who played the leading role in the strike, had begun his apprenticeship early in his college career. He had been one of the "backroom" leaders who had eventually brought order out of the chaos of the Youth Festival strike. He had refused to assume leadership in that strike when appealed to, as he did not believe that it was a "realistic" cause. If students wanted to attend the Festival, why should they not just go off and see it without making an issue of it and striking? However, when the situation got completely out of hand he stepped in, with a number of the other "real" leaders, and helped to restore order. He had also taken a leading part in the July 1962 strike. These two strikes gave him a great deal of experience in dealing with the students, the educational authorities, the government, and the police. His appreciation of basic issues, his astuteness in sizing up situations, his charismatic leadership, and his imagination in regard to tactics were the main reasons for the success of the strike.

The Central Student Action Committee decided at once that there would be no hierarchy of command—no president, secretary, or other formal offices—for they did not want any factions to arise. All were to be equal, and each was to be in charge of a different aspect of the demonstration. Each meeting was presided over by a different member

22. Rao, p. 135. This novel shows how students recognize the steps that can be taken at college towards a political career: "This would make them a leader among the students and from there it was possible to get into politics, travel around the country, and acquire power."

of the committee. As the strike wore on, the members who had shown themselves to be trouble-makers, or who were losing their morale, were made to preside or speak at meetings, or were given other jobs which would both keep them busy and give them responsibilities that would renew their identification with the group. The secret meeting place of the leaders was in the Central College Hostel.

The leaders worked tirelessly, getting little sleep and little food because of the irregular demands of their work. Sometimes they held nine or ten meetings a day. In addition to organizing the infinite number of details concerned with the tactics of the agitation, they had to travel continuously, not only around the city colleges, but also to those in the mofussil, to keep all the students closely in touch with the movement. When they travelled to the mofussil colleges, it was always at their own expense. They seldom got to bed before 2:00 a.m. and were at work again at 5:00 a.m. As the strike wore on, the hard work and anxiety began to tell on the committee members. Quarrels multiplied and tempers became frayed. It even got to the point where members would "fly at each others' throats" at the committee meetings. This inner dissent was more wearing on them than their struggle to maintain student morale and enthusiasm, yet they managed to contain their disagreements and present a constantly united front before the students and the public. With very few exceptions, the student body maintained complete confidence in the leaders and their decisions, in spite of the fact that two of the leaders were thought to be Communists and were watched suspiciously by the others.

The strain on the leaders during the strike can be illustrated by Mr. X. He was completely dedicated to the cause and mentioned several occasions on which he had been willing to die for his beliefs. Although technically a law student, he was also working as a clerk in a bank. From 5:30 to 10:00 o'clock each morning he would tour the city in the committee taxi, meet students, arrange details of procedure, and attend committee meetings. From 10:15 until 5:30 he had to be at work. Then, at 5:30 he would speak at one of the mass meetings of students, for he was a popular speaker, and much in demand. Perhaps he would also meet with the Citizen's Committee or with members of the government. After the public events were over, the Central Student Action Committee would meet for several hours. These meetings were never over before 12:00 or 1:00 o'clock. By that time all restaurants would be closed, so that there was no chance of getting a meal. Mr. X lived mainly on tablets and tea for the thirty-seven days. He was labelled a Communist by outsiders as well as by members of the Committee, although he was a Socialist. His bank tried to victimize him, but was prevented from doing so by his co-workers, who were in sympathy with the strike.

Toward the end of the strike the leaders had the uneasy feeling that the students were becoming demoralized. They themselves were exhausted, and many of them were hoarse from public speaking. Mr. X said in an interview that the leaders could not have gone on much longer, and that he was amazed that they had been able to withstand the strain for as long as they did. He found the experience unforgettable, and said that he probably would never go through anything quite like it again.

The Mysore State Student Action Committee continued to function for a short time after the strike and then disbanded. Leaders who were interviewed were confident that, although there was no continuing organization among the students of the different colleges, should a new emergency occur, leaders would arise from the student ranks who would be able to carry on another successful strike.

The leaders of a strike face many problems. In the first place there is the difficulty of timing the demonstrations so that the potenial participants are ready to take part, and so that the general situation in which the strike is to occur promises some hope of success. Then there is the need to mobilize the participants. This is particularly difficult if they do not form part of a tightly organized group. In the case of the 1963-64 strike the leaders were able to unite students from many scattered colleges into a tight enough unit to make the movement successful. Another problem is establishing an efficient communication system. This is necessary, for misleading rumours must not be allowed to develop, and participants must be well informed on the tactics to be used and on the stage negotiations have reached. Conduct must be kept orderly so that demonstrations do not get out of hand. The leaders of the 1963-64 strike believed that they would never achieve their ends unless the demonstrations remained peaceful, but they had to contend with the excitable nature of students once they began to agitate. They also had to contend with the problem of previous records of violence, of the typical intrusion of goondas into the "fun," and the possible provocation of the police. Keeping student morale at a high level creates another difficulty, especially when some of the students fear that their participation might result in the end of their college careers. The sympathy of the public must be retained. Finally, tactics must be used which will force the government to yield to student demands.

The first problem in mobilizing the students for action was that of timing—to know when to demonstrate. It has already been noted that the "real" student leaders did not think the issue of holidays a serious enough one for agitation at the time of the Youth Festival. They did not consider it a problem that would appeal to enough of the students, and they did not think it was basic enough to their needs to make them unite. However, in July 1962 and December 1963, the issue of raising tuition fees was clearly of great importance, both to the students and to their parents. Had the raise gone into effect, a number of students would have had to leave college, and countless potential students would have been denied a higher education. As many of the public officials, merchants, and lecturers were also parents or guardians, it was evident that the students would receive sympathetic support from many quarters. The timing of the strike was sound in that the public had been stirred up over the issue for a long time and was ready for action. Agitation actually began in a mofussil college in Hassan, the same place in which the 1962 strike had begun. The unrest spread from there to other towns and cities. On December 11, the Central Student Action Committee was formed, and it announced that the strike would begin on December 12.

The second problem of the leaders was to mobilize the students. Student demonstrations have usually begun in Bangalore, in the Law College, Central College or the College of Commerce. The students of St. Joseph's College were said to have initiated the Youth Festival strike. Since then disicipline has tightened, and few students from that college are now prominent in agitations. The first three of the above-mentioned colleges are close enough to each other to enable word of impending demonstrations to travel swiftly from one to the other. Moreover, the first two colleges are strategically located on the borders of the symbolic protest centre—the Mysore Bank Square.

A description of the way in which students were induced to join the 1962 strike will illustrate the method commonly used at the beginning of an agitation.

Leader X: After we had decided to strike we announced that it would begin on the next day. We had to inform the students, so I went early at 7:30 to the Law College, when the first morning classes were beginning.

I knew that if I could get the first batch of students out, the next classes would follow.

I went into a class and the professor told me to get out. We had a loud argument. I said, "Let the students decide whether they will listen to me or not. This is a matter that affects them all, and they have the right to decide!" Finally he agreed to give me five minutes, after the Principal of the college had addressed them. So the Principal spoke first and told them that they should not agitate as the proposed raise in fees did not affect them. Then I spoke. I told them that it was all very well for the law students, we would not be affected by the raise. We were well off and could afford our education. But a raise in fees would mean that hundreds of poor students simply would not get an education.

They agreed to walk out with me, and we went across the street to Central College, and then to the Government Arts and Science College, across the street from Central College, and all the students came out. We were completely unprepared for the large numbers who left class. Soon we had about 10,000 students to deal with, and absolutely no equipment. What could we do? We divided them into three groups in the Central College Compound, and a few of us addressed each group.

We had no money, so we collected funds from them. Then we could print pamphlets, and get loud speakers and other equipment to keep the strike going.

The Principal of a women's college described how the leaders of the Action Committee influenced her students to leave class in the 1963 strike.

My students give very little trouble because they are kept busy with many practical courses in the home science degree, and because I tell them that it is a great waste of time to agitate, and that they may get into serious trouble if they do.

The last few years we have had a "chapel" period at the beginning of the day. One girl will say a prayer, another read an item of news, tell of some important person's life, or give a short speech. I had thought that this period had made quite a difference in our relations. It had made us all feel closer to each other.

But one day when we were in Chapel a young man suddenly appeared on the platform beside me. I had no idea who he was or why he was there. He never spoke to me but began haranguing the students in a very emotional way: "Sisters, join us! We are fighting for your cause—we need your help!" After he had been talking for just a few minutes, nearly all the girls just got up and followed him! They went over to join the other women students across the road. It was so funny to see them disappear so suddenly!

59

In spite of the fact that the issue was one that affected all the students, and that the leaders were dynamic speakers, completely convinced of their cause, rounding up all the students was a lot of work.

Leader X: Each student had to be convinced. When we explained the issues they would understand. But we had to go around to every college. The girls were the hardest to convince because the principals of the women's colleges were very strict, and were against us. I knew a lot of the girls because we had all been in the Indo-American Association so that I was able to convince them, and, through them, the others.

The abstention from classes was thus not a spontaneous mass exit, but rather a gradual movement. Lecturers in some of the more remote colleges said that it was about five days before they were aware that the strike was serious. During that time their students were in a state of confusion; some had heard that the strike had begun, others that it had not. Some wanted to join, others wanted to stay in class.

The third problem was to maintain meaningful communication with the students. In 1963 this involved keeping in touch with about 45,000 students from all parts of the state. As there was little money to spend on equipment, the main device used was the grapevine. In a city the size of Bangalore, with few telephones and an inadequate transportation system, the student grapevine is extraordinarily effective. This is evident from the fact that students from the centrally located colleges always agitate before word or influence or pressure affects those from the more distantly located institutions. Its effectiveness was shown in the Youth Festival strike: students would announce publicly the location of a meeting, and when the police arrived at that place, they would find it empty. They would hear later that the students had had a widely attended meeting in another part of the city.

Bicycles were used by the students to spread news of a strike. In the 1963 strike, the Action Committee was able to afford the services of a taxi (equipped with a loud-speaker) which they drove around the city announcing meetings, and giving news of the latest developments.

Daily processions and mass meetings held in different parts of the city were the main means of mobilizing the laggard students and of keeping them enthusiastic and informed. They were also the means by which the leaders constantly emphasized that the demonstrations were to remain peaceful, and that the strike would continue until their demands were met. In a tense situation it was inevitable that rumours unsympathetic to the strikers would be circulated. But the leaders were able to keep the enthusiasm of the students at a high level, and at the same time, to maintain discipline over their behaviour.

The fourth, and perhaps most difficult problem for the leaders was the keeping of order. The Youth Festival strike seems to have lost control of its actions for two main reasons: the leadership was weak and inexperienced, and the students who joined the strike were, for the most part, those who wanted to have some pleasure and excitement. Very few of those taking part had the support of their parents, and there was no open public acceptance of the strike.

The leaders of the 1963 strike were much more experienced and were in earnest about making it a success. They were convinced that the only way that they could win was to keep the agitation peaceful; they were aware of how easily violence could start, and how quickly the movement could get out of hand. At the beginning Leader X declared that the Vidhana Soudha would be out-of-bounds for the students because it symbolized government resistance. When students had congregated there during other agitations, rumours would circulate quickly among them that the ministers were ignoring them. Then they would "almost automatically" pick up stones, and violence would begin. The Maharini College was also a place where disturbances could easily start because of the "Roadside Romeos" who hung around the gates. Other "bad elements" also roamed the adjacent streets, ready for trouble, so that this area also was declared out-of-bounds. The Action Committee also decided that if the women students wanted to agitate, they must do so in their own compounds. The committee would not allow them to join in the public processions, for this might be a provocation to the goondas, or to the "Roadside Romeos." Moreover, the public might not approve of girls taking public action, and it was essential to keep the public on the side of the students.

The leaders also refused to allow any outside interests to capitalize on the student agitation. Several political parties tried indirectly to benefit from these situations by offering, publicly, sympathy and support, but the leaders refused to accept money from them, or even to allow their members to speak at the public meetings.

Finally, a "vigilance" group of some nine hundred volunteer students was organized, and they maintained order during the processions and meetings. A number of them were armed with whistles so that they could control the traffic as well, when necessary. The leaders knew that there was much less likelihood of incidents occurring if students, instead of the police, handled the situations.

A very sympathetic Chief of Police probably helped a great deal in keeping the strike orderly. He managed to get the complete confidence of the leaders, and the "vigilant" group worked well with him and with the other police.[23]

During the thirty-seven days of tension there were only two minor incidents that were not peaceful. On December 19, during a large procession, some students surrounded a man wearing a "Gandhi" hat (a symbol of the Congress party) for half an hour until he removed it. Near the end of the strike there was a small incident of stone-throwing at Tumkur, which the Mysore State Student Action Committee loudly condemned and repudiated.

The fifth problem was that of maintaining the morale of the strikers. This was accomplished by daily meetings, by processions during which slogans were shouted, by postcard campaigns in which all the students were asked to flood the Chief Minister's office with cards, and by the careful handling of rumours.

Some of the leaders did not approve of using undignified methods, such as shouting defamatory slogans about members of government, but they knew that they were useful for rousing the students for action and maintaining their enthusiasm. The local press was co-operative in assisting the students to keep the issue in front of the public. The publicity they gave the strike was one of the main incentives in moving students to participate in hunger strikes, for the names of those fasting were recorded, and photographs of the participants were published. The strike received international notice in some of the important foreign publications.

Leader X did not want the students to go on hunger strikes, for he thought this was rather cheap publicity; he said that the students were hungry enough without starving themselves further. However, the hunger strike had been one of the main symbols of protest in India, and was so widely used that it was inevitable that the students would want to follow it. Only students who were carefully screened by the committee were permitted to fast. On December 22 the first four students went on a 48-hour hunger strike in front of the Vidhana Soudha. Two of them were members of the Action Committee, for they had reason

23. The Chief of Police restored their confidence after rumours had circulated that some people had tried to get the police to start trouble with the students so that their discipline would be undermined.

to believe that one of the other fasting students, the son of a member of the government, might have been induced to participate in order to break his fast, and so bring disgrace on the students. The committee insisted on changing the hunger strikers every forty-eight hours, for should they fast longer, the police had the legal right to feed them forcibly. Members of the committee said that fasting was not too difficult for them, for they were used to going without food when doing committee work, but the cold was very difficult to bear. The strikes took place during the coldest part of the winter, when the temperature often dropped down to 45 degrees (Fahrenheit) at night. The police would not allow the students tents or any other shelter. This was a new attitude to hunger strikers, for tents had always been allowed on previous occasions. Fellow students were also prevented from bringing them water from a nearby tap. Two of the members of the Action Committee continued to fast with each batch of students who followed the first hunger-strikers, in order to be on hand if any trouble arose. The hunger strikes brought the students a great deal of public sympathy. Hundreds of people came to see them and pressed as close as they could to sympathize with the students. Several photographs in the local newspapers showed these pathetic students, wrapped in shawls and blankets. One group had a bust of Mahatma Gandhi and portraits of great Hindu religious leaders and of the former President Kennedy for company. When women students joined them later, they brought a portrait of Mahatma Gandhi's mother with them.

After about fifteen days the hunger strikers in Bangalore were joined by five women students. Two of these were graduate students; the others were from Maharani College. The leaders had not wanted them to fast, but they insisted that the cause of the strike was just as much theirs as it was that of the men students. Women students had gone on a hunger strike several days before in Shimoga. It was completely revolutionary for women to fast publicly; in fact it was probably the first time that women had ever gone on hunger strikes in India, or perhaps in the world. They encountered many difficulties, including opposition from the authorities of the women's college in whose compound they had decided to fast. One of the first women to go on strike described her experiences.

As we two graduates had been students at Maharani College we thought it all right if we fasted there, but the Principal would not allow us to stay in the compound, and said that if we wanted to do such a silly thing we

63

should "go and join the boys in front of the Vidhana Soudha." So we went there, and although the police were very gentle with us, we were forced to sit in a certain spot, some distance from the boys who were on strike. We were each given twelve blankets, but it was so bitterly cold at night that we could not sleep. They would not allow us a tent, nor any other shelter, and there were very heavy mists in the early mornings, so that we got very wet. My sister tried to hold an umbrella over me to protect me when I became ill, but they sent her away. In the daytime it was terribly hot. At first we were near a small shrub, and that gave a little shelter, but they moved us away from it. We were so far away from the boys that we could not talk to them at night, so the two of us were alone in the dark. The policemen would come and tell us stories of all the snakes in the bushes, or ghost stories, or tales of people who had been murdered or sacrificed in that place.

My mother didn't know that I was going on strike. She is an old lady, and I think that if she had come near the place, particularly when I took ill, I couldn't have carried the fast through. My sister, an advocate, was allowed to come to see me after she had insisted that she must see me as I was ill, but she was not much help as she disapproved of my fast.

Huge crowds of people came to see us. They were kept at a distance by the police, but I could see that many of the older women were crying. The crowd on the whole seemed very sympathetic, but some of them edged up as close as they could and threw wrappers from chocolate bars near us, to make it look as though we had broken our fast!

I had not been eating too well before the strike, as my husband was away, and I had been very nervous about it all for some days. I think it was that, and the fasting, that made me ill. After a little while I kept vomiting continuously. The Action Committee wanted their doctor to see me, but the police insisted that their own doctor should attend to me. He gave me pills, but I could not swallow them as it would have meant breaking my fast. We were allowed water, but they had put salt in it, and it was very hard to swallow.

A lecturer who went to the Vidhana Soudha when the girls were fasting said that the "tension" of the people was terrifying. He thought that any slight incident would have precipitated violence among them.

After the first two girls had finished their fast in front of the Vidhana Soudha, the Chief of Police persuaded the Principal of Maharani College to allow the next batch of girls to fast in the college compound, as he was afraid of what might happen to them if the crowd got out of hand at the Vidhana Soudha. However, the girls were even more isolated and alone at night in the college compound. There were no boy hunger-strikers nearby for company, and the compound was large, with many trees and bushes and no lights. Women constables from the railway police were sent to stay with the girls, but they were so cold, and so afraid of "ghosts" that they slept in the classrooms and left the girls pretty much alone. The girls were haggard from their sleepless nights, although they had been selected very carefully for stamina by the leaders of the Action Committee. The Principal was not encouraging. When some of the women lecturers stayed as late as they could in the evening and returned to college as early as they could in the morning, so that they would be near the girls for as long as possible, the Principal indicated that she was not pleased. When they went to inquire about the girls' health, or did not take anything to eat themselves in the canteen, as they could not bear to when the girls were hungry, the Principal resented these actions, and implied that all sympathy with them should stop. Nor would she allow the students to sit with them, take them magazines, or sing to them to help pass the time. It was reported that she visited the girls late at night and told them that there were snakes, ghosts, and "demons" about. She argued that it was cold, and suggested to the girls that they spend the night in the classroom, or go home with her to her warm house. Better still, she said, she would see that they got safely home in a car. When these tactics did not succeed, she asked the lecturers to keep watch over the girls to make sure that they did not break their fast on the sly.

At Mysore the girls who went on hunger strikes received more sympathetic treatment. Both the Vice-Chancellor and the Principal of the Women's College visited them repeatedly to see that they received water, that their health was good, and that they were not too cold. In addition to this, the girls were allowed tents.

On January 13 the Action Committee announced that an undisclosed number of students would go on an indefinite hunger strike, from 5:00 p.m. on Tuesday, in nine districts of the state. At that time there were ninety-one students fasting in front of the Vidhana Soudha, and by January 15, there were one hundred and six.

At the daily mass meetings, both in Bangalore and in the surrounding towns, the students were continuously reminded that the agitation *must* remain peaceful. The original issues of the strike were always repeated, and new educational problems were added to the list of grievances. Reports were also made on the progress of negotiations with the government.

The leaders were aware that the students were young and not too well versed in educational matters. They therefore kept the issues on a

65

very simple, clear level, for they thought that if the students knew too much, or began to think too deeply, differences of opinion might arise among them. Thus, the main issues of the strike were repeated day after day in black-and-white terms.

At the daily processions, usually preceding or following the meeting, new slogans which typified the situation at the moment were taught to the students. When the strike first began, the slogan "We want justice" was widely used, but this gave way to "Down with Kanthi," when the Minister of Education failed to listen to the students' demands.

By December 17, the leaders realized that the students in the mofussil colleges were getting so emotionally roused that they might get out of hand; so in order to relieve local tensions that might have flared into violence, they decided to organize jathas of students to walk to Bangalore from their respective towns to join in a mammoth procession in that city on December 20. This was a strategic move, for it not only allowed the students to release their frustrations in an exciting mass demonstration, but also gave a spectacular slant to the agitations. The endurance of the students on their long treks—they would not accept any lifts—and their sacrifices in undertaking them, would make a deep impression on the other students, as well as on the public. It would prove, along with the fasting, that the students were willing to suffer for their cause. The jathas of students set out, some walking the whole distance, others coming to within thirty or forty miles of Bangalore by bus and walking the rest of the way. The students from Mysore walked the whole eighty-six miles to the city. They were met by students and sympathisers along the way, who would walk with them until they were joined by more sympathisers. They arrived "beaten with fatigue" in Bangalore on December 20, some barefoot, most with swollen feet. Several had fainted from exhaustion along the way. In spite of this they insisted on marching, and after being garlanded by the Bangalore students, they spearheaded the mass procession.

This procession had been very carefully planned. Thousands of students marched in it, and it was so long that it took twenty-five minutes to pass any one spot. It had been well publicized, and the students had induced the Chamber of Commerce, many of the merchants' associations, and the labour organizations to see that the city kept complete hartal. Shops, restaurants, cinemas, and hotels all closed, and the workers and clerks became part of the audience. The hartal was so complete that the students found it difficult to get food or drinks when the procession was over.

The parade began at 11:00 a.m. Five hundred cyclists formed a vanguard and rearguard. Next came the students from the mofussil colleges to keep order. They were recruited from the different colleges so that they would know the students and keep any "anti-social elements" from joining the parade. They also regulated traffic. No student was allowed to carry a stick, or anything that might lead to trouble. The students marched five to fifteen deep along the main streets of Bangalore. They carried banners and placards with original inscriptions and caricatures. As they marched they shouted "deafening" slogans, cheered wildly, whistled, and clapped. Some groups danced part of the way, timing their steps to the rhythm of the slogans. The procession covered twelve miles in four hours. The Chief of Police personally supervised the procession, and later he praised the students' orderly behaviour.

A few days earlier a number of high school pupils had gone on strike, and had organized their own "Action Committee of Mysore State High School Students." They wanted free education and the exemption, for a six-year period, of Hindi as an examination subject. They also demanded that the boards of private colleges be ordered to stop collecting money from the students for buildings and equipment. On the day of the mammoth procession the high schools were empty, and the pupils formed their own procession. They marched to Cubbon Park, the goal of the students' procession. The Chief of Police notified the college leaders as they approached the park, and they stopped their procession in front of Mahatma Gandhi's statue to avoid becoming involved in any trouble that might be fomented by the high school pupils.

By this time the high school procession had got out of hand, and the pupils had begun pelting stones at the restaurant in the park, and breaking street lights. The estimated cost of the lights that were broken was Rs.2,000. The pupils then roamed about the city, accompanied by a "liberal sprinkling of street urchins," stoning buses and more street lights. Had the college students mixed with them, they might have joined in the stone-throwing, or been blamed for the damage. The student leaders were convinced that the high school students had been urged to demonstrate that day to tempt the college students into trouble.

That night the college students held a huge public meeting attended by 30,000 students and citizens.

Other tactics were used to encourage the students to continue the strike. Telegrams were sent to Prime Minister Nehru, the Chief Minister, and other ministers of the state to tell them of the students' demands. Leaflets were distributed to parents, urging them to write to the Chief Minister to ask him to reduce the fees to the old level.

The elaborate organization of the strike cost money. At first this came from the students, who went without meals or coffee to donate to the central fund. Soon money began to come in from other sources. Many people gave anonymously. No funds were accepted from organized groups, for fear of their influence, the one exception being the Cricket Association, which did not personify any harmful vested interest. In addition to donating funds, this association allowed students to collect money for the strike at their popular winter matches. Students also collected from passers-by, as they marched in processions. On the day of the big procession, even labourers donated as much as a day's wage, so strongly did they believe in the students' cause. The leaders estimated that the Central Committee in Bangalore spent Rs.10,000 on the strike, and that Rs.50,000 was spent in the state. Scrupulous accounts were kept and publicized.

In the 1963-64 strike, complete co-operation was established for the first time among the students of all the non-professional colleges of Mysore University. The leaders went into Bangalore often to consult with the Central Action Committee. They were warned not to believe or trust any rumours, but to take their information directly from the committee. They kept in touch by telephone, by telegram, and through members of the Central Committee who were always willing to travel out to address student meetings or consult with the local committee.

The strike began in Mysore City on December 14. The town hall maidan is the symbolic meeting-place in that city. In the other towns the students usually met in the grounds of the district offices. On the third day of the strike, women students from the Maharani and Manasayangothi Colleges joined the agitations in Mysore. They seem to have been much more venturesome and daring than the women students in Bangalore, for they joined in the men's processions and attended public meetings.

On January 7 they held a separate procession of their own and then joined a joint meeting with the men students. At this gathering they vowed to keep their tresses "untied and unkempt" until the end of the strike, and one of the leaders said that each girl would be an "irrate Draupadi" who would not rest until the government gave in. This announcement was greeted with "thunderous applause." On January 11 four of the girls went on a 48-hour hunger strike, as the committee would not allow them to fast indefinitely. The same day the girls declared that they would not wear slippers until the strike was over. On January 14, they spearheaded a procession of 10,000 students, most of whom were walking barefoot.

In the meantime, the men students had also been making sacrifices. On December 31, they had decided to go through the ordeal of growing "diksha" (beards) until their demands were met. They, too, went on hunger strikes early in the agitations. By January 7, ten post-graduate students were on a token 24-hour hunger strike, and the fifth batch of ten students had begun a 48-hour strike. As had been the case in Bangalore, each move of the government to discredit the student protest was met with renewed demonstrations.

Students from the professional colleges also encouraged the strikers by going on sympathetic token strikes and marching in some of the processions.

On January 11, three men students began a fast to the death. On January 13, 590 student volunteers controlled the "Mysore City bandh." This took the form of a mammoth procession and a completely successful city-wide hartal. Not only did the commercial houses close, but tongas and taxis stayed off the roads, and the city buses stopped in the afternoon. On the same day there was a mass meeting of workers in support of the students. On this occasion, the Mysore branch of the All-India Trade Union Congress criticized the government and expressed support for the students. Various other citizens and members of Parliament also publicly supported and sympathized with them.

On January 17, when the students in Bangalore announced the end of the strike, the Mysore students were in a state of confusion. Some of their leaders asked them to return to class; others appealed to them to continue the strike, for they were dissatisfied with the government's announcement that they would return to the 1960-61 level only for one year, pending the report of a special committee on fee structure. Finally, the local student Action Committee agreed that the strike would continue until the leaders had received clarification from the government. Even leaders from the Central Action Committee, who came to Mysore to try and influence the decision, were not allowed to speak at the students' meetings.

One of the tactics that the Mysore students were going to use, had the government not capitulated, was an intensive village-to-village "no-taxation campaign." That is, they would persuade the villagers not to pay taxes until the students' demands were met.

The same patterns of protest occurred among the students in the other towns. Those places mentioned in the press from time to time were Kolar, Tumkur, Mandya, Hassan, Chitradurga, Chikmagalur, Mercara, Shimoga, Bellary, Devangere, Tiptur, Robertsonpet, Kanakapura and Srirangapatna. Often as many as 1,500 students would parade in these towns. High school pupils sometimes walked with the students when allowed, but there was always the fear that they had been encouraged to do so by people who wanted to embarrass the students.

Shimoga was distinguished by having the first girl students to go on hunger strikes. Seven began to fast on January 7 and on that day the town observed complete hartal in sympathy. On January 9 the sixth batch of men students and the third group of girls began fasting.

The only violence in the whole campaign occurred at Tumkur on January 13, when the police lathi-charged students for throwing stones during a teachers' conference attended by the Minister of Education. Earlier, the students had tried to stop his car. This incident, in which a policeman was injured, was strongly condemned by the Central Student Action Committee, and some of its members met the Minister to express their regret. More violence was avoided at Tumkur at another time, when students thrashed a student for breaking the dome of a street lamp. Considering the violence that usually accompanies student indiscipline, and the length of time over which students had to maintain morale and avoid incidents, these disturbances were relatively insignificant.

Social Controls

The 1963-64 strike lasted over a much longer period of time than the other two strikes, and so there was more time for different interests to express their opinions and actually go into action for or against the students. As government action was again the cause of the strike, it was the government which took the main part in trying to control the students.

The strike was an ideal issue over which the opposition parties could embarrass the government, for the latter controlled the educational budget and passed the laws regulating education. It was thus responsible for deciding the fee structure in all the government colleges. It could also indirectly influence the fees of the private colleges by controlling grants if these institutions did not fall into line. The Chief Minister and the Minister of Education were the spokesmen for the government, and their speeches were given much publicity in the local press. They seem to have underestimated public support for the students' demands. On December 20, for example, a press announcement said that the Minister of Education felt that he was being "picked on," and dismissed the attacks on him as "temporary aberrations of children." Even as late as January, the Chief Minister, in a speech at Tumkur, said that the students did not understand the situation, and that their behaviour was shameful. The Minister of Education was a Lingayat who had come from the "New Mysore" area which had been taken over by Mysore in the 1956 re-division of land. Student fees had been higher in that area, and had remained the same when it was incorporated into the state of Mysore. The minister therefore felt that the fees of the students of the University of Mysore should be raised to the same level. The students' claim was that, on the contrary, fees in the new areas should be brought down to the 1960-61 Mysore level.

The Chief Minister at first ignored the agitation and advised the students, through the press, to call it off. He did not ask to see their representatives, and they would not approach him until he sent for them. He referred to their strike as an "unfortunate, sad but insignificant agitation." On several occasions during the strike he was out of station. The day after the students began hunger strikes, he left Bangalore and did not return for ten days. The student leaders thought that this was to prevent his being held responsible for any violence that might occur. They had so little faith in the government that they always took members of the press to their meetings so that there would be a check on what the government said to them privately and what they said later in public.

The opposition parties showed their understanding for the students by trying to give them financial support, by expressions of sympathy in the press, through heated debates in the Legislative Assembly, and by going on hunger strikes. Two members of the Opposition and a journalist began a hunger strike in front of the Vidhana Soudha on December 24 to give moral support to the students, and to focus the government's attention on the need for an early settlement of the matter. However, the students would not recognize their gestures, as they were afraid that these sympathizers would gain political control over their agitation; they meant to keep it a purely all-student affair.

On December 15 the government announced that the colleges would close for an "early Christmas recess" in order to allow the situation to cool down. Later they said that the colleges would remain closed until January 6, to include the usual "cricket" holidays on January 3 and 4. They warned that any students who did not return to college when the colleges re-opened would be liable to be disqualified from scholarships and freeships. This would mean the end of many a college career for poor students. However, student morale held, and when the colleges re-opened, some were completely empty and others had only a handful of students. Only one private women's college, Mount Carmel, opened with a normal attendance and continued to function that way for the duration of the strike.

On January 2 the government acceded to the students' demand in regard to freeships and scholarships. This would raise the amount of money paid by the government and other sources from Rs.17 lakhs to Rs.27 lakhs. It would mean that out of the 45,000 students in the university, 17,241 would get freeships and another 6,263 would obtain scholarships.

At the same time they made another plea for the students to break the strike, repeating that if they did not do so, freeships and scholarships would be withheld. They also threatened not to postpone the examinations, for which the students had not yet prepared because of the strike. However, since the leaders were not satisfied with this partial concession to their demands, they called for an intensification of the peaceful agitation until all demands were met.

The next threat of the government, on January 10, was that the colleges would be closed indefinitely if the strike was not over by the following weekend. This might mean the loss of a year for many students. Again the students replied with a call for an intensification of their campaign.

The Citizen's Committee, which was formed about this time, seems to have been able to bring the government and the students gradually together. From January 12 they held many meetings, sometimes with the ministers, sometimes with the students.

On January 17, after a prolonged special session of the Cabinet, the Chief Minister announced the government's decision to accede to all the students' demands. He said that this would cost the State Exchequer some Rs.50 lakhs more a year. He announced that a three-member committee would be set up to bring in a report on the fee structure. Karnatak University received the same concessions, and thus a uniform scale of fees was established for the two Mysore universities. The Bangalore students returned to their classes the day after the announcement, but some of the students from the mofussil stayed out for a few more days.

Throughout the strike the government seems to have completely underestimated the strength of the student movement, the skill of the leaders, and the pro-student sentiment of the public. Each of the government's threats was met by an intensification of the agitation, and usually by new demands from the students.

The police appear to have played an exemplary role in this strike. Reference has been made to the way in which the Chief of Police assisted the students to maintain order in every possible way, and of his sympathetic attitude toward them. Plainclothesmen moved among the students, trying to learn of their plans, but the students retaliated by organizing their own group of "spies," who identified the plainclothesmen and kept the leaders informed on police movements.

The main problem of the educational authorities in both the 1962 and 1963 strikes was that, as it was the government's role to make the decisions concerning the structure of fees, the educational leaders themselves could do little to bring about a settlement. However, they doubtless had some power in the background.

In the 1963-64 strike several of the private colleges tried to re-open before the strike was over. Mount Carmel was the only one that was completely successful; others were not so successful, even though they threatened that if the students did not return to class they would close indefinitely. Some remained empty when the time came to re-open and in others only a handful of students attended classes. One principal sent circulars to the parents, appealing to them to persuade their sons and daughters to return, and threatening to close if they did not do so. A Christian college finally closed to avoid any agitation or destruction to the college premises. Two other private colleges cancelled their mid-session examinations because not a single student turned up to take them, although hundreds of boys were seen standing outside the college premises at examination time.

Little publicity was given to the different educational associations during the strike. Doubtless they met often and worked hard behind the scenes, but only a few of their attempts to remedy the situation were mentioned in the press. In January the Mysore State Council of Education urged the government to restore the cut in the education budget. On January 9 the Affiliated College Association, an association of principals, appealed to the students and parents to end the strike. They said that the students who went back to college would have an advantage over the striking students in getting admission to technical and postgraduate courses and research positions.

Interviews showed the strain of the strike on the principals and members of staff. From past experience they knew that if the situation got out of control, "anything might happen," from property damage to injuries to students, or to themselves. Some members of staff were afraid of the potential violence; some were deeply concerned about the condition of the hunger strikers; some were sympathetic to the students, particularly those whose children or relatives would benefit if the students' demands were met. A few actively supported the students. Two who did so were dismissed after the strike, but later reinstated. Many lecturers, however, were unsympathetic to the strike, and later showed their displeasure toward the students in devious ways. The lecturers had to be in their classrooms when they were open; otherwise it would have been a "lock-out," and not a strike. Some had to sit in empty classrooms day after day, waiting for students who never turned up. Everyone found it a very tense, frustrating time.

Another goal of the Central Student Action Committee was the gaining of public opinion and support. Since many of the men and women belonging to the voluntary associations of the state had sons or daughters, who were either in college or were potential college candidates, it was not too difficult to gain their sympathy for a reduction in fees. A number of them supported the students directly through their different associations. This was the first time that the students had enlisted so much formally organized public support.

Members of the trade unions were particularly vocal in trying to assist the students' cause. A delegation met with the Minister of Education to ask him to be sympathetic to the students' demands, but as in the case of political influence, the students replied that they would appreciate trade union support if members went on a token strike (as some workers wanted to do), or showed their sympathy publicly in other ways, emphasizing they must do it in a way that completely disassociated the students from their effort.

A number of business firms sent the Student Action Committee copies of resolutions that they had previously sent to the government, expressing their sympathy for the students' cause and urging the government to accede to student demands.

Members of the various opposition political parties were also very active in promoting the students' cause in different ways. The Kannada Communist and the Swantra parties were particularly eager to identify with the students. Appeals to the government to grant the students' request were sent to the Chief Minister on December 25 and 27. On January 2, in the town hall, the different political parties organized a joint meeting which passed a resolution of sympathy and support for the students. The Mysore Pradesh Youth Congress, the Bangalore Bar Association, the Basavangudi Welfare Association, and the Akhila Bharatiya Vidyarthi Parishad were all organizations mentioned in the press as having supported the students. Several members of the Municipal Corporation also publicly expressed concern over the agitation when it began, and the Mayor played a leading role in the Citizen's Committee.

In Mysore, members of the city's Municipal Corporation expressed sympathy for the students' cause, and one member urged it to send a deputation to Bangalore to plead for the students.

The most influential group was undoubtedly the Citizen's Committee formed on January 11, and headed by the Mayor. It included representatives from all the political parties, from all the major interests of the city, and from among the parents themselves. It was the first time that the leading citizens had gone into joint action. Their main purpose was to negotiate between the government and the students. They gained the confidence of the students at once, and press accounts show that they were very influential in persuading the government to meet the students' demands. They began by holding a large meeting of parents and students, at which they paid tribute to the peaceful, constitutional way in which the students were behaving. The leaders of the Student Action Committee replied that they welcomed their action, as they felt they could not bear the responsibility of the agitation much longer. Nor could they be responsible for the students' behaviour after a certain date. Although they did not admit it publicly, they were physically at the end of their tether and felt that they could not bear the strain much longer. The Citizen's Committee had many consultations with the Chief Minister, the Ministers of Education and Finance, and the secretaries of all the departments involved in the issue. Finally they negotiated meetings between the Chief Minister and the students. At the end of the strike they issued to the press a statement praising the students and the government for their conduct during the demonstrations.

The commercial interests of the city also gave public support to the students. As has been mentioned, a complete hartal was observed in

Bangalore on December 20, the day of the mammoth procession. All the mofussil towns with colleges also went on one-day hartals in sympathy. In Devangere life was virtually paralyzed, as the entire city responded to the students' call for a "Devangere bandh." There are two reasons for shops, restaurants, markets, hotels, and cinemas closing when disturbances arise. One is that proprietors still remember the damage done by students during the Youth Festival strike, or have heard of the destruction that occurs when student demonstrations take a sinister form. The second reason is that should they not close when asked to by the students, they may be the butt of student anger during the disturbances, or in future demonstrations.[24]

All these gestures were of great encouragement to the students, for they felt that as time went on, there was a growing, rather than a declining support for their agitation.

The local newspapers gave the strike a great deal of publicity, and even the international press carried articles on it. The local newspapers carried many front-page headlines, and often included photographs of the students in action, or holding discussions with members of the government. They also printed many long press statements by members of the government, student leaders, and prominent citizens. The names of the student leaders were constantly publicized, as were the names of all those on hunger strikes, even in the mofussil colleges. Debates on the issue in the Legislative Assembly were reported at length, including statements and/or protests from the members of the Opposition.

The leaders of the Student Action Committee called their own press conferences, at which they could pose as authorities on many educational matters, as well as on the issues of the strike. It was a relatively new experience for them to receive this publicity. At these meetings they criticized government statements given to the press, and gave the public their own interpretation of events.[25]

24. Chancal Sarkar, *The Unquiet Campus*, p. 25. "Shopkeepers, cinema proprietors, and newspaper offices have learned (through painful experience) that it is wise to keep in their good graces because arson, assault, and rioting can be as likely as hunger strikes."

25. *Deccan Herald*. For example, on December 18 they said that 2,000 out of 23,000 students would be affected in the P.U.C. by the increase in fees, not 200 as the government had stated. On December 25 they told the press that they disassociated themselves with the hungerstrike that was being carried out by members of the Legislature, and that the agitation was entirely and exclusively that of the students. They were able to protect themselves further on December 27 by refuting the idea that there was a "hidden hand" behind the agitation, and on January 1 the leaders appealed to the students through the press not to be panicky because of any government announcements, but to continue the strike "with vigour and enthusiasm."

The press played a very important part in assisting the students by announcing meetings, clarifying the attitudes of the different sides, and keeping many members of the public on their side. And because the press gave the students publicity and prestige, it played a major role in maintaining student morale.

On January 17, when the strike was over, the following editorial in the *Deccan Herald* congratulated the parents for their support of the students, paid tribute to the students for acquitting themselves creditably, and praised the police for handling the situation with "tact and wisdom."

TRIUMPH FOR ALL

The students are entitled to congratulate themselves in a spirit of restrained jubilation in that their cause has been vindicated, and on their conducting themselves throughout the anxious period in a commendably disciplined manner, resisting the temptations of the mute voices of mischief which augurs well for the future. . . . Without the spontaneous though silent support of the public, comprising the parents and guardians of the striking students and which the Government rightly sensed in time and responded to with imagination, the strike would have entailed total failure, leaving a trail of bitterness, disappointment and frustration. . . . All have won. . . .

The students must adequately and effectively realize that their brinkmanship which, because of the combination of circumstances has come off, will not always succeed and that their fundamental duty is to pursue their studies with single-minded devotion, further cultivating that sense of discipline which they have manifested for constructive employment in large spheres and in good causes, for to-morrow is theirs. . . . The sympathetic sense of restraint throughout shown by the Government toward the strike situation, and particularly for the understanding instructions to the police force which acquitted itself with credit, deserves the public's appreciation and gratitude. . . . And now our student population must at once again redirect themselves urgently and effectually to sympathetic application and reverent study.

Conclusions

An analysis of the three most important strikes among the students of Mysore University shows trends indicating that the spontaneous demonstrations at the time of the Youth Festival strike were gradually organized into a cohesive, effective movement.[26]

In the first place, the 1962 and 1963-64 strikes were well organized. Plans were made carefully ahead of time by a committee of experienced leaders. These plans included methods for organizing state-wide participation by all the students of the arts, science and commerce colleges in the University of Mysore. A Central Student Action Committee was formed early in the 1963-64 demonstrations to co-ordinate and control all demonstrations in the state.

In the second place, the student leadership was exceptionally strong and imaginative. The leaders were old enough and had forceful enough personalities to enlist the devotion of the students for the cause, and to maintain a high rate of morale for thirty-seven days. They were experienced enough to choose an issue that was popular both with students and with a large part of the public, thus gaining a great deal of public support. They added minor items to their demands as the strike went on, in order to hold the interest of the students. Many of these leaders had also been in charge of the 1962 strike. At that time they knew when they were "licked," and capitulated to the government, for they feared that they could not hold the students to a peaceful demonstration once violence had occurred in Shimoga. The 1963-64 strike was perhaps unique in the history of student strikes in India in that it did remain peaceful over a long period of time, except for a very minor incident in Tumkur. This was in complete contrast to the Youth Festival strike, which grew out of control almost as soon as it began. The general feeling of uncertainty regarding the maintenance of order among the students, particularly in view of the known history of student violence in India, was evident in the fears of the public, the concern of the government, and the increasing tension of the leaders.

In the third place, many more students took part in the two later strikes, because most of the students believed in the issue of the strike,

26. *Statesman*, August 27, 1965. Further evidence from student demonstrations in other parts of India shows that student outbursts have gradually become so well organized that they can affect government policy. This was seen in the recent reaction of students in Madras State. They were preparing to convene a Tamil Nad Students Conference to decide their future course of action in relation to the adoption of Hindi as the national language. Their main object is to work for the early replacement of English by Tamil and other regional languages. One of their main aims will be to iron out their own differences of opinion on the language issue, so that they can present a united front to the government.

and because there was a more organized way of putting pressure on those students who wanted to remain in class. The only large blocks of students who did not join the strike were from the Christian colleges where discipline is strong. Mount Carmel could retain an almost normal attendance of women students because of the strictness of the Principal, its rather remote position from the other colleges, and because the leaders did not encourage women to take part publicly in the strike. Thus, there was less incentive for them to leave class. This may be the reason why leadership among the women students was not very strong in the 1963-64 strike. The first two women to go on hunger strikes in Bangalore had tried to rouse their fellow graduate students for some time, but their efforts did not meet with much enthusiasm. Two reasons may account for this lack of strong leadership among women students: one is that Maharani College, whose students were usually the leaders, was put "out of bounds" by the student leaders to minimize their problem of keeping order. Thus, the girls would not be influenced by the usual crowd of excited students milling around the compound gate and standing in the adjacent streets. The other reason is that the Principals of two of the women's colleges were unusually strict, and any potential participant was afraid to disobey them. It was said that a student from Mount Carmel College was expelled for going to the Vidhana Soudha to sympathize with the women hunger-strikers when all students had been forbidden to do so.

Although the government still did not handle the strike situation with acumen or tact, they were quite firm in withstanding the students' demands. They tried at first to ignore the leaders, and treated the strike as beneath their contempt, but finally had to take it seriously and capitulate to the claims of the students.

The educational authorities also played a more influential part in trying to settle the strike behind the scenes. Principals met with government officials. Private colleges were more prepared and had learned when to close (so that damage would not occur on their premises), and when to put pressure on their students to remain in class.

The public, who did not have much time to form opinions during the Youth Festival strike, was so well informed about the impending rise in tuition fees that it was able to move into organized action more rapidly. This time the people were largely in favour of the students' fight, as were many parents and relatives. Many voluntary organizations, such as trade unions, came out publicly in favour of the strike. Parents,

79

who had been in sympathy with the 1962 strike, but had, at that time, told the students to stand aside and let them handle it, now made no mention of taking control when they organized a Citizen's Committee. The press, too, was much more in favour of the students, praising especially the peaceful nature of their demonstrations. On the whole, the attitude of the public showed that peaceful student demonstrations had become an accepted way of handling issues of immediate concern to the students themselves.

There are many ways of disciplining, either directly or indirectly, students who take part in demonstrations. They are often arrested, particularly if there is violence, but in the past they have usually been kept only a short time and then released. An exception to this was the group of ten students who were arrested, along with about two hundred other people, because of their participation in the anti-Hindi riots in Madras State in the winter of 1965. They were arrested some months after the riots, under the Defence of India Rules, as it was feared that more trouble would arise on August 15, Independence Day. They were detained until fear of renewed agitation was over.

More subtle methods of retaliation include the prevention of students from graduating. Students from the Law and Commerce Colleges are usually the ringleaders in Bangalore. After the Youth Festival strike, only 17 per cent of the students passed their examinations in law, and only 8 per cent in commerce; the usual number of passes is around 35 to 40 per cent in each discipline. Informants were sure that students had been penalized in this way because of participation in the strike.

After the 1963-64 strike the head of a department in which two of the women students had gone on hunger strikes refused to give the students in question "attendance." All students must attend a certain number of classes before they are allowed to write their examinations. These students lacked only about 5 to 10 per cent of their attendance, partly because of illness. The Principal of the college, and other lecturers were willing to let them have their attendance, but the head of the department refused. This meant that they had to wait a whole year before writing their examinations. He told them that their behaviour in fasting had been immoral and disgraceful. The same professor also refused to give attendance to one of the men students who had taken part in the strike, although the student in question had missed only 5 per cent of the classes.

There are other subtle ways in which students can be punished. The

Principal of one of the women's colleges had been very much against the strike, and was said to have "persecuted" the girls who had gone on hunger strikes in many small ways. She made their lives miserable and sometimes reduced them to tears. It was said that she expelled one of the girls from the hostel for taking part in the strike. The Principal of the Law College tried to restrain his students by threatening that they would not receive recommendations when they graduated. Some of the student leaders claimed that they were all on the "red" files in the police office; this is a serious matter, for these files can be used for reference if people apply for government jobs.

Informants also said that the central government is trying to legalize the arrest of all students who lead demonstrations or protests. Jailing or expelling students may be a deterrent, but since only a few can be punished in this way, most of the students do not receive any sort of punishment for participation.

How, then, can indiscipline be contained or eliminated? The central and state governments are now in a very difficult position, and there is no agreement on how the situation should be handled.

Members of the Study Committee of the Congress Parliamentary Party on Education to-day expressed concern at the *growing indiscipline* of students. . . . Members expressed sharply divergent views on recommendation of a conference held by the Chief Minister last year which had suggested firm action to curb strikes. More powers to Vice-Chancellors to deal with indiscipline, ban on political meetings on the campus and curbs on political interference in educational affairs. (*Times of India*, August 24, 1965.)

Some wanted these suggestions to be vigorously implemented, but the others were probably alarmed at the thought of too much suppression of student action. In *The Hindu*, a letter to the editor deplored the ruthless suppression of students by the Madras government after the language agitation, and pointed out that it had made students even more restless.

Many students who took active part in the last agitation have been dismissed from colleges on one pretext or other. Many have been turned out of their hostels without notice. The houses of many student leaders are ransacked by the police, and severe warnings issued to them in spite of their repeated denials of indulgence in unconstitutional activity. Scholarships have been withdrawn.
    The colleges, obviously under pressure, are demanding written promises from students that they will not take part in any agitation in the

future. Even some teachers who have sympathized with the student move-ment have been mercilessly dismissed. Several colleges have received notices from the Government asking them to show cause why the Govern-ment grants should not be withdrawn.[27]

An intensification of rustication (expelling) has also been threat-ened; although this has been successful at different times in the past, it is risky now that the students are well organized, for thousands of students might demonstrate if popular leaders were expelled.

One of the more recent attempts to curb student action occurred in New Delhi on November 17, 1966, in regard to a national protest meet-ing of students. The march had been prohibited by the government, which feared that it might set off a new wave of violence similar to that which broke out on November 7 during demonstrations banning the slaughter of cows. Also, more violence might flare up in different parts of India, such as that which had occurred for several weeks, earlier in the autumn, in northern and central India. However, as the preparatory committees disregarded the prohibition, policemen were sent to guard the boundaries of the capital from the in-coming students. They watched bus terminals, railway stations, and the roads to detain the students. As an added precaution, all schools and colleges were ordered closed to prevent the students from using the campuses as jumping-off points for their planned demonstrations.[28]

The extent to which the government must go to prohibit student meetings of this nature is an indication of the way in which student agitation has at least partially got out of hand in India.

27. *The Hindu*, July 22, 1965. Letter from V. Mitter and K. Kesavan, representatives of the Supporters of English at the Indian Institute of Science, Bangalore.
28. *New York Times*, New York, November 18, 1966.

2

The College Setting

Many suggestions have been made in the past few years as to the part played by the college environment in encouraging student agitation. Overcrowding, insufficient guidance, the transition from high school to academic life, and pressure to get high grades have all been considered contributing factors by different writers.

Lecturers, too, have come under criticism. We hear more about the growing distance between teacher and student, and in the United States, professors have been charged with giving more time to government and other outside agencies and to their own research than to their students, thereby increasing the impersonality of teacher-student relations. An analysis of many interviews with lecturers in different parts of southern India during a year of research in 1962 and during the summer of 1965 suggests that, although the lecturer may share some of the responsibility for the restlessness of his students, a good part of his effect on them is due to their effect on *him*.

The way in which the lecturer defines his role, and the way in which the attitudes and behaviour of the students affect his career have so far been almost completely ignored. Perhaps the most basic change that has affected the position of the lecturer lies in the change in the purpose of higher education. The main function of the university is no longer considered to be the development of character, and education is no longer thought of as a "preparation for dignified leisure rather than for productive work." Nor is it considered to be the prerogative of a privileged and limited élite.[1] Rather, the whole purpose of higher education has been altering gradually, so that a college degree is now looked upon as a normal channel to careers, by those able to afford it, and as a "must" for those who are striving to gain more prestigious occupational positions.[2]

The recent increase in the numbers of students going to college means that those receiving higher education now come from the lower as well as from the higher strata; thus many tend to be concerned with the practical aspects of education. That is, they expect that it will bring them better jobs than they could have obtained had they not gone to college. Another reason for the increasing desire of young men and women for higher education is that jobs tend to be the main locus of security in highly industrialized societies, for when the structure of the family and kin groups change, neopotism declines, and safe entrance into traditional family occupations can no longer be counted on. As one's occupation becomes recognized as the means of achieving security in the modern world, education and/or professional training become increasingly important. School and college thus become the "decisive agencies managing the status and life chances of the individual."[3] In this way, university teachers and examining bodies who determine who shall succeed and who shall fail play a very important role in the student's career. This may be one reason why the tensions of students are often released on them. Thus, a change has come about in the whole purpose of higher education. "No longer is it a question of handing on an unchanging, or only slowly changing, body of knowledge and belief. On the contrary, education in modern societies has more to do with changing knowledge than with conserving it, and more to do with diffusing culture to wider social circles, or from one society to another, than with preserving and transmitting the particular culture of a particular group."[4]

The need to meet these new educational conditions has been a heavy burden for all countries. The highly industrialized countries have adapt-

1. Peter F. Drucker, "The Educational Revolution," pp. 15, 16. "[The] highly educated man has become the central resource of today's society, the supply of such men the true measure of its economic, its military, and even its political potential."

2. Jean Floud and A. H. Halsey, "Introduction," in A. H. Halsey, Jean Floud, and C. Arnold Anderson (eds.), *Education, Economy and Society: A Reader in the Sociology of Education*, p. 2.

3. H. Schelsky, "Family and School in Modern Society," in Halsey, Floud, Anderson, pp. 416, 417.

4. Jean Floud and A. H. Halsey, "Introduction," in Halsey, Floud, Anderson, p. 3.

ed more quickly to these conditions. They were better prepared for educational change and expansion, and as they had produced the new industrial system, the recent emphasis on education was more in line with their way of life. In most of the developing countries a modern educational system had been grafted onto cultures to which it was quite foreign.

In India the present educational system was introduced in colonial days, and did not develop as a natural expression of Indian life. It still retains many remnants that apply more to the British culture than to the Indian. At the same time the British failed to introduce a love of scientific inquiry in many fields, and so the conception of scholarly research has been slow to develop.[5] This has meant that academic curiosity and the desire for the advancement of knowledge have not been one of the prerequisites for an academic career; this in turn has proved to be a handicap in developing scholarly attitudes among the students. It may be one reason for their general lack of interest in their studies. As in other developing countries, the need for a rapid increase in educational facilities arose in India at a time when the country had neither adequate financial resources, nor enough trained personnel to carry out the reforms. There was still a very high rate of illiteracy.[6]

EDUCATIONAL PROBLEMS

The increase in the actual number of students in India has probably been greater than in most countries. This increase has been accompanied by a sharp rise in the number of colleges and universities.[7] However, there are still insufficient colleges for the number of students who want to attend, and there is increasing pressure on the existing colleges to overload their classrooms. Another problem in this connection is that,

5. D. D. Karve, "The Teacher in Higher Education," p. 7. " . . . till about the early years of this century, all universities were nothing more than syllabus-drawing, examination-holding and degree-giving organizations. The actual training of the undergraduates was carried out by the affiliated colleges, situated at considerable distances from the universities. There was very little post-graduate teaching and practically no research activity. The proper functions of these academic bodies were thought to be to help the students in the passing of an examination and the acquisition of a degree with consequent improvement in the type of employment. Scholarship, research, and the intellectual life in general had no place in the picture. University teachers were simply non-existent, and college teachers who specialized in some branch of their study or wrote books which commanded the respect of other scholars were the exception rather than the rule."

6. Humayun Kabir, *Education in New India*, p. 9. Out of the population over five years of age in India, 14.6 per cent were literate in 1941. This figure rose to 18.3 per cent in 1951.

Report of the University Grants Commission, p. 4. By 1961 the percentage of literate Indians had risen to thirty-five.

as in most countries, certain professional fields such as medicine and engineering are the most sought after, as they yield good incomes and have high prestige. Nonetheless, because the number of seats in the professional colleges is limited, many a disgruntled student finds himself forced to take an arts or a science degree that neither he nor his parents desire. This disappointment often causes frustration.

Still another factor that is disturbing both to students and to lecturers is the increasing influence of politics in the universities. The fact that politics now often decides staff appointments and promotions leads to factional quarrels and loss of morale among the staff.[8] "Some teachers

7. *Report of the University Grants Commission*, p. 12. India has also shown a marked increase in its college students in the past few years:

	Men	Women	Total
1955-56	563,904	77,489	641,393
1958-59	747,107	115,432	862,539

In the period 1958-59, out of a total of 1,252 colleges, 146 were exclusively for women.

Handbook of Indian Universities, pp. 3, 5. The total number of universities is now fifty-five, but at the time of Independence there were only eighteen. This means that thirty-seven universities have been built in India since Independence. The total number of students enrolled in all the Indian universities in 1961-62 was 980,380. Fifty-one thousand other students in the same year were enrolled for a Master's degree, and 4,500 were enrolled in the same year for the Ph.D. degree (a total of 1,035,880 students).

Report of the University Grants Commission, pp. 3, 4. In 1959 it was estimated that in the United States the university population was over seventeen per one thousand people. In India it was about 2.5 per one thousand of the population. However, if these figures were taken in terms of the relative numbers in both countries who were literate, then the figures might be different, for in the United States over 95 per cent of the population is literate (1961). Another comparison is with the United Kingdom. The university population there is approximately the same size as in India in relation to the total population, although there exists almost universal literacy in that country.

Some idea of India's problem of obtaining qualified teachers and lecturers is shown by the estimate that, in order to carry out the educational plans of the third Five Year Plan, 61,000 *additional* teachers and 37,000 *additional* lecturers must be trained. (*The Hindu*, Madras, October 29, 1961.)

8. Chanchal Sarkar, *The Unquiet Campus*, pp. 14, 15. Sarkar puts this point bluntly: "The attitude of the government to the universities in most states is obtuse, short-sighted, and illiberal. And, whether one likes it or not, the influence of governments on universities is decisive. They supply the funds; they nominate important sections of the universities' deliberative and executive bodies; they are responsible for the legislation under which universities work; and, too often, they advise the chancellor on the exercises of his functions, including the choice of vice-chancellor . . . , in their personal as well as official capacities, members of a government often exert tremendous pressure on universities in matters of appointments, promotions, and admissions. . . .

"In state after state the government's power of nominating members to the senate and syndicate has been used to put in ministers and mere politicians, often people whose own educational qualifications are dismally low. . . .

"Governments and politicians have not only interfered with universities and destroyed their status and authority, they have also wrecked that subtle thing in them which is described as 'atmosphere.' "

Many newspapers and journals speak of this control. For instance, *The Hindu*, Madras, August 15, 1961. "It would appear that the first thing on which the eye of a politician falls is the university."

make college "politics" their major preoccupation. This malady affects the small, teaching universities to an even greater degree. Here the non-teacher members of university and college bodies find ready allies among the frustrated teachers. In this atmosphere university elections are characterized by much manoeuvring and behind scene deals."[9]

This situation is at least partly due to the gradual rise of some of the lower castes to political power. The Lingayats and Vokkaligas, formerly agricultural castes, now hold the top political positions in Mysore State. Control over the educational system has seemed to them to be essential for survival. Their infiltration into the field of higher education has been greatly deplored by many who feel that they have not sufficient knowledge about education, and are introducing reforms which are too rapid and too sweeping. One of the most respected educators in India comments on this problem: "Nothing can be more devastating for the future of education in the country than educational conditions and ideas being dictated by political authorities. . . . Frequent and ill conceived changes in the educational pattern might ruin a whole generation. . . . Politicians turn themselves into educational experts and try to experiment with the educational system in accordance with their whimsical ideas."[10]

These college politics are deeply disturbing to many students, for they are fully aware of the intrigue and corruption that have penetrated the educational system. Rumours circulate easily in the intimacy of the college. Students, younger staff members, and even the clerical staff are mines of information. The local press publicizes many cases of litigation in the courts between members of the staff and the higher educational authorities. This tends to undermine the authority and the dignity of the university and its staff in the eyes of the students.

If administrators and teachers in universities imagine that their petty intrigues, their tussles for elected offices, their flattery of authority,

---

9. M. S. Gore, "The Crisis in University Education," pp. 347, 348.
See also the *Deccan Herald*, November 4, 1961. "Politicians who either by training, attitude or record of public service are fit to be members of university bodies, manage to get themselves into advantageous positions from which they wield a powerful influence over the teachers there."
Report on the Problem of Student Indiscipline. "Members of various political parties directly interfere in the internal affairs of the university and lead students astray by holding before them wrong ideals of leadership and significance."

10. Dr. L. Mudaliar, Vice-Chancellor, Madras University. Quoted in the *Deccan Herald*, Bangalore, September 20, 1961. Dr. Mudaliar was referring to the changes in curriculum that have often been introduced very hurriedly into schools and colleges.

their inability to stand up against unfair practices, their lack of interest and competence in academic matters, their attempts to instigate students for private ends and their lapses of conduct go unnoticed by students, then they are deceiving themselves.

How deep the extent of demoralization among teachers is, I have tried to convey in these articles. Lack of pay and status and dispiriting conditions of work have a great deal to do with it. But there is also disillusionment about selections and promotions, about academic freedom, about the administration in universities and about the scant understanding which unpleasantly partial groups like politicians and government have of their work.[11]

Yet another urgent problem faced by Indian universities lies in the medium of instruction. Serious controversies have arisen over the retention of English versus the introduction of Hindi or a regional language. A few universities have chosen Hindi or their regional language, but the staff has had to face the problem of finding adequate text-books and other materials in these languages.[12] The retention of English means that many are forced to lecture in an unfamiliar language. A good deal of the boredom of the students in class probably results from having to listen to lecturers using poor English and talking with almost impossible accents. Later they have to write down the little they have gleaned from the lectures in this foreign language in the emotional tension of the examination room.[13]

The organization of the syllabus also contributes to student dissatisfaction. A central board plans the courses given at the colleges, and sets and corrects the examinations. The main purpose of this system is to assist universities to maintain high standards in an era of rapid expansion, when it is difficult to obtain qualified lecturers, and to eliminate the possibility of the lecturer being pressured into inflating the grades from families who can "persuade" him to do so. On the other hand, the system encourages students to depend on learning by heart certain set passages from texts or lectures in order to pass the examinations.

11. Sarkar, p. 19.

12. *Handbook of Indian Universities*, pp. 57-59.

13. Aileen D. Ross, "Some Social Implications of Multilingualism," pp. 212-36. The relation of bilingualism or multilingualism to student indiscipline needs a much fuller discussion than it has had in this study. A great deal has appeared in the various Indian newspapers and journals on the problems created in India by the great variety of official languages. The article describes the number of languages learned by a sample of students, as well as some of the problems they have faced in trying to learn in an unfamiliar medium of instruction.

See also: Anees Chishti, "Role of Language," pp. 19, 20.

The system, then, is an authoritarian one in which the lecturer is not free to develop his own style of teaching, his own courses, or his own intellectual initiative.[14] The frustrations arising from this lack of independence tend to increase his hostility toward the administration. It also encourages students to put pressure on the lecturer to dictate accurate notes in class. Many an enterprising lecturer who has tried to introduce interesting, related materials has been forced by his students to return to the note-dictating routine.

Students will be even more anxious to have notes dictated if the lecturer speaks English with a difficult accent. However, some lecturers who were interviewed felt their students had such a poor knowledge of English that if they did *not* dictate their notes, the students would never pass the examination. Most of the lecturers interviewed thought that much of their lecturing was a complete waste of time. One woman lecturer said that she kept her finger on the line she was dictating so that she would not repeat, for she was too bored to think of the meaning of what she was saying. Dictating notes was greatly deplored by older lecturers who were used to smaller classes and more interested students. Note-taking tends to increase the restlessness of students for two reasons: it bores them, and they see little point in sitting hour after hour, writing notes that could be much better bought in the "bazaar," or borrowed from other students.

The educational system therefore tends to increase student restlessness because it fails to capture the interest of many students, or to encourage them to develop a keen interest in knowledge.

The examination system, too, puts a great strain on the student.[15] His success depends on his performance in two examinations: the intermediate, which is written at the end of the first two years at college; and the B.A. or B.Sc. examination, which comes at the end of the fourth year.

> To understand the Indian college system one must comprehend the pervasiveness of the final examination in all its ramifications . . . the whole classroom operation, the preparation of teachers, the use of books, are all

14. Gore, p. 342. ". . . this system makes the job of the teacher an uncreative one. In his concern for covering 'portions' for the examination, he misses the intellectual excitement of developing a theme, experimenting with new interpretations, and in the effort, contributing to the subject which he is teaching. . . . The emphasis is on the mastery of a text, not the exploring of a subject."

15. Kabir, p. 157. "The fact that the possession of a degree is an essential condition for employment whether under government or in private offices of firms, except at the lowest levels, has aggravated the evils created by the emphasis on the final examination."

consciously or unconsciously controlled by the omnipresent final examination. Thus, the method of instruction naturally adopted by the teacher is one which helps the student to get exactly the information he needs and to memorize it. Such things as tutorials and seminars where students present their own ideas, discuss, and argue over them, papers where students must on their own look up materials and organize it logically using their own intelligence, quizzes whose marks will not affect the final grade—all of these are "off the main track. . . ." Thus, the system of external final examinations in India leads to certain types of teaching, certain types of studying in which the premium is put on memorizing certain details thoroughly and foregoing personal opinion or original thought in regard to the material.[16]

Since the results of the examination greatly effect his future, and since two years of work can be wiped out in one day if he is indisposed on the day he must write, the emotional tension raised by the fear of failure may result in an unnecessarily poor performance. It may also account for the fact that so much of the student indiscipline in India begins in the examination room. The strain on the student is shown in the following interview with a Vokkaligan student.

> I worry a lot about my examinations, because if I do not pass I cannot get a good job or marry. My mother, sisters, and my uncle will be terribly disappointed and sorry if I do not get a degree, and I am sure that if I fail my father will not let me repeat my studies. Everyone will be very angry with me. I am very worried about my future for it depends on my getting a degree.

The lecturers whose positions are insecure are very worried lest their students get low marks or fail. Stories have been told of some who take sweets to the examination room to encourage their students to write well. If a certain percentage does not pass, the blame may fall on the lecturer. He may not be promoted, or he may be penalized in a more subtle and practical way.[17]

Another factor that may help to explain student indiscipline is that

16. *Handbook of Indian Universities*, pp. 32, 33.

17. Lecturers may not have actually been dismissed because of their students' failures. But, as it has happened to high school teachers, there is always the possibility that the college lecturers may be the next victims. For example: "Four hundred and eighty-nine trained graduate teachers were punished in Patiala and Ambala divisions on account of the poor examination results of their students. Forty head mistresses and about two hundred headmasters of various high and higher secondary school in the state were served Show Cause Notices because of the poor results of their students." (*The Hindu*, Madras, June 9, 1963.)

the age at which the student enters college is lower in India than in most Western countries. This has a great bearing on his adjustment to college, for he is less prepared for the impersonality he often finds there.[18] Nor does it make it easier for lecturers to treat the students as adults. Some parents are so anxious to get their children through college and ready to earn money that they "fake" their ages so that they can begin school at an earlier age. Thus, some arrive at college before they are socially and psychologically prepared.

Writers have often deplored the lack of suitable equipment in many Indian colleges. Libraries are often nearly empty; even when they are relatively well stocked, they are not always used, as many of the students have not formed reading habits at home. For example, a total of only two hundred books was taken out by students in one year from the well-stocked library of a large Christian college. Moreover, if students can pass their final examinations by memorizing class and bazaar notes there is little incentive for them to delve further. The libraries often tend to be difficult places to read in, for they are even more of a gathering place for chattering students than in other countries.

Playing fields, equipment for games, and trained personnel are often lacking. Thus, the great majority of the students have little opportunity to get rid of their excess energies through organized sports. One lecturer in a college of over one thousand students said that only about one hundred students play sports; the others watch. Many students take a vicarious interest through listening to games over the radio. Sometimes a cricket match will be broadcast all day, and at that time a student with a radio will have his room full of friends, while others without radios will stand in groups outside cafes that have them to follow the game.

Other college activities of a more cultural nature are not very much in evidence. A few students are interested in dramas or debates, and many debating competitions are held between colleges. On the whole, though, students do not arrive at college with wide interests in cultural matters, and once there, they find little incentive for developing them.

There is a wide difference of opinion as to whether students do much

18. *Report on the Problem of Student Indiscipline.* "The atmosphere of the University should be one of ordered freedom in which the forms of private and public behaviour of students are influenced by their own mature judgment about conditions appropriate to the responsible position of the university students. But boys and girls enter our colleges at too early an age and are unable to act as responsible free agents; the colleges have often to organize their life as though they were still high school students. In such a situation 'discipline' tends to become a product of regimentation."

in the way of social service work or not. The government has dropped its scheme of having all students do a compulsory three months before graduating. The National Cadet Corps does some service in the villages. In one women's college a number of the senior students had spent several evenings a week for several years teaching the adults of the neighbouring village to read.

This comparative lack of amenities, or of interesting extracurricular activities, however, must be seen in relation to the student's expectations. Since the great majority of Indian students have been brought up in a milieu where they have not been exposed to the more highly organized, often commercially-centred ways of spending leisure time, they do not feel the "deprivations" of their own colleges as would a student from a highly industrialized modern society. The novelty of being in the midst of a large number of students, and the new adventure of getting to know peers from different communities are, in themselves, psychologically rewarding experiences. Certainly there is no dearth of "chatting" on Indian campuses, and much tension may be drained off through this media. However, a later chapter will show that many of the students of this sample felt that their social lives were not satisfactory. The frustrations that some felt in this regard could easily be released in collective action.

The way in which a student lives while at college may have a great influence on him. Residential life may be a newer and more profound experience for Indian than for Western students. A greater proportion of the latter may have had experiences in "group-living" in boarding schools and summer camps. In 1961-62 it was estimated that 18.2 per cent of the total number of university students in India lived in hostels. Here, for the first time, they are on their own, and must make their way. However, it is estimated that, as in Western universities, there are not enough hostels for all the students who need them. An intensive campaign has been under way in India during the last few years to build more hostels and thus give the students a more favourable environment for their studies, but as the total cost of living in a hostel is from Rs.75 to Rs.120, many of the students cannot afford to stay in one. Moreover, although this price is high for the student, it is low in terms of catering to them, and therefore the equipment and food is not always of a high standard. In the first year that a student goes to college he may be living with three others in one small room.[19] Some hostels are

19. *Handbook of Indian Universities*, p. 41.

reserved for students of a certain community; others are mixed. In Bangalore the Lingayat community has put up a number of hostels, but in the early 1960's there was only one that had been especially built for Vokkaliga students.

The rules of the hostels are often very strict, although they vary from college to college. In one Christian college the boys must be in at eight o'clock at night. If they do not obey the rules, they cannot go back to the hostel or even to college the next year. The boys used to be able to climb over the walls to get out, but now new walls have been built which are impossible to scale. In the Radahkrishnan hostel the regulations are very strict; for example, the boys must be up at 5:30 a.m. to exercise and bathe. The rules in the girls' hostels are even stricter than they are in the hostels for men: the girls are usually expected to be in by 6:30 p.m. and are only allowed to go once a month to the movies, and, very occasionally, for a walk with another group of girls. Their time in the hostel is therefore very dull. Hostels usually seem to have a good deal of influence over the boys or girls who live in them, particularly if students are there for four years. One warden said that most of the students, particularly those who come from the villages, must be taught such things as manners, cleanliness, and how to get on with the other members. After a few years they are usually much better dressed and smarter in their appearance. There are probably many more subtle things that they learn as well, and so hostel life is a very important break from complete dependence on their families.

Some of the girls interviewed said that they had a lot of fun, even though the rules were strict, for they found the environment much freer than that of their own homes. One informant said that the boys from the villages often went a little wild because they could not adjust to the sudden freedom from family and community restrictions.

THE LECTURER'S DEFINITION OF THE SITUATION

This chapter has suggested that some things in the college environment may be disturbing to students. Student-lecturer relations must now be considered, for it is through the lecturers that the students do, or do not, receive the inspiration that will lead them to real intellectual effort. Changes in the educational system have necessarily also affected him, and given him a new self-conception. This, in turn, has affected his relations with his students, possibly abetting their indiscipline.

In describing the conditions in his college, a lecturer who has had many years of experience claimed that it is not the students who are indisciplined, but the lecturers. He described how the majority of the lecturers in his college were late for their classes, or did not turn up at all. When they did lecture, it was often in the easiest way. Some collected a few rupees from their students and used the money to get a clerk to type out their lecture notes which they then gave to the students. After that they felt that they did not need to be in class except to take attendance, and show the principal that they were present. Other lecturers marked passages in a text and got one of the students to dictate to the others, which permitted them to abstain from attending at all. The first ten to fifteen minutes of a class are often lost, for the lecturers who do begin on time cannot make themselves heard when, in other rooms, students with no lecturers are making noise. This also causes frustration among the eager first year students, who gradually lose their enthusiasm in their disappointment at the indifferent attitude of their teachers. When lectures do begin, attendance must be taken, and this lasts about ten minutes. Then, some teachers leave the class ten minutes early. Thus, lectures often last about half the time they are supposed to. The lecturers often go home after class and are not available should students need help or advice. The Principal of this college has now ruled that the staff must arrive at eleven every morning and remain at college until 5:30 p.m.

This illustration certainly does not apply to all lecturers in India, as there are many devoted teachers, but it does illustrate one of the universal problems of education—that of keeping the system dynamic enough to enable the teachers to develop their own capacities and so give the active leadership that will make colleges places of high morale and lively participation.[20]

In few countries did the individual look up to his teachers in the past as the Indian looked up to his "guru," and this respect was transferred to the first British professors, many of whom were of high intellectual calibre.[21] Even a generation ago, students had a high respect for their professors, and although sometimes they cut classes, they would never think of making a disturbance in class, or of being rude to the lecturers.

20. Everett C. Hughes, "Level, Direction and Style of Effort," p. 5. "Teachers who have taught too many courses, from too many text books, for too many years, may be useless as models and as reinforcing advisers or companions in learning."
21. Kabir, p. 152. "Unfortunately, teachers today do not command the respect and affection of their pupils to the extent they did in the past. For this, they alone are to blame."

In the colleges today, however, there is scant respect, even for principals, unless their personalities command it. In other words, the position is no longer held in high esteem, and it is only the person fulfilling the role who can command deference from his students. Several cases were mentioned in which students would have reacted in a violent way during a strike had they not liked and respected their principal.

There are many reasons for this change in attitude to the educator. One of them, not confined to India, results from the increased demand for education, which has caused colleges and universities to admit so many students that the close, personal relationship between teacher and student has largely vanished, except on the graduate level. In many countries the decline in the prestige of the lecturer is also due to the change in the type of person who now lectures. This, in turn, has been caused by the change in job opportunities in the highly industrialized countries. In India the lag in catching up with the problem of the "educated unemployed" has forced many men and women to take up teaching on the school or college level because they cannot get other jobs.[22] Another factor which explains this lack of regard towards lecturers is that in India there is a large proportion of students who now come from rural, low-income, and non-Brahman homes. These students were not brought up with the traditional attitudes of respect for the guru, and they seek degrees for the jobs they will bring, rather than from any deep admiration for learning. Still another reason is that the students are fully aware that the individual lecturers have little control over their educational careers, for they do not set or correct their examination papers. One informant said that the whole university could be run without teachers; the students could simply buy "bazaar" notes, learn them by heart, and write the examinations without any further aid. The attitudes towards lecturers change when the students know that the latter are often not adequately trained.

> Most university teachers today teach in the same way and by the same methods that were current twenty or thirty years ago, when they themselves were students. Some of them were not capable of falling in with modern techniques, while others have neither the time nor the energy to attempt new experimental methods. . . .
> Most of the students [of this survey] complain about the extreme in-

22. Howard Becker, in Halsey, Floud, Anderson, p. 98. Becker suggests that a system that favours the selection of "disgruntled failures" for teachers will not get the "teaching enthusiasm, which may be more important than a degree."
See also: *Report of the University Grants Commission*, p. 18.

adequacy of the teaching staff. Eighty per cent have found only a few of the teachers successful in creating an interest in the subject. . . . [23]

All these factors could certainly contribute to the informal, and perhaps indirectly, to the formal indiscipline of students. In one interview the following remark was made: "Students behave badly in class. They cheek their lecturers. The boys often talk about their clothes and laugh at them, and at the way they lecture."

However, the effect of the lecturers on their students cannot be understood fully unless we know how the lecturers themselves define the situation in terms of their own careers, and in terms of the students' behaviour. It has already been pointed out that the backlog of educated unemployed is still so great that many graduates are literally forced to become lecturers, whether they like it or not. It is to be presumed that there is a large percentage of the teaching staff who do not define this type of career as satisfactory; this group tends to become disgruntled and frustrated. Women lecturers who teach for a few years before marrying, and have very little interest in their courses, could be added to this group. The devoted teacher in India is probably as willing as his counterpart in other countries to forego higher salaries, a better standard of living, or an honoured position.

Many lecturers may define their slow rise up the academic ladder and small yearly increments in salary as satisfactory, as long as they can do the work which they love, particularly if they are able to teach in government colleges which provide pensions. Nevertheless, although the teaching profession has never been a very lucrative one, changing middle-class aspirations and the higher standard of living that accompanies industrialization have spread the desire for monetary rewards; thus the salary of a lecturer in India is more important in defining his prestige and position today than it was formerly.

I had greater respect for my teachers twenty years ago than my students do for me. My teachers were poorer and more shabbily dressed—we respected them because they did their duty towards us enthusiastically—our welfare was their main concern. For most of us, on the other hand, the student's welfare is only of secondary importance. We do not much care whether they understand what we tell them. We do not bother whether they fail or pass, because it will not bring any material gains to us.[24]

23. *Report on a Survey . . . of the Students of the University of Bombay*, pp. 50-56.
24. V. S. Mather, "Nothing Wrong with Our Youth," p. 40. See also: *The Report on the Problem of Student Indiscipline.*

The actual financial position of lecturers varies from one area of India to another, according to the salary scale of the state. In general, salaries are lower in southern colleges than in central and northern ones. Most observers feel that low salaries constitute one of the main reasons for the deterioration in the level of ability of those seeking academic positions.

> [The colleges] have to recruit their teachers mostly from those who cannot go in for more lucrative careers in other fields. . . . The remuneration paid to the large majority of college teachers in non-government colleges is so modest that the profession has failed to attract the best product of our universities, to say nothing of those who have received advanced training in Western universities. The universities, with their higher scales of pay, are in a somewhat better position, but the college teacher, who is responsible for the training of over ninety per cent of Indian undergraduates is still regarded as only a little better than a high school teacher.[25]

The side effects of low salaries have also been detrimental to the calibre of the teaching staff, for many lecturers and professors must supplement their incomes by tutoring, or by working at other jobs, particularly if they have large families to support. Some double their salaries by lecturing in colleges which have morning and afternoon shifts. Others supplement their salaries by taking various part-time jobs. Some who lecture in more rural areas keep cows, or grow their own vegetables. The result is that they have little time or energy left over for studying, and are often exhausted when they arrive at college. They cannot take the kind of interest in their students that leads to good teacher-student interaction. Sometimes lecturers in other countries must also supplement their salaries by working outside the university, but in India the situation is aggravated by the ever-present fear of loss of job, and by the difficulty of getting promotions. The long-term result of financial worry is that the lecturers, once married and supporting families, become more and more absorbed with the problem of financing growing children, with paying for their education, and with arranging their marriages. They gradually lose even the little interest they may once

25. D. D. Karve, "The Teacher in Higher Education," p. 8. Sarkar, p. 21. "In private colleges in Madras, for instance, a Professor's grade is from Rs.250-500, a Lecturer's Rs.150-300 and a Tutor's Rs.85-125. The U.G.C.'s recommended improvements are, respectively, Rs.400-700, Rs.200-500, and Rs.125-200. In a Government College . . . Chief Professors get Rs.500-1,000, Professors and Additional Professors Rs.250-700, Assistant Professors Rs.150-250 and Tutors start at Rs.80. It seems fantastic that a country . . . pays its university and college teachers a fraction of what it pays civil servants of corresponding age and qualification."
See also: M. S. Patel, "Modern Trends in the Teaching of English in India," p. 93.

have had in their students; by the age of forty they are of little use as teachers, and merely repeat the same notes year after year.

> Our system of education has thus institutionalized the role of a non-creative subject teacher who functions much the same way as a high school teacher would—reading, explaining, annotating paragraph by paragraph the textbooks which his students have to learn for their examinations. His interest in students is judged by whether he dictates "notes" and memory points on "difficult" and "important" portions——i.e., the ones more likely to appear in the examination paper—of his syllabus. He rarely uses the college library and no one really expects him to have seen recent issues of professional journals.[26]

The insecurity of the lecturers increases when they compare themselves with those who return from abroad with degrees. Not only does this comparison suggest they are lethargic, but the lecturers with degrees from abroad pose an additional threat to their promotions and to their positions.

Small salaries mean poor living conditions, including little privacy, noisy surroundings, and poor health. In referring to a recent survey of the living conditions of students Sarkar, in *The Unquiet Campus*, writes: "If [a survey] were carried out for teachers, particularly those in private colleges and even in government colleges and the universities, results, I am sure, would be as shocking. Life is hard for college teachers."[27]

A small proportion of the more privileged lecturers and professors make extra money by correcting or setting examination papers, but entry into this lucrative occupation is carefully guarded and not many can benefit from it.

Working conditions, too, may be hard. The college lecturer normally teaches fifteen hours per week. The beginners may not be able to protect themselves from an even heavier load. They often have to remain six, seven, or eight hours a day at college, even when they have no lectures to give. Very few have private offices, or even share an office. Their spare time must be spent in a common-room which is not equipped for comfort, and is so crowded that it is impossible to study or read seriously. Sanitary arrangements, too, are often quite inadequate. In one college there was not even running water, and the lecturers had to go to neighbouring houses for a drink.

Few colleges have adequate equipment. Often the classrooms are so

26. Gore, p. 347.
27. Sarkar, p. 21.

dark, partly because of the need of shade from the sun, that it is difficult for students and lecturers to read their notes. Lecturers must often put up with a great deal of noise, for doors and windows must be left open on account of the heat. In addition to making themselves heard above the noise of restless students in and out of class, they must also contend with the loud, raucous "caw" of crows, the chattering of monkeys, or the thunderous roar of the monsoon rains.

In some states the insecurity of the lecturers in government colleges has increased, for these people can be transferred at any moment to any other college in the state. The reason for this is to make sure that even the most isolated mofussil college has its quota of good teachers. In practice, however, it often means great hardship, and a good deal of extra expense for the lecturer who has to keep up two households instead of one. In Bangalore a woman lecturer was transferred to Mysore and had to leave her husband and small son in the former city. In another case the husband's business was transferred to Madras; his wife, a lecturer, was sent to another city, and the children remained with relatives in Bangalore. In still another case, an elderly woman lecturer, just about to retire, was transferred to another city, and her family had to remain in Bangalore. In one unfortunate instance a highly qualified professor was transferred from a college, where he was considered an inspiring teacher by a number of graduate students, to a small mofussil college where his students, consisting mainly of village boys, had no idea of going on to graduate work.

Women lecturers have a particularly difficult time when they are posted to colleges in small towns. Single women are not expected to live alone in India, and so must always have a relative with them to maintain their respectability. As their salaries are very low, and they may even be expected to send money home to help their families, it is difficult for them to maintain an adequate standard of living. Moreover, as their leisure time is confined to women, and there are few educated women in the towns, their social lives are not satisfactory.[28]

28. In a letter in the *Deccan Herald* (Bangalore, July 4, 1965), a doctor pleads for greater consideration for the living arrangements of unmarried nurses. His remarks would also refer to unmarried lecturers. "[They] are many a time solely responsible to their families and have to look after them. They have, more than not, many dependents on them consisting of old parents, younger brothers and sisters, nephews and nieces and are thus as much as, if not more than, in need of family quarters. . . . Economically an unmarried nurse is more at a disadvantage than a married nurse who can combine her income with that of her husband. The latter is more in a position to rent a house outside. Thirdly it is more inconvenient and dangerous for an unmarried nurse to stay out than for the husband-protected married one."

Given these conditions and the setting within which the lecturer must work, it is small wonder that there are many references in the press, and in private conversations, to the disgruntled, frustrated lecturers, to their low morale, and to the fact that the profession does not attract the most competent and alert students.[29]

Attitude to work may make a great deal of difference in a lecturer's morale. If he accepts his lot, and is relatively competent, his position is assured, and he has little incentive to "keep up," or raise his teaching standards. A number of informants spoke of the dullness, conservatism, and boredom of the lecturers. One said he knew few staff members who were proud of their work. Deshmukh has spoken of this lack of motivation: "The real difficulty is that at present not enough of the teachers and research workers take intellectual work seriously; not enough of them do serious work of their own, either in their research or in their teaching. Too many of those who do research, do it in a perfunctory and indifferent manner without real conviction as to its worthwhileness. Many of those who once had it have given up all interest in research, even though some of these still go through the motions of research. Too many have so lost interest in their subjects that their teaching has become boring to themselves and their students. Little attempt is made to keep track of the development of their subject and the same antiquated lecture notes are used year after year—not that a better performance in this respect would be easy, given the poverty of the teachers and the spotty character of most college libraries."[30]

Indian writers have also noted disillusionment and loss of morale among Indian lecturers.

> The most depressed and pessimistic section, I found, were the teachers. Some senior people were unashamedly fatalistic. They traced the malaise in the universities to a general decline in integrity, morals and character in the country and thought that the old breed of teachers, students and administrators had gone, never to return. . . .
>
> Younger teachers were cynical, whether coolly so or passionately. The satisfaction of teaching large classes they rated very low, promotions they

29. *Report of the University Grants Commission*, August 21, 1965. The Committee did not find the morale of the teachers and students very high in the different universities visited.

See also: *Economic Weekly*, p. 862. "In the University especially, the self-pity which once characterized the Brahmans is now widespread . . . what is more significant today is the widespread demoralization among teachers. An afternoon spent with them can be most depressing."

30. C. D. Deshmukh, "The Present State of University Education in India," p. 15.

did not think came in recognition of creditable work nor did passing large numbers through "grace marks" do any good. Academic freedom and autonomy they considered myths.

This, I think, is perhaps the most dangerous and painful disease in Indian university education today—those working it have no faith. Teachers have their shortcomings—in some cases they may even obstruct progress—but the fact cannot be blinked that, as a body, they are gravely disillusioned and apathetic.[31]

Many lecturers begin with as much idealism as do Western lecturers, but for a large majority of them the combined problems of the situation gradually sap their first enthusiasm.

It is by no means an uncommon experience to encounter a tired and hopeless Indian university teacher in early middle age, who, as a young man in an Indian or British university was full of enthusiasm for his work, impelled by bright or even deep ideas, which he pursued with intense industry and even dedication. When one meets him in his early middle age, he has done practically nothing with his talent or his training. When one asks him what happened, he tells a melancholy tale. He began his career full of life but after a time his vitality faded. The head of his department was resentful of his qualifications and his intellectual vivacity. He could not get the books or equipment he needed or he got them so long after applying for them that he had lost interest. His colleagues, who had advanced further in their process of stultification, offered neither the stimulation of their own ideas nor an understanding and responsive audience for his own. Bit by bit, under the weight of growing family responsibilities and the allures of college and university intrigue, his mind wandered away from the problems which had once fascinated it. The result: one more depressed, saddened, or embittered middle-aged teacher, who in his turn, will guide other bright young men of the succeeding generation, on the path of intellectual dullness and indifference.[32]

Given the conditions for lecturing—the need to follow a set curriculum, the lack of incentive for using one's intellectual imagination in the developing of courses, the system of dictating notes, the absence of incentive for research or original writing, the lack of library facilities, and

31. Sarkar, p. 7.
32. Deshmukh, p. 16. ". . . overwork, anxiety about the economic situation of one's family . . . the lack of adequate facilities in the home or at the college to work on one's subject, have much to do with this condition. The poor preparatory education of [most of] the students also contributes. Yet, all these factors are insufficient to explain why bright, sometimes brilliant and often promising young men, as many Indian college and university teachers were at the start of their careers, sink away into boredom, intellectual dullness and sterility."

the necessity for spending long hours at college with little to do—it is no wonder that many lecturers are bored with their work. This is particularly true of women lecturers who have, as yet, few possibilities of extracurricular activities or outside distractions. Even holidays are not a time of recreation or relaxation. Some lecturers do not even want them, for they cannot afford trips. Most of them live in homes where there are no separate rooms and no peace and quiet. They cannot spend their time at college, for they have no office of their own to work in, and in any case there is little incentive for studying. Holidays can thus be just as boring for lecturers as they are for students, who have little or no money to spend on entertainment.

Lecturers, therefore, have many anxieties and frustrations, and it would be impossible for them not to pass these on directly or indirectly to their students: "A large amount of student frustration can be traced directly and indirectly to indifferent teachers and unprogressive teaching methods . . . when incompetent teachers dictate indifferent notes from start to finish, it is beyond the bounds of a joke, perpetrated on students with the connivance of the present system."[33]

Many lecturers were also discouraged by the fact that their relations with the students seemed to be deteriorating. They could see no remedy for this situation, as the flood of students entering college was increasing year by year, with no sign of abatement.

THE STRAIN OF INDISCIPLINE

The effect of the lecturer on students is indirectly influenced by indiscipline, for his relation with the students will be largely determined by the way in which he defines the students' behaviour, particularly in relation to himself.

Both the formal and the informal indiscipline of the students causes a great deal of strain for the college staff, particularly for those who cannot handle the students in class, or have had to face the violence of student riots. The Principal of a small women's college in the south told of how she had had to go on a holiday after her first encounter with organized indiscipline. Her women students had been obedient and docile until the men students in the adjoining college had tried to get them to join in a strike. "I was very nervous, I did not know what they would do. Individually, the students are all right, but in a group they

33. *Report on a Survey . . . of the Students of the University of Bombay*, p. 35.

cause damage. The boys had pushed one of their professors onto the floor during the trouble last year, and broken all the equipment in the chemistry lab. I went away for a few days after the strike was over, I was so exhausted."

In this case there had been no violence, but so much had already occurred in different parts of India that there was always the chance that it would break out. Time and again the strain that the lecturers are under was shown in that same sentence: "I didn't know what would happen." It takes a great deal of courage to stand up to a mob of students. The demonstrations after the liberation of Goa in 1962 were not particularly emotional in Bangalore; in fact, only about two hundred students actually demonstrated, and even they were not very enthusiastic. Nonetheless, when the men students from the Central College (they are the customary initiators of demonstrations) marched along to the Women's College shouting slogans, the teaching staff who had gone through the Youth Festival strike felt that anything could have happened. The Principal went down to the compound gate to tell the students that the girls could not leave class as they were writing examinaations. "The boys were very polite, but I did not know what would happen." Still greater anxiety and strain occur for the staff when a strike lasts a long time. The anti-Hindi strike in Madras State in the winter of 1965 lasted several months. This was a long ordeal for principals and lecturers, as well as for the higher educational authorities, the government, and the police.

It was the first time that the women of two private women's colleges in Madurai had joined in an agitation, although the men students had had a long history of conflict. The fears of the staff had been accentuated by the destruction that had accompanied these demonstrations; one lecturer had seen groups of students moving towards the station, armed with shovels, sticks, and stones.

The colleges had been closed by the government when the first violence occurred, but not before the Principal of one women's college had had word that the men students were on their way to burn as much of the college as they could and to destroy the chemistry lab. The staff sent home as many of the students who were in residence as they could and for several days made the rest of them sleep in the classrooms, as the hostels were too difficult to protect. They did not allow the girls any lights, so that the men students, who were roaming around the grounds every night flashing lights on the buildings, would not be able to see where they were. Finally, one night the Collector arrived at 2:00 a.m., saying that he had word that the students were again coming to raid the buildings, and so all the girls must be sent home immediately. When the colleges were re-opened, the girls returned but would not go into class. They sat all day in the compound in the boiling sun, many of them fasting. (In this particular strike the fasting seems to have been symbolic rather than realistic, as many men and women students were said to have eaten when not under observation.) By this time the college was protected by soldiers, as well as by the police, and one of the class-rooms was a miniature arsenal, full of rifles, extra ammunition, and tear-gas bombs. The Principal had also been receiving many anonymous letters of a "terrible" and threatening character. No one dared to go out after dark. The strike continued for some weeks, and principals and lecturers lived under the threat that the college might be attacked. The days were also wasted, for the staff was too tense to profit by the free time occasioned by the absence of the students. When the students finally returned, the staff had to continue lecturing well into their vacation time to help them catch up in order to pass the examinations. Thus, they had hardly any holidays before the next college year began.

The irritating nature of strikes is illustrated by another demonstration which took place, this time in a men's college. When all the colleges were ordered re-opened after a three weeks' strike, the men students returned, but, like the women students, would not go into class. Instead, they organized a procession around the college compound that lasted from 8:30 in the morning until 5:00 in the afternoon. While they marched, the students never stopped shouting slogans, which became particularly vicious when they taunted the police on guard outside the compound wall. The lecturers had to sit in their classrooms for the lecture periods with everything in readiness—note-books, chalk, etc.—alone and harassed by the continual, deafening noise. Again the strain was difficult to stand. When would the students erupt into violence? When would the first stone be thrown, the first window broken? Any incident could precipitate violence and police retaliation. Finally, the staff could stand it no longer, and the college was closed down for five more weeks. All the other colleges in Madurai closed at the same time.

The strain has been heightened by the fact that many lecturers feel student indiscipline is increasing. This seems to be particularly true of women students. Several principals in different parts of India have said that their girls never agitated openly before, or took part in strikes.

Their protest in the past has usually taken the form of abstaining from class and staying at home, but during recent demonstrations they have been very excited and rowdy. They also have participated more in hunger strikes, although they usually fasted within the college compounds.

Most lecturers are afraid that they will not be able to control their students in class, partly because they recognize their own incompetence. Women lecturers are particularly unsure of themselves, especially when lecturing to boys. Several instances were cited of their being unable to answer the students' questions, or to get sums right when writing on the blackboard. One began to weep when a bright student asked her a question she could not answer. After that the boys stopped asking her for information. Most of the women lecturers are afraid that they will not be able to manage their male students. Their control over them is not as great as that of male lecturers, partly due to the fact that they tend to lecture in low, monotonous voices which are very hard for the students to hear. If their English is poor as well, even attentive students get restless. Also many men are unable to speak English well enough to explain material to their students, and when asked questions they simply refer them to their notes. Some are terrified that their lack of ability to speak English well will be found out.

Another factor that reduces the ability of the women to hold the attention of their students is that they are often even less interested in their students than are men lecturers. They go to college, lecture— which usually means dictating notes which they themselves often do not understand—then go home. As one of them said, "They could just as well be typists." Part of their attitude results from the fact that the great majority of them lecture only for a few years before marrying. The turnover is great, and so there is little opportunity or incentive to improve. In the meantime, they pass the time lecturing and waiting for a husband. This is the main reason why they do not give their work the devotion that the task demands.

> The teachers, having no love of their subjects, cannot communicate any love to their students, and the uninterestedness of the students only makes the teacher bored. Teacher and student are caught in a vicious circle which, if it breaks at all, breaks into a downward spiral because of the difficulties which students so often encounter in understanding lectures in English and textbooks in English.[34]

34. Deshmukh, p. 15.

Women lecturers suffer a great deal from anxiety because the lecturing situation represents a new world for them: their upbringing within the intimacy and the protection of the family has in no way prepared them for the formality and impersonality of the classroom, nor for its publicity. They have been brought up to play a passive and subordinate role, and it is difficult for them to take leading roles in their relationships with students, either inside or outside the classroom; indeed, they often speak of their shyness with students. The traditional separation of the sexes, which means that men and women lecturers are not able to mix socially, poses another difficulty for women lecturers. Even at formal social affairs, the men and women may eat at separate tables, and the women are supposed to sit on the girls' side of the hall at college functions. This separation makes the job a lonely one when a woman finds herself the sole one in a department or college.

The male lecturer also finds it difficult to face a room full of girls when he has had no training in social contact with them, for they do not know how to respond. In one interview, a lecturer remarked, "What bad luck it was to be appointed to a girl's college! I felt like a fish out of water in the midst of this ocean of girls. I could not scold them; if I did, they giggled at me."

HANDLING INDISCIPLINE

The main problem for the educational authorities and staffs of universities is that they have no idea when the demonstrations will arise, or what form they will take. It has already been noted that the intensity of the action varies in different student agitations. Some demonstrations seem to arise with only slight provocation, spread rapidly, and erupt into violence. In other cases the students are much more rational and will negotiate with the authorities.[35] Agitation is particularly difficult for a woman principal to handle in a women's college because she is completely unused to violence, or to handling unrest.

Many professors and members of the public who have witnessed the students in action have been bewildered and horrified at the extent of their hostility and violence. In one college where the students had gone on strike because of the alleged rudeness of a clerk to the secretary of the union, the Principal afterwards said that he had never seen anything

---

35. Neil J. Smelser, *Theory of Collective Behaviour*, p. 225. "The degree of intensity depends on the degree of strain, on how effectively leaders can mobilize an aggravated group, and on the effectiveness of counteracting social controls."

like it in all his years with students. The boys were completely uncontrollable. No lecturer could approach them. One, who felt that he had good rapport with them, tried talking to them in the compound. Soon other students gathered around and started swearing and yelling at him until he left. When the Chaplain spoke to some of the Christian boys, the mob got vicious and yelled at him, "Go home, white man." He was later warned to keep away from the students as they were plotting violence against him. To the staff, the unexpected and frightening thing was that the boys were so beyond control that they were unable to respond to any rational appeal.[36]

The way in which the principals and lecturers of various colleges handle student indiscipline differs. Some colleges are fortunately situated on the outskirts of a city so that the students are not near such temptations as movies and restaurants, and they are also far away from the centre of most student disturbances. It is, therefore, not as easy for students to find outlets if they cut classes. Even if the boys ventured the bus distance to a movie, it is doubtful whether many girls would dare to take the risk of being reported by a neighbour as having been seen in a bus.

This was the case of a private college of arts and science in one of the Bangalore suburbs. It was even too far away for student leaders to go there to entice the college students out, unless a major disturbance was occurring. The atmosphere of this college was good, as there were only about six hundred students, and their relationships with their lecturers were more personal. Moreover, the Principal handled any potential indiscipline by giving the students a holiday if he feared any trouble. In this way he avoided any destruction of property. This technique was also used by the Principal of one of the colleges whose students were ringleaders in any trouble that arose. If he felt that they were worked up, or if he heard their leaders haranguing them about taking part in a procession or demonstrating, he would immediately declare a holiday. He told his staff to continue to teach as long as any students remained in class and were listening, but to stop at once *as soon as* they grew inattentive or restless, and dismiss them. As a result, no damage was done to his building, although his students joined many demonstrations. The Principal's philosophy was:

36. Sarkar, p. 22. At the time of the Youth Festival strike at Mysore the "teachers expressed their amazement at the transformation in their students . . . they had not imagined that people could so change . . . individually quite decent, [the students] had shamefacedly confessed they did not know what had come over them."

When you know you're licked, admit it. When you see that the students won't obey, you must give in. For example, I arrived at college just as the students' meeting to celebrate Goa was under way. I was surprised to see the boys huddled in the compound. I thought it might be because a favourite teacher had been transferred. When they told me that they wanted a holiday because of Goa, I agreed at once. There is no trying to do something that the boys are against. If they won't do what you want you must give in.

A Principal of a Christian college avoided a good deal of trouble by anticipating the reaction of his students at the time of the Youth Festival strike. He and the Vice-Principal acted as soon as the demonstrations began. They called in the potential leaders and told them that if they took part they would be expelled. Then they went to see the parents of the students and told them to keep the boys at home, and away from Central College and other danger spots. Large notices were put on the school-boards saying that if any students were seen near the riots they would be expelled. Classes continued while the riots were going on, although few boys attended. When holidays were declared officially to allow the situation to cool down, one of the lecturers immediately organized an operetta and kept the boys busy practising in it throughout the holidays.

In another private college, again a little isolated from the other colleges, the Principal was on good terms with the students. If they became agitated in college he cracked jokes with them, put them in good humour, and gradually ushered them outside the compound. He told them that if they wanted to strike the compound was the proper place to do it. It is a co-educational college, so when the boys began to mill around in front of the building, the women students were told to leave in small groups by the back gate. In this way their mixing with the boys, which might have caused trouble, was avoided. He did not telephone the police when an incident occurred (principals are supposed to inform the police at once), but waited until things had quietened down. Then he telephoned them and reported that they had a little incident, but that now all was quiet. By handling the situation thus, he avoided becoming a symbol of authority whom the students could hate.

In another case, the popularity of the Principal saved his college from a strike. This man was a bachelor who gave at least half his salary to help the poorer students, and was well liked by them. At one point, he tried to change the system of examinations, but the students resented this. At the final examination only about 25 per cent of them turned up. They sat for an hour without writing, then left, turning in blank papers. The general opinion was that had the Principal not been so popular with the students, they would have gone out on strike.

On the other hand, it is little wonder that some principals are intimidated by their students. In one case over a hundred students beseiged their Principal in his office, demanding that he put off their examination for a week. They said that they would not let him go until he agreed. He finally conceded, but his staff felt that he should have been firm, for having once won their way in this manner, the students would demand the same concessions at the next examinations.

The head of another college was very much disliked by the boys and had no control over them. On one occasion when they had an honoured guest at one of their evening functions, the boys threw eggs at the Principal; unfortunately the guest also was hit. This Principal was replaced, and the new Principal and Vice-Principal kept good order, because not only were they very strict, but also they were respected and liked by the boys. It was said that only a glance from one of them was enough to make the boys obey. The students did not even dare to smoke in front of them.

A gathering of students for the purpose of watching sports or entertainment is a potentially dangerous situation. One college function provided a particularly anxious time for the staff of one of the colleges, as it was the first time that the women students had attended an evening affair with the men. The women sat on one side of the hall with the women lecturers. Behind the seated audience stood three or four rows of tightly packed students. The Principal and older professors sat in front, looking nervous. One had the feeling that they would not have known quite what to do if violence had started. When the entertainment began, the boys clapped and roared at the scenes they did not like, at unpopular actors, and at girls who danced badly. As they became more and more excited, the standing students pressed forward. At any moment trouble could have begun. However, the evening was saved by the lecturer in charge of the events, who had had enough experience to know that he must watch his audience carefully. As soon as he thought that the spectators were too excited, he would remove an entertainer, or stop one act and bring on a different one.

Lecturer: Sometimes we have to stop an entertainment, for if the boys don't like it they get restless, and begin throwing small stones at the actors or making disturbances. I knew last night that if there was one minute's lag in the events, so that the audience was not kept busy, there would be trouble, but I was pleased that the women students were in the audience without causing trouble.

Firmness, popularity, the respect of the students, and a sense of timing—knowing when to give in, or when to distract students—these seem to be characteristics that can partially contain, if not entirely eliminate formally organized indiscipline. The same qualities can also be important in minimizing informal indiscipline in the classroom. Persons interviewed said that there was always confusion in a class if a lecturer could not hold the attention of his students. When the lecturers are incompetent, the students may call out and tell them to leave the class, or may take part in some mischievous, noisy behaviour.

> *Informant*: Some lecturers are not able to control the boys at all. They will call him names or draw cartoons of him on the board. One we had could not keep us in order. We would go to class until attendance was over and then leave, or, if we stayed, we would hoot and shout and roll rocks along the floor.
> One day we garlanded the lecturer and carried him around the corridors. He couldn't go to the Principal about it, because he would have perhaps lost his job if they knew he could not control us.
> We used to laugh loudly too at the way in which some of our lecturers pronounced English, or the words they used. Or we would insist that they must explain the portions in Kannada. Some of our lecturers would get so annoyed, or feel so helpless, that they would walk out of class.

However, there are also many lecturers who can hold the interest of the students. One such lecturer found the Principal waiting for him outside the classroom door after his first lecture in the college. Since the students in that district carried knives, and the lecturers were so afraid of them that they did anything to appease them,[37] the Principal was amazed that the lecturer had had such order on his first day. He told him that he could command any salary he wanted in that district, as the students were so difficult that all the principals were looking for staff who could keep them in order.

Some of the lecturers avoid indiscipline by getting rid of those students who are potential underground leaders, or those who are inclined to be rude or noisy in class. This can be done by allowing the students

37. Certain lecturers have even condoned cheating during examinations, for a student may lay his knife on his desk with the blade open as a symbol of what will happen to anyone who tries to interfere with his cheating.

to leave class after attendance is taken. One lecturer told of how he got out of trouble when his students were in an excited mood. "When a crowd of students mills around outside, shouting for the students to come out, I turn to the class and ask, 'Do you want to join them?' If they say they do, I leave the class ahead of the boys, thus maintaining some dignity in the situation. Otherwise, great confusion might arise in the class, with the students shouting and arguing with me and eventually walking out. Moreover, the noise outside is usually too great at such times to permit lecturing."

The strain of both the informal indiscipline in the classrooms, and of the publicly organized student protests, is augmented by the fact that most lecturers think both are increasing, not only among the men, but also among the women students. Lecturers feel helpless in dealing with it, for they have no hold over their students. They do not control the rewards and punishments entailed in allotting grades, and they cannot even protect themselves from the system. If the supply of lecturers in India were at all equal to the demand, lecturers could complain and initiate action without too much fear of losing their jobs. Unfortunately, however, the economic system is so out of balance that it produces much unemployment among the more highly educated Indians, and many lecturers are too fearful of losing their jobs to have the courage to face up to attacking their employer (usually the government).

To what extent, then, do the Indian lecturers contribute to the indiscipline of their students? There is some evidence that they have taken some active leadership in student revolt, as have lecturers in the United States, where faculty "rebels" have encouraged students, both by their attitudes to certain issues, and by speeches in which they have encouraged the students to protest, or have blamed them for their apathy.[38] However, not many have done so, and for the rest, unless they have the charisma which enables them to gain the admiration of the students, or forceful personalities which will brook no nonsense, they often inadvertently encourage indiscipline through their inability to exercise control. The difficulty of their position, caught as they are between a system which allows them very little initiative, and students who are difficult to handle, undoubtedly affects their definition of the situation. Their self-conception is also affected, and all this has repercussions on the students and increases their restlessness.

The morale of lecturers will undoubtedly rise as more educational

38. Lewis S. Feuer, "The Decline of Freedom at Berkeley," pp. 78-87.

reforms are carried out, and as means are established for raising the lecturers' professional status. This, in turn, will enable them to cope with their students more adequately. It is obvious, however, that even more adequate teaching, and better relations between lecturers and students, will not, in themselves, go far toward eliminating student indiscipline, unless the more basic problems of change which are upsetting many role and career conceptions are also solved.

THE STUDENT'S DEFINITION OF THE SITUATION

A summary of the points that have been made might suggest there are so many problems for students in Indian colleges that it is remarkable that indiscipline is not more general and continuous. How does the student actually define the situation? Does college life tend to increase his disposition to indiscipline, or does it merely offer a channel through which frustrations engendered from other factors can be discharged?

This chapter has shown that, on the whole, the student's part in the educational system is to take down notes as accurately as he can, and then learn them by heart. This does not help him to learn to think creatively, or to organize and analyze ideas. The final examination becomes a test of memory, rather than of "understanding or judgment," and the whole situation produces "a tendency to amass information without understanding."[39]

Another problem is that this system does not encourage the students to learn regular habits of study. The great majority neglect their work during the year and then try to make up for what they've missed by working at high pressure during the months preceding the examination. This often causes severe strain, which may be accentuated by the fact that examinations are usually written in the hot season of the year. At one college many of the girls fainted during examinations.

This concentration of work at one time in the year has other undesirable effects: "Since, during the major part of the year, the energies of the pupils are not fully employed, they seek an outlet in various kinds of activities, some of which are definitely anti-social."[40]

The examination system is made worse for both teachers and students by the fact that it is sometimes inefficiently run, and that rumours often

39. Kabir, p. 156.
40. *Ibid.*, p. 156.

circulate about uneven grading.[41] Many lecturers feel that they could assess the students much more accurately themselves: "It is very discouraging to have to send our students' papers out to be corrected by other people. Sometimes they seem to correct in such a peculiar way. Students fail who shouldn't, and then we have no recourse." One problem is that the date of the final examination may be changed, and this also adds to the student's nervousness. Still another is that classes may commence late, at the beginning of the academic year, and then it may be difficult for the lecturers to cover adequately all the portions of their courses.

The students' belief in the educational system is further shaken by the fact that some of them take devious means to ensure that they pass. By tipping clerks, or by other means, they may be able to find out who is correcting their paper. The fact that the university is no longer completely respected or trusted is evident from the way in which many students have copied their lecturers and have brought cases of supposed injustice before the courts, which often judge in their favour.[42]

The students interviewed for this study were asked to list their "likes" and their "dislikes" of college life. Contrary to expectation, after all that has been said about boring lectures and the cutting of classes, their courses were first on the men's and second on the women's list of preferences. Only four men and three women put them on their list of "dislikes"; but whereas the courses ranked highest for men, the lecturers came fifth on their list. On the other hand, lecturers also topped the list of "dislikes" for both men and women. Some said they could not stand them.

Another criterion that helps to assess the students' definition of college is the extent to which they cut classes. Presumably an interested student would want to attend regularly, and one who thought little of college

41. This is a serious problem for all countries that have mass education. In India, as there are sometimes as many as 10,000 to 15,000 papers to correct for one examination and markers may be few, fatigue may creep in and bias the decisions. The Indian government sometimes steps in and changes the level of marks by giving "grace marks" that raise the grades of all students. Students may feel that they are being unfairly treated if their particular college is not given grace marks.

42. *The Hindu*, Madras, February 17, 1963, tells of a case in which a student claimed that he had been refused admission to a college when students with lower marks had been admitted. He won his petition. In another case a student who had been found cheating twice was debarred from writing an examination. The court issued directives to the university to allow him to appear. (*Deccan Herald,* Bangalore, December 8, 1961.) In still another case a student who had failed an examination requested that his marks be retotaled. He then filed suit against the college for the "mental agony" caused by the long silence of the authorities on the matter. These instances are only a few of many which are now taken to court rather than to the academic administrators.

would try to absent himself as much as possible. Students in the Banga-lore colleges must attend 60 per cent of the lectures, or they are not able to write the final examinations. As the majority of work is done in the classroom, and little, if any, individual work is required in the form of term papers or essays, there is no penalty for cutting classes, as long as it is not discovered. The main reasons the male students of this sample gave for cutting classes were boredom, being urged to do so by friends, or wanting to go to the movies. One Brahman student emphasized his impatience with the situation. "Everything is dull, boring, and has no charm. Going to a movie is the only way to get pleasure. But there are not enough movie houses to fill all my time! A co-educational college would give me pleasure and relief. What is there in a college full of boys and scientific apparatus!" If the bored student remains in class, he seeks diver-sion by talking, or by causing a disturbance. Some interviewees thought that if the college did not insist on attendance, the students, because they were bored, would skip classes. A few of the older students cut classes, not because they were bored, but because they worked, in addi-tion to attending college, and had no time to waste. Thus, if the lec-turers gave notes which were of little use, they would miss them. There were some very serious students who were by no means indisciplined, but cut classes because they could not tolerate the agony of taking down dictated notes, hour after hour, day after day. There were also some bright students who knew they could pass without attending class, as they could work on their own. However, the large majority of students who cut classes were either bored, or wanted entertainment.

Out of a sample of eighty-four women students, fifty-three said they cut classes. The most important reason given by them was also boredom. A girl might cut a class by herself if she was bored, or if the lecturers were uninteresting or "incompetent." Or she might go with a group of girls, and sit under the trees in the compound and chat. Some of the reasons girls gave for cutting classes were ill health, and going to the movies. Still other reasons were given: they missed their classes to attend family ceremonies, to keep other engagements, or to be with friends. On the other hand, the thirty-one women students who did not cut classes defined college as a place for serious study. They spoke in terms of their interest in their work, of the duty they felt toward their parents to attend classes, and of their feelings of guilt if they missed a class. Several felt that it would be a waste of their parents' money to stay away from class.

Through the colleges and universities, students in India should be able to build up a new set of values more in tune with the nuclear age, but as yet, the great "urge to education" as the solution for national and individual needs does not seem to have helped the students achieve a new identification in terms of college life. "Our schools and colleges today have sadly failed to create an environment for the student in which his desires and aspirations could be properly channelized and he is able to grow into a fully integrated personality."[43]

The satisfaction of Indian students with their college education, and with the opportunities they have for extracurricular activities, cannot be judged by the Western ideal, which stems largely from the traditional, rather mythical conception of Oxford and Cambridge. The changing composition of the student population, with many now coming from low-caste or rural backgrounds, means that students now have a totally different expectation of what college life should be like. Oxford and Cambridge are completely beyond their cultural and class comprehension. Thus, the lack of playing fields or of sports equipment for students who have never expected or wanted to play games may not be felt as a serious loss. The lack of college equipment and facilities, too, may be inconsequential. Nor are the students accustomed to being provided with organized entertainment. Thus, the way in which they define their college experience will doubtless be different from the way in which it would be defined by Western students.

Some of the students of this sample adapted relatively easily to the college environment, and even enjoyed it no matter what the shortcomings, while others never adjusted to it. The way in which resistance to college and its effect on students cause indiscipline will be considered in a later chapter.

The student's definition of the college situation thus varies according to many background factors, and to his interest in his work. It could safely be said, however, that a student who goes to college merely to get a degree, or to help pass the time before getting married, and who associates with a group of peers who are also uninterested in academic work, tends to use the college environment as a place in which to enjoy himself. He may join in the "cheeking" of lecturers; on the other hand, he might get rid of his more basic frustrations and grievances through some sort of active protest.

43. *The Hindu*, Madras, August 25, 1962.

*Caste, Family,
and Religious
Background*

The Indian government has probably tried harder than the government of any other country to break down barriers between the different strata of its society in order to bring about more equality among its people. The main dilemma has been that, in trying to help some of the lower castes to reach a higher or more equal position, the government has inevitably strengthened some caste differences. In Mysore State, for example, the attempt to assist the lower castes by dividing all the communities into "Forward" and "Backward" communities has emphasized the divisions between them, and caste identification has tended to become the basis for political patronage.[1] This has threatened the security of some of the castes who had formerly had greater advantages in the field of education, and so felt safe in their higher occupational positions. On the other hand, it has given some of the former lower castes a feeling

---

1. *Deccan Herald*, November 22, 1961, p. 5. "It is common knowledge, and indeed a matter of everyday experience, that the administration in this State is being moulded on communal consideration for the benefit of those in power . . . in the selection of the candidates for Congress tickets, eighty per cent of the seats are shared among the members of the two or three powerful communities, who form only about thirty-five per cent of the population."

See also: M. N. Srinivas, *Report of the Seminar on Casteism and Removal of Untouchability*, p. 133. Srinivas says that in the first popular cabinet in Mysore State, the ministers were chosen on a caste basis, and each had a secretary from his own "sub-sub-sub-caste." "Shri Hanumanthayya wants to rule strictly and impartially, but he must realize that the electors do not want it. They want him to confer favours on the people who have elected him." Srinivas claims that in no part of India can provincial politics be explained without referring to caste.

of greater security, particularly those which have been able to climb into safer positions in the governmental hierarchy.

Students from four communities, the Brahman, the Christian, the Lingayat, and the Vokkaliga were selected for this study to test the effect of caste background on indiscipline. The abbreviations *Br.*, *Ch.*, *Li.*, and *Vo.* are used here to refer to these students. A detailed explanation of this sample, and the methodology is contained in Appendix I. Two of these groups, the Brahmans and the Christians, are now classified as Forward communities in Mysore, whereas the Lingayats and Vokkaligas have been placed in the Backward category. This means that the latter have more privileges in education and jobs than the former. The Brahmans and Christians can obtain only a few freeships and scholarships and so must make their way mainly through their own ability and energy. Moreover, as the Lingayat and Vokkaliga castes now have the highest number of representatives in the State Legislative Assembly, ambitious students belonging to these castes are able to get assistance from people in influential positions. In this way, being "Backward," with its attendant privileges, helps to keep these two castes economically and politically powerful. Along with this power has gone the ability to penetrate even deeper into the life of the universities. "Caste and community still remain troublesome, inhibiting factors in the universities. In Mysore, where the entire state machinery is geared to caste, it is not surprising that caste should play a powerful role among both teachers and students."[2]

This movement of new castes to power has made the struggle for education and for control of the educational system very severe, for much depends upon it. Since caste influence is so strong that it has seeped down through other organizations and is even reflected in the elections of the student unions, it is small wonder that the division into Forward and Backward communities has had the effect of producing insecurity and frustration in the communities which have little power.

The figures for the elections of 1957 and 1962 show that the Brahman

---

2. Chanchal Sarkar, *The Unquiet Campus*, p. 12.
   For further information on the importance of caste power in the universities, see: Selig Harrison, *The Most Dangerous Decade*, p. 11.

caste does not have a great deal of political strength in Mysore.[3] This has, directly and indirectly, gradually affected their economic power and their prestige, so that many Brahmans have moved down the occupational hierarchy from the higher administrative and educational positions. A number have even been forced into such menial occupations as domestic service, skinning cattle, and making leather goods, jobs which were formerly allotted to the lowest castes. This decline in their status is largely due to a strong anti-Brahman movement that began around 1900, and has grown in strength since Independence.[4] Many Brahmans have felt the future to be so hopeless that they have left Mysore to seek their fortunes in other states. Those who have remained are pessimistic about the future. Most of the Brahman students interviewed were not even dreaming of trying to get important jobs after college; rather, they

3.	ELECTION RESULTS IN MYSORE STATE — 1957 and 1962*	
Community	Number of Members	
	1957	1962
Lingayat	61	59
Vokkaliga	59	56
Scheduled castes and tribes	12	11
Brahman	9	11
Muslim	7	6
Christian	3	1
Other	57	64
TOTAL	208	208

*Information from an informant who worked in the elections

4. M. B. Nanavati and C. N. Vakil, eds., *Group Prejudice in India: A Symposium*, p. 167. Its aim was to undermine the favoured position that the Brahmans had always held, and which had been supported by the British. During their regime, the Brahmans, due to their "intellectual" heritage, were given a proportionately larger number of the top administrative and educational positions. The non-Brahmans have gradually been able to displace the Brahmans in these areas by taking over political power. Theoretically, the movement encompasses all non-Brahmans, including all other caste Hindus and all religious groups such as Christians and Muslims. The movement has always been stronger in the south than in the north, and strongest of all, perhaps, in the state of Mysore.

One of the surprising things about the anti-Brahman movement is that the Brahmans have not yet organized to resist it, even in the face of the fierce competition of other castes. One reason for this seems to be that, as they have largely maintained their original rather rigid sub-caste divisions based on language and religion, they are not a united group. Informants said that even the Brahman members of parliament did not stick together on parliamentary issues. Another reason lies in the fact that their higher level of education has tended to broaden their outlook, so that they are less orthodox and more individualistic than other castes and so less inclined to hold to the traditional caste customs and loyalties. In the third place, their inability to maintain their position of power and prestige in the last decades has turned them into a bitter, discouraged group. They sometimes refer to themselves as the "Jews" of India because of their feeling of persecution.

felt that if they were able to get any jobs at all, they would be in the low status positions of teacher or clerk. On the other hand most of the Lingayat and Vokkaliga students considered that their futures were bright, for they knew that when seeking employment they could rely not only on financial assistance from the government for education, but also on help from influential caste members.

The Brahmans in Mysore, then, feel very insecure and see little hope of rectifying their position. Their greatest fears centre around education, for although they are still proportionately much more highly educated than the other castes, the latter are catching up, and the rise of some of them to political power means that they can now "call the tune" as far as governmental privileges are concerned. Before the Mysore government introduced a hierarchy of Forward and Backward castes, merit and high marks counted, and the Brahmans received a good many scholarships. Now these go to the Lingayat and Vokkaliga students, although these students may get lower marks. Many Brahmans cannot attend college as they cannot afford the fees. Nor can the Brahmans, with little political power, use caste nepotism as a means of protecting their share of seats in the colleges, or later, of jobs in the civil service.[5] Since appointments and promotions in the colleges and universities of Mysore are now almost completely under government control (except in private colleges), they see one of their former important occupational channels slowly closing to them. A radical change in the caste background of those in the top positions of the colleges and universities has already occurred. Brahmans are now seldom selected to head the new colleges that are springing up. Few of them are now heads of departments in the existing colleges,

5. Through age concessions to the Backward castes, members of these groups have until they are twenty-seven years of age to get government jobs, whereas the Brahmans must be under twenty-four years of age. One result of this is that Brahman parents often push their children much harder so that they will attain the necessary qualifications for a government job at the earlier age.

Figures were not available for the caste composition of the students in all the colleges of Bangalore. However, statistics from two colleges indicate that there is still a much larger proportion of young Brahmans attending college than of members of the other three communities:

	Brahmans	Christians	Lingayats	Vokkaligas	Total
Women's College					
Third-year students	187	17	19	7	329
Co-educational College					
Men and women	563	18	61	146	817

and their control over promotions within the colleges and universities is almost nil.[6]

Christianity has been looked on as a foreign religion in India, brought in by the British conquerors, and forced on the Indians by missionaries.[7] In the minds of the Hindus, all Indian Christians are lumped together as one group, and they see little difference between Roman Catholics and the Protestant sects. In reality, however, the two form distinct groupings and have as little feeling of identification in India as they do in Western countries. However, the two groups are alike in that they are more urban and Westernized than most of the other communities. They are also ahead of most castes, except for the Brahmans, in literacy and in their command of English.[8]

After Independence the Christian Indians lost the favoured position which they had held during the British regime.[9] In the process, they lost many of the explicit and implicit privileges accorded them by the British. Their feelings of isolation when faced by a potentially antagonistic Hindu majority which felt them to be outsiders prompted the Anglicans, Presbyterians, and Methodists to amalgamate into the Church of South India. Thus, one section of Christians closed their ranks at this crucial epoch. They have continued to run their schools and colleges

6. Many cases were cited by informants of Brahman professors whose students of other caste background had been promoted to ranks above them in the colleges. These illustrations show how a plan, which was implemented in order to help the lower castes achieve more equality, has resulted in lowering the efficiency of the educational system, for, as more and more Brahmans have been replaced by men from the less educated castes, less capable men become lecturers, and are replaced by equally incapable ones. An article by a correspondent in the *Economic Weekly* has this to say about the situation:

Correspondent: "Profile of a Southern State," *Economic Weekly*, July 21, 1956, pp. 859-62: "It is well known that over the last three or four decades the University has been trying to blow its brains out, and has succeeded in its task. . . . Mysore University is one hundred per cent a limb of the government. . . . All non-Brahman castes are 'Backward,' including the all-powerful Lingayats and Vokkaligas. . . . Even in an 'A' vacancy, a better qualified Brahman may be turned down in favour of a non-Brahman who has the minimum qualifications for the post. . . . In brief, the mode of selection has ensured the weeding out of the brightest in favour of the duller. . . . A young non-Brahman with not even five years of service frequently supersedes his Brahman teacher with a teaching experience of ten to fifteen years. . . . Each instance of supersession adds to the collective demoralization of the Brahmans. Slowly the group came to be what they are to-day—embittered, self-centred, and negative."

7. Nanavati and Vakil, pp. 90-102.

8. Kingsley Davis, "Adolescence and the Social Structure," *Annals of the American Academy of Political and Social Science, 1944.* Quoted from Jerome M. Seidman, *The Adolescent: A Book of Readings,* pp. 169-86. Davis says that whereas the 1931 Census gave the number of Christians in India as 1.77 per cent of the population, he estimated that they would be 1.91 per cent of the total population in 1941.

9. R. A. Schermerhorn, "Where Christians are a Minority," pp. 497-509. This article gives an account of the early and present history of the Christians in India.

which, because of their higher standards and stricter discipline, are sought after by many Hindu parents.[10] The Christians do not form a very large group in Bangalore, and the Protestants and Roman Catholics do not seem to be very closely united.

The Anglo-Indians belong to both Catholic and Protestant faiths, but have always been considered a group apart by Christians as well as by Hindus. This is due partly to their having mixed blood, and partly to their having taken over many British customs in food and dress. They are faithful followers of such British festivals as Christmas. Most of the Christian Indian women wear saris, but Anglo-Indian women wear the Western type of dress. They consider England to be their spiritual home, and many have migrated to that country since Independence. This exodus has confirmed the Hindus' stereotype of their not being completely Indian, either "biologically," or in their loyalties, and thus the prejudices against them have intensified. In their interviews, the Anglo-Indian students showed how this affected them. *Ch. 120*: "Caste feelings are quite strong in the colleges. The Indians think we are different from them. They ridicule us and make fun of our culture, dress, and the way we live. They think we are lower than them. They rarely invite us to their homes."

10. *Ibid.*, p. 502. "Education assumed a salient position among Christians. The leaders . . . founded hundreds of schools, colleges, and institutes where a new generation of clerks, teachers, ministers, priests, and white-collar workers were graduated for new positions in a changing India. . . . What was perhaps unexpected, or if not unexpected, unprepared for, was the rush to Christian schools of Hindus, Parsis, Sihks, Muslims, and aboriginals. The overwhelming importance of English instruction as a prerequisite for upward social mobility stimulated increasing numbers of non-Christians from wealthy or ambitious families to attend mission schools in the early twentieth century, beginning a trend that continued even after the departure of the British. Particularly influential in this process was the novel emphasis, at least in India, on the education of women in Christian schools."

Observation of many of the Christian colleges seems to show that they are better equipped to introduce the Indian students to the modern world than are most of the other Indian colleges. In the first place, the discipline is stricter, with more emphasis on work, and a more serious attitude to study. They are also likely to follow many more of the non-academic standards of the Western world, laying a greater emphasis on sport, dramatics, school uniforms, and better libraries. They are more likely to exchange teachers with Western colleges, and the Western teachers bring back some of the atmosphere of college life in the highly industrialized countries. Many of the lecturers in the Hindu colleges are there because they cannot get other jobs, so they may not be as devoted to their students. Many of the leading teachers in the Christian colleges are dedicated people —priests, nuns, or older single women—who have given their lives to teaching.

It seems probable, too, that the women lecturers in Christian colleges are more feministic, more independent, and readier to accept change than most Hindu women lecturers.

Finally, the Christian religions have greater possibility of changing with the times. For they have a modern rationalization and interpretation of life. They are thus able to offer stronger psychological support to the students through their traditional period.

Several of them said that they were forced to migrate to the United Kingdom because they could not get jobs, particularly in the civil service. This has made them feel even more insecure and more anxious to leave India. Under the British they had safe occupational niches in the railways, and in some of the minor civil service posts, but since Independence, their economic position has tended to deteriorate. They have a fairly low standard of living, and so, although many families can manage to send their children to the Anglo-Indian schools, few of these children can go on to attend college. Out of the five Anglo-Indian students in their final B.A. or B.Sc. year in the Bangalore colleges, four were interviewed.

The standard of living of most of the other Christians is also relatively low, but their higher educational standards, and their closer identification with the Western way of life have given them a high standard of aspirations. Parents often impoverish the family in order to send their children to college. As they know that their children must have very high marks in order to get a seat in a professional college, a good deal of pressure is put on them to study. Like the Hindus, they do not like their sons to do menial work, and so many Christian students go through the discouraging and frustrating experience of sitting around after graduation, waiting for a "good" job to turn up. Having been classified by the Mysore government as a Forward caste, along with the Brahmans and a few wealthy sub-castes, the Christians have few educational and job privileges. Many of them are sure that the government is against them. Their feelings contrast with those of Christians in such states as Madras and Andhra, where there is no strong caste control in politics.

The Lingayat community originated in the twelfth century in South India as a religious offshoot from the main body of the Hindu religion. The Lingayats are now regarded as a Hindu caste. This community has always been very strongly united, having had "an ecclesiastical organization comparable in thoroughness to that of Catholic Rome."[11] This organization was maintained through its priestly sub-caste, which performed political, economic, and religious functions for the group. Over the years, the Lingayats spread rapidly in the south, chiefly in the

---

11. H. V. Nanjundayya, *Mysore Tribes and Castes*, p. 81. The Lingayats worship Siva through the symbol of the linga, a phallic symbol which is worn on a cord around the neck. The movement was a religious protest against the power of the Brahmans. In a way it was a movement of Dravidians against the Aryans from the north, as well as a protest against the combined power of the king and the priests.

Kannada-speaking areas. They were originally peasants, but were gradually able to get more education as they moved into the cities. They became merchants and entered public administration, the professions, and other urban occupations. At the same time, they gradually took over many of the customs of the prestigious Brahman caste, such as vegetarianism.

Around 1900 a movement started within the caste to try and raise the Lingayats from their depressed condition. One of the major aims of this movement was to increase Lingayat power by inducing the government to bring the Kannada-speaking areas of the neighbouring states of Bombay and Hyderabad within the jurisdiction of the state of Mysore, for these areas contained many Lingayats. In 1956, when Mysore and several other Indian states were reorganized on a linguistic basis, these areas were incorporated into Mysore, and the Lingayat population rose to 20 per cent of the total. This changed the Lingayats from "a loose sectarian alliance of sub-castes into a united regional force." It also enabled them to outnumber the Vokkaligas, formerly the largest caste. The latter now constitute only 15 per cent of the population.[12]

The Vokkaligas belong to the chief cultivating caste of Mysore, and are often said to be the most distinctly Kanarese of all castes, for they have no historic or other ties outside the region.[13] Although many of them are still very poor, those who have become wealthy could be called the *nouveau riche* of Mysore, for even after a generation in the city, they are still unsure of themselves amongst the more sophisticated urban people. Their rural roots are strong, and they tend to retain their rural properties after moving to the city because they prefer to return to their native villages on retirement. On the whole, the Lingayats are more urbanized, have more education, and are wealthier. On the other hand, the Vokkaligas, having remained largely in rural areas, have not had as much education and so have not been able to take over the more prestigious and remunerative positions. These factors, plus the greater numerical strength of the Lingayats, explain why they hold slightly more power in the State Legislative Assembly of Mysore.

It was during World War II that these two castes gained political power in Mysore. The wartime rise in food prices made many of them wealthy, and this, in turn, encouraged them to aspire to higher positions of power and prestige. After Independence they became rivals for politi-

12. Selig Harrison, *The Most Dangerous Decade*, pp. 111-14.
13. Nanjundayya, p. 81.

cal power in Mysore; their aspirations rose, and they began to seek more education. It is now often possible for the sons of Lingayats or Vokkaligas to enlist the aid of a caste politician, even if they do not belong to one of the powerful families.[14] This is not as easy for people from the other two communities. Such advantages, combined with the greater possibility of obtaining scholarships and freeships as members of a Backward community, enable the Lingayats and Vokkaligas to face the future with less anxiety than students from the other communities.

These, then, were the four communities from which a sample of students was drawn, in order to get some idea of the importance of community background in relation to student indiscipline. The smaller proportion of Christian, Lingayat, and Vokkaliga students made it difficult to get an even sample from each group. There was only a small number of Vokkaliga women students due to the fact that so few women from this caste yet attend college. This is one of the last castes to permit its women higher education.

In spite of variations as regards feelings of security among the students of the four communities included in this sample, caste and religious background did not appear to be important factors as far as student indiscipline was concerned. A later chapter will show that in a sample group of students who had actively participated in formal indiscipline, both the men and the women students came from the three castes, as well as from the Christian religion. The only exception was the case of Vokkaliga women. In this sample, none of them qualified, according to the criteria of this study, as "Participants." However, this might have been due to the fact that as has already been mentioned, very few young Vokkaliga women are given a college education. The women students of this caste were by no means behind the others in indulging in informal indiscipline.

However, although caste or religious background did not appear to be a variable that had much effect on indiscipline, it was significant in increasing the anxieties of the students in regard to their education and careers.

CHANGING RELATIONSHIPS WITHIN THE FAMILY

Three main aspects of the students' changing relationships to their families were thought to be significant for student indiscipline. In the

14. From a correspondent: "Profile of a Southern State—Mysore." *Economic Weekly,* July 21, 1956, pp. 860-64.

first place, the traditional responsibilities of sons and daughters are bound to change in an industrial society. New, more formal responsibilities will arise, which may bear heavily on children until they have been released from some of their former family obligations. This can cause considerable strain which may, in turn, lead to indiscipline. Secondly, as the students move out into the world, new interests and relationships will tend to separate them from their families. The degree to which this was occurring in this sample of students was tested through ascertaining their affection for their families, and their desire to live with them after marriage. In the third place, family quarrels and/or disagreements would be expected to increase as the students became more independent, and the young people would tend to resent the more traditional behaviour expected of them at home. Problems of this type might upset the students and make them more prone to releasing their tensions at college.

FAMILY RESPONSIBILITIES

One of the fundamental changes that takes place with the coming of urbanization and industrialization is a shift in the rights and duties of the different family members. Not only is the individual obliged to reorient his obligations in terms of his gradually widening circle of contacts, but the changes taking place within the family redistributes his responsibility and/or changes the emphasis of the obligations and rights of different roles.[15]

One of the basic tenets of the Hindu religion is that of personal duty toward family and kin. This concept is so deeply rooted in the Hindu philosophy of life that any denial of these duties may arouse deep feelings of guilt. On the other hand, feelings of resentment, insecurity, and antagonism may arise on the part of those whose expectations of aid

---

15. Aileen D. Ross, *The Hindu Family in Its Urban Setting*, p. 88. "The forces of industrialization and urbanization bring a gradual change in the expectations of responsibility. On the one hand, they shrink to the immediate family of parents and children, but, on the other, they widen to the community, and they even become national or international in scope; so that finally a stage is reached at which even close relatives in need are considered 'public' problems rather than personal ones. Attitudes correspondingly change as outside agencies—such as governments—take over, so that public assistance gradually ceases to be a stigma, and people accept it without shame or guilt, as 'naturally' as they formerly accepted the help of close relatives. This change will, of course, not come evenly or easily, particularly if individuals are brought up to the traditional deep sense of family responsibility which is firmly implanted in the Hindu joint family by religious sanction."

have not altered, and who find that they are not treated in the way that they had expected.

The traditional concept of family responsibility has been one of the reasons for the solidarity of the joint family in the past, and has served the function of knitting the members, and of even more distant kin, into a strong system of mutual responsibilities and obligations. In the traditional Hindu family this included an expected hierarchy of those who would give assistance.

In the Hindu system of family obligations, the sons are expected to look after their parents in old age and illness. If there are no sons, then it is the duty of daughters. After daughters, obligations in order fall on brothers, uncles, aunts, and finally any other relatives. Typically, too, these duties were not thought of as burdens, but as privileges. In fact, it was a matter of pride to be the son or daughter whom the parents chose to live with in old age.[16]

This traditional pattern is one of the last to give way when industrialization forces other changes, and its laggard nature makes it difficult to remodel a society on a modern basis.

Nepotism remains a dominant source of corruption in social and political life. This is in part due to the carry-over of exclusive family loyalties into the life of a nation. People reared and trained in a joint family system find it difficult to conceive of duty as transcending family and sub-caste loyalties. A development of democracy requires the recognition of a large area of life separated from family ties and based on the rule of law. The rule of law has to be impersonal if it is to be impartial. From this angle, the old and emergent patterns of family structure need to be examined.[17]

In the traditional Indian family, the sons were financially responsible for the support of their parents in their old age. As soon as they began to earn, they were also supposed to assist in getting together the doweries of their sisters, and in seeing that their brothers got jobs.[18] With the development of formal education, these obligations were extended in the higher castes to include the education of younger brothers, and later, education of sisters. These are now considered normal responsibilities.

16. *Ibid.*, p. 70. See also: Irwati Karve, *Kinship Organization in India*, p. 136.

17. A. P. D. Barnabas, "Patterns of the Rural Family," p. 30.

18. *Ibid.*, p. 79. "One important aspect of family obligation is the way sons take over financial responsibilities as soon as they are earning. They are expected not only to contribute to the family purse when living at home, but to continue to send money to the family when they move away for a job, even though earning very little themselves."

The increase in higher education for women can be construed as an indication of the growing financial responsibilities that parents and brothers have to assume.

This sample of college men and women, like a group of interviewees in a previous study, varied extensively as regards their positions in this spectrum of changing responsibilities. Some had moved far away from the traditional patterns, both in the geographical sense of having moved away from their villages or kinsmen, and in the psychological sense of having taken over new ambitions which forced them to concentrate all their efforts on building their own careers.[19]

The data from the sample showed that daughters are now tending to assume some of the responsibilities formerly borne by sons, such as helping their families financially. It is only recently that women of the higher and middle castes have worked outside their homes, and so have been able to help. The higher cost of living for urban, as compared to rural families; the later age of marriage, which leaves the girl with a number of empty years after college; and the increasing demand for white-collar workers, due to the expansion of commerce and industry, are all responsible for this change in the young woman's role.

The longer period of time that daughters spend at home before marriage gives them a stronger sense of identity with their own families. Child marriage weakened this bond and enabled the young bride to develop a sense of loyalty and responsibility to her husband's family, while still in the formative stage of her development. Now, however, most educated girls do not marry until after they have finished college, or, as is becoming more typical, not until some years after college, when they are bound more closely into the system of obligations of their own home. Thus, it might be hypothesized that at least part of the family disorganization today could be attributed to the fact that a girl with a college education, who marries at twenty-five, has quite a different problem as regards changing her kinship loyalties and taking over a sense of responsibility to her husband's family, than did the child bride. Indeed, a system of bilateral obligations typical of the modern Western family gradually seems to be developing in India, and the daughter often feels the responsibility to aid parents or siblings as strongly as does the son.

New trends are influencing the people of the middle class in India. It is this class which is feeling the greatest income pressure, for with

19. Ross, pp. 67-90.

increasing industrialization, real money income is declining, while aspirations continue to rise. It is probable, therefore, that the burden of responsibility of the middle class young man is getting heavier. He tends to marry an educated girl who presumably has more needs and desires than an uneducated one. Thus, in spite of the fact that his sister now sometimes shares part of the financial burden for a few years, and his wife may work after marriage to help the family budget, the increasing needs of his family may be far ahead of his ability to fulfill them.

The responsibility the male students of this sample felt toward their parents varied considerably. Some had a deep emotional attachment to them and could not imagine not caring for them forever. Many said that they would willingly and gladly look after them and would be proud to do so. Others felt it to be a duty. Their parents had brought them up and educated them, so their children had a moral responsibility to them. Still others qualified their terms of assistance. Some said that it depended on the jobs they got: "You cannot contribute to the family income if you are married and only earn a little." Some of the students said that they could not help financially now, but would do so later, if they were able. Such qualifications are a change from the rigid requirements of a traditional family system.

Eighty-five male students said they wanted to take complete financial responsibility for their parents when the latter grew old. These attitudes may not be too significant, because when the students replied, often their first impulse would be to speak in terms of their training. Whether they would carry out this responsibility when the occasion demanded it is another matter. However, there may be some significance in the fact that forty-seven of the students said they wanted only to help support their parents. This might be due to the fact that there were sometimes other brothers to assist. On the other hand, it may support the trend shown by the students who said that they did not feel that it was their responsibility to support their parents financially in their old age. Ten students (one Brahman, six Christians, two Lingayats, and one Vokkaliga) reported they did not feel it to be a moral duty to do so. Five of the students had no parents, and twelve did not answer the question.

Some differences were found in the attitudes of the students from the four communities. Whereas twenty-three Lingayats and thirty-nine Brahmans wanted to support their parents completely, only nineteen Vokkaliga and four Christian students wished to do the same.

Students from poor families who had suffered from poverty, and who had witnessed their father's struggle to support the family were particularly anxious to help. In one case, the father augmented his pension by working, which brought his total income up to Rs.60 per month. He paid his son's college fees, and gave him Rs.6 for pocket money each month. This student considered it his "essential duty" to look after his father, who had sacrificed so much for him, and he was determined to care for him, even if he had to remain unmarried to do so.

Several students seemed to feel that if they did not assume these responsibilities, some sort of retribution might befall them: "If I do not help I will not survive." Some felt an almost overpowering moral obligation to their parents, particularly if they were only sons, and emphasis was often put on seeing that the parents lived a happy life in retirement. Several loved their parents, but were not sure enough about their own futures to know whether or not they would be able to help them. One said that if he got a good position and a handsome salary, he would be willing to help.

Parents often reciprocated by being particularly careful about the welfare of the student upon whom they depended, as they knew that if he failed them they would have no one to look after them in later life.

The tradition that the eldest son should take over the major family responsibilities if a father dies or retires, or when the son, himself, begins to earn, is still rigidly adhered to. "The time at which sons begin to make money usually coincides roughly with two of the major family expenses, the marriage of daughters, and the education of the younger sons. The eldest son being the first to earn will have to contribute more than the others, especially if he is much older than his brothers. When he becomes head of a family his main responsibilities will be similar to the father's—supporting the family, educating his younger brothers, and marrying his sisters."[20]

Students from this sample had not questioned this obligation as yet, although the eldest son was sometimes able to escape it. Sometimes this burden is very heavy. *Li. 26*: "I have great responsibilities to shoulder in the family as I am the eldest son. My father is ready to retire now, so it is time for me to render service to the family. I must shoulder the responsibility by helping to educate my brothers and sisters in order to keep up the long-standing prestige of the family. I will only marry after my last brother is settled in life. This will give my parents some peace

20. Ross, p. 79.

of mind for a few years. So I have made up my mind not to continue my studies, because we have not enough money for the fees."

In one family the father was dead and the eldest son, with his wife and three children, lived at home with the mother. His brother, his three sisters, and the three daughters and two sons of another sister all lived with them. *Br. 14*: "My brother has to look after them all. It takes about Rs.500 a month to do so. He has nothing extra for illness or crises. The first sister's marriage cost about Rs.8,000, and the family finally has managed to clear that debt. They now have to face Rs.8,000 for the second sister's marriage. After that there are two more sisters still living at home who have to be married off."

The obligation of the eldest son to take over the family responsibilities is so strong that in one case the elder brother's insistence that he should live separately caused a grave problem. Another case showed that, even under extreme pressure from the family, the eldest son would not take the burden of obligations expected of him.

Br. 102: After he graduated, my brother got a job at a salary of Rs.150 per month. Father insisted that he pay the family Rs.100 from this sum, and keep Rs.50 for his own expenses, but my brother had other ideas. He wanted more money for himself, to buy clothes, a bicycle and other things. So the trouble started. Father insisted that he give him the Rs.100. When my brother pleaded that he could not afford to give him that much they quarrelled, and Father told him to clear out of the house. My brother was always a sensitive fellow, and a little hot-headed and independent, so he walked out and we have not seen him for five years.

This shows that the responsibility to help the family financially is something you cannot escape, unless you leave home. I don't think Father should have demanded money as a right. He used to always shout at my brother, "Did I not feed you, clothe you and help you stand on your own? Now that you can be independent you are ungrateful; a dog would have been more faithful." From my father's point of view we were really very badly off, what with the high cost of living, school fees, bus fares, and clothes, and so Father thought my brother was hard-headed, irresponsible, and selfish. On the other hand my brother had had so many miseries that he thought that at last when he was earning he could have some good clothes and other things. So both were right.

The change in attitudes toward responsibility to relatives varies considerably, according to such criteria as urbanization, affection, past assistance, and the degree to which the family has changed from a joint to a nuclear type. Several informants insisted that many nuclear families no longer feel responsible for, or want to look after their relatives. In fact, they often refuse to do so. It has been the tradition in many rural families to send the children to relatives in the city to board. The latter may even pay their educational costs. This custom is now beginning to cause great inconvenience to many city families, for it is impossible for them to add extra people to the household in a small city unit. Resistance to this pattern is thus beginning to appear.

Twenty-five of the male students (seventeen Brahmans, one Christian, seven Lingayats, and ten Vokkaligas) said they wanted to support their relatives if they needed help. Twelve (nine Brahmans, one Christian, and two Lingayats) said that they would not. Twelve other students (four Brahmans, two Christians, four Lingayats, and two Vokkaligas) said there was no need to do so. Perhaps most interesting of all were the eighty-six students (twenty-three Brahmans, twenty-two Christians, seventeen Lingayats, and twenty-four Vokkaligas) who said that they had no relatives to help. This might be an indication of the extent to which families are changing from the joint to the nuclear form. However, it may be that the question was interpreted too narrowly by the students, as assistance can be of many types. "Relatives were not only taken in to live, or fed, looked after when ill or old, and given financial assistance, but also they were given much advice and sympathy. In recent years educating nieces or nephews, or getting them jobs or government posts, is an important part of the family obligations of middle and upper class families."[21]

A close bond of sympathy or affection for their relatives increased the student's desire to help them. A number of students declared that they hated their relatives, for they had not helped their own families when they were in difficulties. Several were contemptuous of them, expected nothing from them, did not want their help, and would certainly not help them. Several warned against any close contacts with relatives: "It is better to keep aloof." Others said they should be treated as friends, rather than as part of the family.

The male Hindu's heavy traditional obligation to his siblings was made evident, to some extent, in the interviews. The students' replies were probably often just as much automatic responses to their deeply instilled obligations as they had been when they replied about the responsibility they felt toward their parents. However, in view of the number of students in this sample, and of their brothers and sisters,

21. Ross, p. 70.

who were actually assisting siblings, it is probable that the sibling tie is still close enough to entail a good deal of mutual help.

In fourteen cases the brother of a student had helped to finance his education, and in six other families it was the brother who had supplied the student with pocket money. In two families, sisters gave the student his pocket money from their salaries. In ten families, the students worked, as well as studied, and a few of these students contributed to the family finances.

The responses of the students were influenced by their feelings of affection for their brothers and sisters, and by the position they held in the family. Younger brothers and sisters did not feel as much responsibility as did the older ones. Students from wealthy families often said there was no need to help. One student sighed deeply when questioned about family responsibilities, and said that he would help educate his sisters, and help them get married "out of courtesy." Others said that much would depend on the salaries they earned; if their salaries were high enough, they would help. Two felt a moral responsibility to do their share later, as their education had been a financial burden on their own brothers.

In all, sixty-one (twenty-five Brahmans, three Christians, nineteen Lingayats, and fourteen Vokkaligas) said they would help educate their brothers, and sixty-six (thirty-three Brahmans, three Christians, fifteen Lingayats, and fifteen Vokkaligas) said they would help educate their sisters. The fact that eighty of the students (thirty-four Brahmans, seven Christians, tweny-one Lingayats, and eighteen Vokkaligas) said they would help marry their sisters might be an indication that they thought this role for girls more appropriate than education. All these figures might have been higher had all the students had siblings, but thirteen of them had no brothers, and six had no sisters; thus, they did not reply to the question.

Only a few Brahman, Lingayat, and Vokkaliga students said they would not actually help, but nineteen Christian students were against assisting their siblings. The fact that, compared with other groups, so many more Christian students said they did not want to help educate either their brothers or their sisters is probably due to the difference in their expected family obligations. The Christian families are much more like Western, Anglo-Saxon families than are those of the other three groups, and the members are brought up with a more individualistic view of life. As a large proportion of the Christian girls work, they are more able to look after themselves. It is probable, too, although no statistics are available, that more of the Christian girls work after marriage. Forty-seven Christian students said there was no need to educate their brothers, fifty-two did not see the necessity for educating their sisters, and thirty-five felt there was no need to help marry their sisters.

The financial burdens of most middle-class Hindu parents are so heavy that they have little or no chance of saving for the future. The great anxiety of the parents to see that their sons well placed follows from a realistic appraisal of the future, for the son must reciprocate by looking after his parents when they can no longer look after themselves. The system has worked on the principle that the parents did not need to save, as their future was secure.

The extent of the dependency burden of some students is shown in some of the Christian families represented in this sample. Two of the students from these families were very wealthy; one of them owned plantations and houses and came from a very rich family. The other came from the richest Christian family in a southern city, and this student expected to receive large amounts of money in the near future. However, at the other extreme were the students from families which were definitely poor. In one case, the father was dead, and the family was aided by a brother who helped by sending back money from another part of India. In another case, there were nine children, and as it had been impossible for the parents to save any money, there was nothing for them to retire on. In still another, the family was always in financial difficulties until the sons and daughters were old enough to earn. Thus, in many of the Christian families, the father had not been able to put aside any money for old age, and if he had no pension, he was completely dependent on his children.

The dependency burden is very heavy for fathers who have low incomes, large families, or must assist relatives. A combination of two or three of these is disastrous, and often bears heavily on the sons as well. In one case, the father had to help finance the education of his brothers, and assist his two widowed sisters financially, in addition to supporting his own family. In another case, that of a Brahman family, the father sent money as often as he could to his brother who was supervising their lands in their village. He was also financing the medical education of his brother's son. When his brother died, the father found himself with his brother's wife and eight children to support, as well as his own nine children, five of whom were girls. In still another Braham family, eight sons had to be education. *Br. 64*: "My father is a godly man; he has never been harsh or hard-hearted towards us at any time. He is happy to support his family. My heart aches when I see him going out of the house every day at five o'clock in the morning, to work. As we were eight brothers, all of us students, you can imagine the difficulties Father had in educating us. He is always kind and hard-working. He is so kind that he prepares coffee very early in the morning and takes it to each one of us in bed. He always allows us to do as we think best, and this includes the way we study. He is always a source of inspiration and joy."

The new trend in the change in women's responsibilities was evident from the fact that twenty of the women students (ten Brahmans, five Christians, three Lingayats, and two Vokkaligas) wanted, or felt it to be their duty, to give part of their earnings to the family. These students also wanted to support their parents in their old age. Two of them did not want to marry, but wished to continue working to support their parents. Five of them said that they were "expected" to help. Eight other students said that, as their parents were well off, they would not need to help. Thus, out of the ninety-one women who were asked whether they were anxious to assist their parents financially, twenty answered in the affirmative. Fourteen of these students said they would even take a job to help their relatives if they were in need. This, too, is a new trend.

These small figures suggest that some young Indian women are beginning to take on the new role-component of financial responsibility for the family and are being drawn into the net of family duties.

CLOSENESS OF FAMILY IDENTIFICATION

Why do some students desire to live independently from their families? It is still exceptional to want to do so.

> Most Indians are not individual enough to start their own homes and plan their own lives, yet the need to have a small home in the pattern of the West has come to be a necessity. . . . The alternatives the Indian faces are to emancipate himself emotionally and establish a home, or to submit to the traditional way of life which ignores the violent changes going on around it, which would sweep away everything which stands in their way.[22]

22. Barnabas, p. 31. Jyotirmoyee Sarma, p. 222. "Since with us, wealth is maintained mostly in the form of land and houses, the division of property becomes a difficult affair. The division of the income on property takes place gradually. This period of transition may continue for several years, and is the hardest in any household. . . . The feeling that the members should continue to hold the house together, and that the present generation of sons should bring their wives into the house, continues to hold sway. . . . With each succeeding generation the relationships between the members become more distant. There is no general rule on how many generations are needed to require that a house be held together. It depends entirely on the convenience and the wishes of the inhabitants."

However, in view of the many pressures which are tending to break down the former joint families into nuclear units, it is to be supposed that this trend toward independence is increasing. The question remains whether this movement is an economic necessity in view of changing ambitions and higher aspirations, or whether it symbolizes the general desire on the part of sons to live independently. This problem is further obscured by the fact that a son may be forced to live with his family after marriage, or a daughter may have to live with her in-laws because of economic factors, or the inability of the families to support themselves separately. About all that can be done to clarify this trend is to describe the attitudes of a sample of students who were asked whether they wanted to live separately, keeping in mind the fact that, not having experienced this situation, their opinions would often be merely reflections of their training. One could also count the number of young men who have formed an independent family unit after marriage. In a former study, information was acquired on the number of brothers over eighteen years of age who had left home. Of the two hundred and seven brothers mentioned by the sample, one hundred and ten were living away from home, often in distant cities; the remaining ninety-seven were living with their families. The separation of brothers from their families had been due mainly to the problem of finding suitable jobs. However, some of the younger men had moved to distant cities in order to escape from painful family situations, or to avoid family conflicts. Other reasons were the desire to be economically independent, the wish to avoid conflict after marrying a woman of another caste, and the feeling that living independently would be a more satisfactory and pleasant arrangement.[23]

The response of the male students of this sample showed that the great majority of them had not yet broken away from the tradition that sons should live with their parents after marriage. Ten Brahman, five Lingayat, and seven Vokkaliga male students wanted to live separately, and for much the same reasons. The main reason was the father's strictness, or the fact that he was too religious or orthodox. Other reasons given were: unhappy families, the disadvantages of the joint family system, the desire to get away from family quarrels, and the desire for independence and a good time. Only five of the Christian students wanted to live with their parents; twenty-four definitely did not, and two did not answer the question. Their attitude probably stems from

23. Ross, pp. 41-50.

the fact that Christian families bring up their sons to be much more independent. They are not expected to live with their parents as are the sons of families from other castes. The twenty-four Christian students who wanted to live separately gave as reasons their desire for greater freedom, their wish to run their own homes in their own way, and the disadvantages of living in a joint family.

The great majority of the students who said that they wanted to live with their parents after marriage showed a strong sense of family responsibility, and often spoke of their feelings for their family with deep emotion. Some were eldest sons, and they felt that they should stay with the family because they had particular responsibilities. Others either loved large families, did not want to marry, or loved their mothers or sisters so much that they wanted to stay with them. A few whose fathers were dead felt that they should stay to look after their mothers. "I want my wife to serve my beloved mother." The remaining students did not have such a strong sense of identification with their families. They felt that there was some good in having separate families, although they themselves preferred to live with their mothers, or with the family. Some thought that certain circumstances, such as getting jobs in another part of the country, might take them away. Others felt it to be a duty to stay with the family, but their fathers were so strict that they would have liked to have escaped from them, or from family fights. Others felt that their parents could look after themselves, or that the burden of looking after a family would be too great after their fathers died. Several students were afraid that the good name of the family would suffer if they moved away, for the move might be interpreted by neighbours as being due to family quarrels. On the whole, then, these students were undecided. On the one hand, loyalties and duties tied them to their families; on the other, their desire to be independent, the strict family controls over their behavior, the desire to be alone more often, and fear of fathers or grandfathers made them yearn to be on their own.

One thing that may increase the opposition to sons becoming independent of their families is the growing insecurity of parents. The latter now have fewer relatives to lean on, at a time when their children are becoming more expensive to provide for, and this makes it more difficult to save for old age. Thus, the increasing independence of their children may alarm them and may cause the parents to try to hold them when they attempt to escape.

The question of whether a student will live apart from his family after he marries is more relevant for male than for female students. A young man is the more important financial support. His living independently implies that he may be trying to get away from family responsibilities.

The equivalent to a son's wanting to live with his family after marriage is the daughter's wanting to live with her in-laws. The former actually has more opportunity for leaving his family, as the daughter's decision depends largely on her husband, but it is important to know whether the daughter's desire to live separately is increasing in view of her growing independence, of her later age at marriage, and of the general influence of an urban society. A large increase in the number of women wanting to live separately would have an influence on the decisions of their husbands to live apart from their families, and so would help to break down the joint family pattern.[24] There is little comparative data to show whether the tendency for young women to want to live separately from their in-laws is in fact more marked than formerly. In this study, twenty-eight students (eleven Brahmans, ten Christians, one Lingayat, and six Vokkaligas) said that they did not want to live with their in-laws. Five others (two Brahmans, one Christian, one Lingayat, and one Vokkaliga) said they would if it was necessary. Twenty-seven Brahmans, eight Christians, eight Lingayats, and one Vokkaliga, forty-seven in all, said that they wanted to live with their in-laws after marriage. The rest of the students either did not want to marry, or gave no answer to the question.

The attitudes of the women toward this subject, as in the case of the men students, varied considerably. Some had a submissive attitude, which came from the traditional training they had received at home, and these felt it was the duty of children to live with their parents when they were old. This view is illustrated by a Brahman student. *Br. 219:* "I think it is the duty of a son to be with his parents when they are old. For instance, when we four children get married and go away, my brother should live with my parents. He will not be filling his obligation, or doing his duty if he just sends money home every month. After all they have done for us I want somebody to stay with them and say thanks to them."

Many are not worried about the problem. The training that girls get in adjusting to their in-laws is shown in the following interview. *Br. 173:*

24. Ross, pp. 41-49. See also p. 289. This study showed a small trend in the desire for young brides to live separately from their in-laws.

"My mother sometimes advises me to look after my mother-in-law and father-in-law lovingly and very happily if I expect God to bless me and my family. When they are old they will need help, and I am prepared to adjust to their temperament."

Those who wanted to live with their in-laws gave a variety of reasons. Some had never questioned the matter. Some felt it to be their duty. Others thought it would be very helpful for a young wife to have the guidance and help of the older members of her husband's family. Other reasons were a preference for large families, the feeling that life would be less lonely, and the fact that the in-laws could help with the children, both practically and financially. In return, the young couple could look after the parents-in-law in their old age and could help educate their brothers-in-law.

Another group was more realistic in its outlook. Five said that they would live with their in-laws, "if necessary." If they lived in the same city or town it would be very difficult to avoid living with them. *Br. 169*: "After marriage there won't be much choice; if we live in the same town it will be the natural thing for us to live together. I don't think I'll have the courage to insist on a separate house. Our society and our relatives would condemn me. Besides, the boys in our community would prefer to live with their parents. I often worry as to whether I'll be able to adjust to my in-laws. I am afraid they will not appreciate me or like me. I am afraid that they may turn out to be very narrow-minded. I like to do things on my own; I am not the submissive type."

One student said that she would prefer to live in an independent family after marriage, but that "if there are old in-laws to be looked after, then I'll stay with them, as it is my duty to do so."

Others did not want to live with their in-laws because they had heard so much about the problems which arose between mothers-in-law and daughters-in-law. *Ch. 228*: "The mother-in-law might turn out to be very cruel to me. The in-laws may not like my views on things. We may not like or dislike the same things, so it is better to have a separate house and keep one's freedom. If my relatives wanted to live with me, my in-laws might not like them visiting us. If I lose my parents I would want to have my sisters live with me, but the in-laws would be sure to object to it, so it is better to have a separate establishment from the beginning. Then my husband and I could both send money to our relatives, and our relatives on both sides can visit us whenever they want to."

It seemed that on the whole, the students worried more about living with their in-laws than about their life with their prospective husbands.

Those who did not want to live with their in-laws felt this way because they had not had a happy time in the joint family, or because they had seen how other people had suffered. *Br. 233*: "Grandmother is very cruel to my mother. She does not even allow her to select her clothes or anything for the home. To say the least, she treats her cruelly. Even my father cannot check his mother, so he says that Mother has to put up with her."

A few students wanted to live separately because they cherished their freedom and independence, and did not want to face the problems of adjustment.

> *Br. 200*: When I marry I do not want to stay with my in-laws, for I feel that I will have to obey them and do as they like. I am fed up with restrictions. I do not want to have more from more people, though I will have to put up with my husband's, as it is my duty.
>
> I love seeing movies, and sometimes worry whether my in-laws will allow me to see them. I would also like to go out in the evenings. I feel I'll be able to adjust myself to my in-laws, only I hope and pray that they won't be the orthodox type who want girls to remain shut up in the house all the time.

A new idea for some of the women students, probably the result of courses in home science, is that they want to have their own homes so that they can decorate them in the way they want, and arrange their time schedules to suit themselves. This might be prevented by the orthodoxy of their prospective in-laws.

On the whole, the girls' attitudes to living separately was a reflection of their experiences at home, of their own personalities, and, for a few, of changing circumstances that had borne heavily on their traditional position in the family.

The attitudes of the men and women students of this sample showed no conclusive trends, and no desire for a sharp and sudden break from their families or future families. The significance of the number who did, in fact, want to live apart, is difficult to estimate, for there are very few studies of student independence in the past that would help to substantiate a trend away from family life and its responsibilities. Perhaps all that can be said is that some of the students did not want to be too closely identified with their families or in-laws when they married, and that if the forces of modernization impinge on the Indian students in the way that they have on students in the West, this trend is likely to increase.

The comparison in Chapter VI of students who took part in organized indiscipline with those who did not suggests that the independence that underlies the movement away from the family also tends to make the student more independent at college. There, this independence finds expression in an increase in formal and informal indiscipline.

One of the basic changes that occurs when the joint family becomes a family of the nuclear type is a change in the structure of authority. The modern child grows up in an environment in which he must learn to be independent and to control his own life. The moral right of parents, and of the older family members to complete obedience and respect from their children was one of the most important traditions in the joint family, and could hardly undergo transformation without a good deal of family strain. The stage at which a young man assumes control over his own conduct is thus a constant family problem, for there are few clear guides to help parents decide when to allow him to make his own decisions. Each new area in which he gains independence may be fought over bitterly, and parents may be slow to relinquish control. Family conflict, then, may be an indication that the children are becoming emancipated from parental control. It may consist of daily minor quarrels which do not disrupt the family relationships, or it may be of such an intense nature that it builds up to prolonged battles of will. It may finally lead to the disintegration of the family. When family members live as close together physically as do the members of most Indian families, even a relatively minor quarrel may involve the whole household. It is possible that disagreements in the joint family are intensified by the fact that the members concerned cannot easily escape each other's company.

The majority of students interviewed said, at first, that they had few, or no conflicts at home. However, this did not necessarily mean that all their families had ideal relationships, or that all the students felt close to their parents, and respected them so much that they were in agreement with them and obeyed them willingly. More intensive interviewing showed that most of the students disagreed with their parents on some points and resented their strictness, but did not dare reveal their feelings because they could not face family displeasure. The traditional family structure is still strong enough that the parents' authority is accepted as inevitable by the children. This situation builds up tensions that are often released in other ways. It is possible that one of the main reasons for students' taking part in demonstrations at college is that they suffer little punishment there for their behaviour, in comparison to the pain they would have to endure in defying their families.

Quarrels at home are kept to a minimum in many of the families because the children either respect their parents and do not want to hurt or challenge them, or have not the courage to express their own views. There is fear, as well as respect, in the father-son relationship, and so a son tends to listen to what his father says without retaliating. Otherwise, he avoids contact with his father as much as possible. When the father comes home, for example, the boy will leave the house.

> *Br. 27*: Father was always very strict. Even now I cannot express my views in front of him, except over some minor matters, for I am afraid to face him boldly. So I don't quarrel openly with him, but only "inwardly." If I disagreed with him I might be sent out of the house. Then I would have to wander here and there without any education. I would probably have to do some sort of unpleasant work, and this would bring a bad mark to the family name. I do not want to take this rash action, so I will obey my parents until my education and marriage are over. Only then will I be able to plan my future as I want.

Of the male students questioned about family conflicts, twenty-eight (twelve Brahmans, eleven Christians, one Lingayat, and four Vokkaligas) said that they had many conflicts and disagreements at home. Thirty-three (twenty Brahmans, one Christian, six Lingayats, and six Vokkaligas) said that they had no conflicts or disagreements at home. Twenty-nine (eight Brahmans, ten Christians, three Lingayats, and eight Vokkaligas) said that they had a few conflicts. This is a very small sample, but it suggests that it is the Christians who have the most conflicts. On the other hand, among the Lingayats, only one person said that there had been many conflicts, and six out of the ten replying said that they had no conflicts.

The reason for this lack of conflict among the Lingayats interviewed was that the six who said they had no conflicts seemed to have very happy, close, affectionate relationships with their families. One said that he had nothing to quarrel about because his parents were wise and reasonable, not rude or strict. Another said that there was a perfect understanding between himself and his parents, even though the family was an orthodox one. Still another Lingayat appreciated the able guidance of his parents. The same relationship existed in the Vokkaliga families in which there was little or no conflict—that is, a perfect understanding existed between the parents and son, or else, as the student was away from home, there was no occasion for quarrels to arise. The one Christian who did not quarrel with his family had been trained to be good by a father to whom he looked up as a very religious and God-fearing man.

The fact that a student does not have family quarrels or disagreements does not necessarily mean that he accepts his parents' authority. He may have found a way to avoid an open clash. One informant explained how this may come about:

> Boys do not disagree with their father because they simply do not bring up subjects on which they know they would not agree, so there are not many opportunities to quarrel. They never disagree with him openly if they can help it. Girls cannot escape the family tutelage as easily, particularly that of the mother. It is also true that boys are generally more often the favourites of mothers, and as the girls are with her over longer periods of time, there are more opportunities for them to quarrel. Also, the mother is not feared as much as the father. It is, therefore, likely that there are a good many more disagreements amongst girls and their mothers than with boys and their fathers.

One way in which many Hindu children avoid trouble with their fathers is by getting their mothers to act as intermediaries. In several families in which the father was said to be very strict, the boy would tell his mother what he wanted, and she would go and ask the father for him. Another way of avoiding family conflict is through secrecy. Sons may obey their parents at home, but do what they like when they get away, thus releasing their tensions and avoiding trouble. *Ch. 144*: "I have to be a good boy at home, but outside the house I am a free man, and can do what I please. I am very free with my friends, and when I am with them I have a good time."

One of the reasons why the son avoids his father is that there is little companionship between them. Students do not usually chat with their fathers, or eat their meals with them. Their relationship changes when the son marries. The father then accepts his son as a responsible person, able to understand and participate in family responsibilities. The father-son relationship is different for students who live in villages, for in this situation the sons are usually more highly educated than their fathers. Thus, the latter dare not push their views too far.

These observations suggest that the traditional basic structure of the Hindu family has not yet changed as much as might be supposed from a superficial glance at the outward signs of behaviour. The Principal of a college said that in the south the family is still so powerful that even a hint that he might write to a student's family was usually enough to make the toughest boy submit.

As has been noted already, the Christian students seemed to have more quarrels at home than did students in the other communities. Some of the disagreements arose over the question of spending pocket money, but the main problem seemed to be that the students resented their parents' control and wanted to be independent. One student felt that he was treated like a small child, as his parents tried to force him to do things which he resented. *Ch. 128*: "Father is very strict, and we are all afraid of him. He shouts at us. I resent his shouting, and the more he shouts, the more I feel like defying him. I don't like authority. When someone tries to impose things on me I defy them." This quotation illustrates what seems to be a basic difference in the attitude of the Christian students toward authority, as compared with the attitudes of students from the other three castes. The Christians seem not only to resent it to a greater extent, but also to show more defiance. One reason for their attitude might be the fact that Christian families spend a great deal more time together and so have more opportunities for quarrelling. They take the morning and evening meal together, and spend more of their leisure time in each others' company. Sunday dinner is as much a family ritual with them as it is with Western families.

However, the actual problems that the Christians quarrelled over were the same as those mentioned by the students from other castes. The amount of money received and the way it was spent seemed to be one of the most constant causes of friction. Other problems included friends, the way in which leisure time was to be used, lateness in arriving home, not studying enough, and friction caused by the strictness of the father. These would probably be some of the main reasons for parent-son conflict in any country.

A father's strictness may seem so unbearable that it may be a major reason for a son's not wanting to live with his family in later life. *Li. 31*: "Our family conflict is due to my father's strictness. He does not allow me to entertain my friends. At present I am not in a position to leave my home; if I did, I would be helpless; so after college, when I feel I can stand on my own feet, I may leave the family. It is quite impossible to suit my father."

The orthodoxy of parents is another reason for conflict. This shows that the younger generation is gradually drawing away from the old traditions. *Li. 108*: "I have some disagreements with my parents over the superstitions they believe in, and in which I do not believe. For example, I am not supposed to travel on Tuesdays, Fridays, or new Mondays, and am not supposed to expect a money order from Father on certain days, even though I may be desperately in need of money. If I leave home on these particular days, everybody is upset, and life is a misery, for I hear later that Mother has taken no food, Father has been wild, etc. We have arguments and quarrels, very often shouting at each other. I don't like it, and don't think I should have to live this way."

"Old-fashioned" parents sometimes do not want their sons to wear new types of clothes. Their attitude reflects antipathy, not only to changes in fashion, but also to a change in the traditional type of dress which they may cherish. *Li. 34*: "My father hates the type of dress I wear. He prefers a dhoty, shirt, or pyjama, but I like the latest patterns and styles which most of the college students wear. Whenever I go to my village during vacation he comments on my dress. I argue with him, and he takes it seriously."

Coming home late was often resented by parents, even on "stuffy" summer evenings when the heat in the home was unbearable. In several cases students were able to slip out and come back unnoticed, but if they were caught they "faced the music."

Finally, several of the students had great trouble at home in trying to follow a career that their parents did not like. If the whole family is against the student, his position is extremely difficult.

Br. 58: I had always loved literature, especially in my favourite language, Kannada, but my parents and brothers wanted me to become an engineer. They were absolutely deaf to my interests, and so I was helpless and was forced to finish the engineering degree. But during those years my interest in Kannada literature increased tremendously; I kept on studying it by myself. So, outwardly in the eyes of the university I had a diploma in engineering, but my inward taste had developed for Kannada literature.

I did not want to spoil my hopes by going into an industrial concern, so I decided not to get a job but go on in literature. Because of this, the whole family turned against me, no one protected or defended me. I was very dejected and disgusted, and became a lonely man in a dark and dreary world of my own. But I still had strong hopes for my future, so with great courage I put my confidence in God, and against all their wishes, joined the pre-university course in my beloved Kannada medium. I was very happy and contented at college, but I had many unhappy moments at home, especially when many of my colleagues got jobs with decent salaries.

My family provides me with two meals a day and I have to pay my fees and pay for my books. They do not care whether I am dead or alive, but I have great hopes and confidence in myself as well as in my future.

Jealousy seemed to be the main cause of conflict between brothers. In this sample, seven of the Vokkaliga students (more than in any other community) suffered from such quarrels. In three of these cases, the family lived in a village, and the brothers were jealous of the student's education, for they themselves were illiterate. They wanted him to stay at home, help them in the fields, and stop studying. In one of these cases the relatives were also jealous of the student, and the combined pressure made him feel that it was impossible to return to live with his family.

Vo. 35: I am the only man in my family who is studying and getting distinction. Neither my brothers nor my cousins are educated. They work in the fields together for the common interest of the family. They think that I am wasting their money because I get money through my father from their earnings. So they are jealous of me. My cousins and aunts are also jealous, first because they are not educated, and secondly because they are not studious. All these people say that my education is a waste. I cannot tolerate illiterates. They never think broadly. They are narrow-minded fools. I am even ashamed of my people.

I am often worried about my future, not because of a job or money, but because of family misunderstandings. I am alone; I will have to live separately because my brothers and my cousins will unite against me, and even carry tales against me. This worries me a lot. Though a villager, I am not going back to live there because I cannot settle down in the family.

When the parents are dead the student is very often dependent on an uncle and aunt, or on other relatives. In one case a student lived with an uncle who had no interest in him, and who treated him so badly that the boy was at the end of his tether.

Li. 8: It is my moral duty to help keep up the good name of our family. I am doing this in spite of the many obstacles in my way. I am suffering a lot at my uncle's; I am struggling like hell there—I often feel like dying. My uncle is a narrow-minded man. My aunt continually tells him false tales about us all. He believes blindly what this bloody, unscrupulous lady says to him. I cannot repudiate what she says, so I receive kicks and abuse from him. Whenever he sees me he glares at me. All I can do is to go and commit suicide.

I could take my share of the property and leave, but if I did our friends and relatives, whose opinion is more important than that of my aunt and uncle, and who don't know of my troubles, might easily think I was in the wrong, and so they, too, would desert me.

My uncle tells his friends that I am a bad boy, and all sorts of wretched things about me. He says to me, "Take your share and go away." He believes all my aunt says about me and my brother. I feel like kicking them both, left and right. Why don't I? Oh God, I cannot even dream of doing it, for I must have their support. What would people think of me if I left?

In another case it was the stepmother who made life so miserable for the student that he felt that he could not stand it any longer.

Vo. 18: I will take no responsibility for my family which I call the "worst family of the first order." My father is kindhearted and good to all of us at home, but my stepmother manages the family. My poor sister is at the age of marriage, but so far we have not been able to find her a bride-groom, mainly because of her complexion, so my stepmother takes advantage of this and treats her as a servant in the house. She does all the work. I suffer too, because she will not give me money. My poor sister is really suffering a lot; I am afraid she may commit suicide. She has said so to me many times. My main responsibility in the family is to find her a bridegroom; then only will I be happy and not feel so burdened. I feel no other responsibility, even for my father, though he has helped us a lot.

I can say that jail life is better than my family life. Burglars and mur-derers don't suffer as much as we do at home. I will certainly not stay at home after my marriage. I am sure that my wife and stepmother would never adjust.

Forty of the ninety-one women students had had a good many dis-agreements or conflicts at home; twelve had had a few, and thirty-two had not had any. Six did not answer the question. Thus, about one third of the women students, as compared with a little over 25 per cent of the men, spoke of family conflicts. However, although the figures for this sample are very small, they suggest that the women who came from the Forward communities, that is, the Brahmans and Christians, had more conflicts at home than those from the Backward communities, the

Lingayats and the Vokkaligas. In other words, the more educated and urbanized students were more likely to have arguments and conflicts than the less educated and rural ones.

The reasons given for quarrels and disagreements between the women students and their families were very similar to those given by the men, although "fashionable" clothes and make-up were more often the cause of trouble for the former. The women stressed the orthodoxy and the "old-fashioned ideas" of their parents, particularly those of their mothers. The fathers were often more advanced in their ideas than were the mothers, and encouraged or supported some of the daughters' new behaviour. This might cause trouble between mother and daughter.

> *Br. 169*: My mother does not like "modern" girls. She wants me to sit at home and do embroidery and paint as she does. Father is very broadminded, and Mother has just the opposite ideas, and so there is a lot of conflict between them, mainly about our upbringing.
>
> I would like to have fashionable blouses made by tailors, but my mother insists on making all our blouses herself. She does not want us girls to join clubs, even though there is one near our house. She's against college education for girls, but Father is very particular that all of us should be well educated, and insisted on sending us to college.
>
> When I feel that my mother will not give me permission to do something I'll ask my father; this makes mother very angry.

Coming home late is a particularly serious offense for a daughter, as she is not meant to be out late, unescorted, for fear of unfavourable public opinion. Money is not as important to the women students as it is to the men, for the women have less liberty to use it. However, it did cause quarrels in regard to buying new saris and jewellery. Friends, too, are not such a problem, as many of the college students were not used to the idea of being with their women friends outside of the college or home environment. Some were rebellious at not having more recreational freedom, such as being permitted to join women's recreational clubs, or to take part in the extracurricular activities at college, due to the scruples of orthodox parents. Going to the movies is a fairly new type of recreation for women. Many women students consider that the movies serve not only as a particularly attractive form of entertainment, but also as a place of escape from lectures. Some girls are now allowed to attend in the afternoon, if accompanied by a group of girl friends. However, some parents complained when their daughters attended movies, while others tried to curb the number of movies the students saw.

The mother was the main person with whom the women students had disagreements. Thirty-two of the girls had quarrelled with their mothers, whereas only fourteen mentioned their fathers. Three Brahman students said they had quarrelled with the grandmothers, mainly over their orthodox views, and five Brahmans said they had disagreements with their brothers. Two Christian students had had quarrels or fights with brothers, and three had had them with sisters. One Lingayat had fought with her brother, and one with her sister. No Vokkaliga mentioned brother or sister as sparring-mate.

This fragmentary evidence suggests that quarrels and disagreements can occur with any member of a family. Sometimes a girl would have a very good relationship with her parents, but would quarrel with her brothers and sisters. The fact that there was no suggestion that the sisters who disagreed with their brothers were always particularly fond of them might challenge the hypothesis that there is always a very close bond of affection between brothers and sisters in the Hindu family.

There were doubtless many quarrels and disagreements between mothers and daughters in the traditional joint family, but as the daughters were married at an earlier age, these quarrels would be on the basis of a strictly superordinate-subordinate relationship. The young girl, being completely under the control of her mother, probably had little inclination to revolt, as there were no alternate patterns for her to follow. Today, however, the student in her last year of college is a more independent person. Her four years at the university have made her conscious of many new ways of behaving, of which her less educated mother may not even be aware. "I quarrel more with my mother now than when I was at school. She is orthodox, innocent, and aged." Through her life at college, her observation of her peers, the information she gleans from her college courses, and even the movies she has seen, the woman student gains many new insights into variations on the traditional woman's role. Thus, it is not surprising that most of the conflicts mentioned by the girls centred around differences of opinion about how a young woman should behave.

In the joint family the fact that emotional ties are strong makes it likely that changes in structure which call for a new sense of family responsibilities, new affectional ties outside the boundaries of the family, and a new independence from its jurisdiction will affect the way in which the student faces his role at college and in the outside world.

The student will get more support for the new problems he faces from a nuclear family that is deeply affectionate, and in which the relationships are not strained. He will get more help from a family that has been closely identified with the Western world, has been urbanized for several generations, and in which the parents are less orthodox, or more liberal. A very strict father, in particular, may so separate himself from his children that he is of little use in helping them meet their problems.

Three basic changes occur in the system of family responsibilities with the coming of industrialization. First, there is the change from a feeling of obligation to the wider kin group, to sole responsibility for one's nuclear family. This is accompanied by a widening sense of responsibility as a citizen. In the second place, new family responsibilities must be assumed, as others are dropped; e.g., new duties such as the educating of brothers and sisters, and the placing of brothers occupationally. Finally, there will be a change in the role-component of women, who will gradually assume an economic role and begin to support themselves and support their families financially. In India, this trend is due to later marriage, a new emphasis on the education of girls, and a rising standard of living. A daughter who works before marriage is coming to think of it as a "natural" duty to help finance her family. The wife who works after marriage does so mainly to increase the family income, not to perform a service to society, or to enrich her own life.

The desire to be independent, the wish to manage one's own home and avoid family conflict or unhappiness, the necessity for finding jobs in other cities, and the fear of elders and mothers-in-law—these are some of the main reasons that make sons and daughters wish to live separately after marriage. On the other hand, certain factors make sons and daughters want to stay with their parents or in-laws after marriage. Some of these are: custom, a strong sense of duty to parents or siblings, deep affection, the desire for guidance, and the fear of loneliness.

Family conflict may be taken as being an indication of the extent to which sons and daughters are becoming independent from their families. On the other hand, an absence of quarrels and disagreements in the home may not be a sign of submissive children, for in order to prevent unpleasantness at home, or to avoid having to defy too powerful elders, students may relieve their resentments in other ways, one of which may be participation in indiscipline at college.

CHANGING ATTITUDES TO RELIGION

Religion is such an integral part of the whole Hindu way of life that any changes in ritual or belief could be an upsetting factor in the lives of students. There is a certain amount of evidence that in modern societies young people are not as religious as their parents. Informants who had lectured for some years in India felt that religion did not mean nearly as much to the young Indian students as it had to their parents and grandparents. If this is so, does it mean that they are losing their moral bearings? Could this be one of the causes of their malaise?

If a religion that has been a vital and integral part of a traditional culture is suddenly challenged by rapid social changes that question its basic precepts, the younger generation may find that the moral values in which they have been brought up to believe are no longer adequate to guide them. Since religious principles and rituals change slowly, there may be a period of time when a young person feels himself to be in a "moral vacuum." This has proved a shattering experience for many young people who have grown up in periods of rapid change.

The four communities represented in this study had different religious beliefs. The Lingayats are a religious sect who worship the Linga—as compared to the Brahmans who worship gods. The Vokkaligas have the same religion as the Brahmans, but unlike them, have no household gods, and some of their rituals are different. The Christian students belong to a more highly organized religion than do the Hindus. Regular church attendance, financial support of the church, participation in the church's activities, and family prayers at home are all essential duties for those belonging both to the Protestant and to the Roman Catholic faiths. Various formally organized groups, such as women's meetings and youth organizations, take part in many of the church's leisure time activities.

The Hindu religion is transmitted from generation to generation through the family, and through stories, dramas, and rituals performed both in the home and in the temple. There are no formal ways of initiating children into the religious rituals, and there is no particular functionary whose special mission is to train them. Nor are there such institutions as Sunday schools. The religious rituals vary from caste to caste, from sub-caste to sub-caste, and even from family to family.

For some sub-castes it is very important to carry out daily poojas, and there are many special rituals at times of festivals. These rituals are carried out scrupulously, particularly in the villages. A good many of the women students from the four communities had received strict religious training at home, usually from the mother who, in nearly every case, was mentioned as the most religious member of the family. *Br. 159*: "I have not yet had my Upanayana, but I go to the temple each Thursday, and on that night I fast. Every day I prostrate myself before God in the morning, as soon as I get up from bed, and at night before going to bed, I so believe in God. My mother is very religious and has taught us all to believe in God. Naturally I have imbibed some of her religious attitudes."

The Christian students of this sample showed a greater belief in, and dependency on their religion than did the other students, although there were some deeply religious students in each group. The Christians nearly all spoke of their families as being very pious and religious, and talked of their own great faith. They all attended church regularly. Twenty-seven of them said that they still practised and believed in their religion. None of them said that they did not believe in it or practise it. On the other hand, fifteen students from the other communities (six Brahmans, five Lingayats, and four Vokkaligas) said they no longer practised their religion. Three Brahmans, seven Lingayats, and four Vokkaligas said that they no longer believed in it. Twelve other students said that they only practised a few of the rituals, and twenty more said that they only partly believed in their religion. On the other hand, eighty-three students (twenty-nine Brahmans, twenty-seven Christians, eleven Lingayats, and seventeen Vokkaligas) said that they believed very strongly in their religion.

Religious attitudes are not easy to analyze, because they are usually composed of a combination of factors. "Fear of God" is an aspect of worship in certain religions, and this accounted, at least in part, for the deep impression made by religion on some of the Christian students. Implied in this is the fear that a person who does not live up to his religious duties will get into some sort of trouble. Five Brahmans said that it was only because they had practised their religion that they had got as far as they had, and they stated that they had escaped trouble by doing religious penances. One was convinced that, as he was having a hard time, he must have committed some blunder in the past, and so deserved his present "Karma," or fate. Another said that it was because of his strict adherence to religious practices that he was earning distinction at college. A Lingayat student who had a deep belief in his religion feared the consequences of not praying every day to his god, and many students said they performed poojas before an examination, promising to give gifts to the gods if they passed.

To a few of the students, the importance of religion lay in the fact that they found comfort in it when they were in trouble. *Br. 68*: "Whenever I feel miserable or disgusted, I go to the temple and meditate; then

I forget all the worries of the external world. My mental peace and happiness is derived from my belief in God." Another relates: *Ch. 130*: "My parents, relatives, brothers, sisters and I are all very religious. We go to church regularly and pray and have great faith in the Almighty. I always feel secure when I pray, because God has given me whatever I have prayed for. If I do not go to church for a few days, I feel that I have missed and lost something, so I go to church regularly and pray." To others, participation in religious services helped to satisfy their desire for recognition and prestige. *Ch. 220*: "We go to church regularly and pray. We always help in maintaining the church and conducting the services. Our family is said to be a good and model Christian family, and we are proud of it, and want to live up to the opinions people have of us."

The fourteen students who no longer believed in their religion had also ceased to carry out the rituals. Some had moved so far from their religious beliefs that they no longer felt a sense of guilt about not performing them. Some of the students who "partly" believed still practised the rituals for the sake of their parents, who would be distressed if they did not do so. Others only performed them when they returned home to their villages. Still others carried them out because it saved trouble with parents, or because they were compelled by their parents to do so. *Vo. 81*: "My parents are very orthodox; they observe each and every ritual. They are so orthodox that once I was not allowed to enter the house until I took a bath when I returned from Bangalore."

The pressure of city life makes it difficult for students to perform the traditional rituals that were suitable for a simpler society. Some of them felt that they simply had no time for them, their days were so busy. Another new situation that appears to be hastening the decline of religious fervour is the fact that students from many religions now mix at college. This makes it impossible for many of them to believe in the supremacy of their own religion. This change has gone so far that some students will not tolerate the practice of traditional rituals by others at college. Instead, they ridicule those who try to cling to them. *Br. 14*: "Many students make fun of my practising religion. They call me names because I wear an old-fashioned hair style, that is, long hair which is not common now, and always dress in the Brahmanical way. Students call me 'Juttu Kudumi' because of my dress. In spite of all the teasing, I am a firm believer in my religion. I am convinced of it in my heart."

Much the same reasons were given by the women students as by the men for believing in, or not believing in their religion. Fear was also present in the attitudes of some of the students: "I get scared if I do not pray every day." Others felt the solace of religion. *Br. 201*: "I do a pooja daily. I have great faith in God. So far, He has answered my prayers. When I have disappointments I always take refuge in the pooja room, and it has always given me relief. No one forces me to pray. It has become a habit for me, and I cannot get out of it. Religion plays an important part in my life, and it gives me a lot of joy and relief."

The hope of some practical gain or good luck was also a part of the religious attitudes of some students. *Li. 236*: "I do a pooja every day before I go to college. If I miss a day I feel very guilty and unhappy. I do pooja to Lord Shiva, I ask him to give me a better memory. All my prayers are answered so far, and I have great belief in him."

A Christian student said: *Ch. 228*: "I go to church every Sunday, and I read the Bible before going to bed. We have family prayers every evening. I have the belief that if we have faith in God, and if we pray, we will come out successfully in almost all our troubles and difficulties. Whenever I am unhappy I pray."

A Brahman student expressed this idea in another way: *Br. 173*: "Every morning I do pooja. When we were small Father made us learn a list of Sanskrit *slokas* by heart, and I repeat them every day. I cannot understand them, as they are in Sanskrit, but if I do not repeat them, I feel uncomfortable and expect something bad to happen to me. If I do repeat them, I feel quite happy and satisfied, and know that I have done my duty. But when I need something very badly I pray in my own words from my bed."

On the other hand, those who only partly believed in their religion often carried out rituals just to avoid trouble. *Br. 169*: "My mother and I often have arguments because she does long poojas, both morning and evening every day, and I only do them on festival days. My mother insists that I do them like her every day. I do not believe in her poojas, and am not interested in doing them. But sometimes, just to stop her from scolding me, I will do one quickly and get it over. When my mother scolds me for not doing them properly I feel angry and go off to college without listening to her; then she won't talk to me all day, or will be angry and rude to me for the rest of the day."

Sixty-five of the women students (twenty-nine Brahmans, twenty Christians, eight Lingayats, and eight Vokkaligas) said that they still practised their religion, and sixty of the students (twenty-six Brahmans, nineteen Christians, eight Lingayats, and seven Vokkaligas) said that they still believed in their religion. Sixteen still practised some of the religious rituals (eleven Brahmans, one Christian, two Lingayats, and two Vokkaligas). Nineteen (fourteen Brahmans, one Christian, two Lingayats, and two Vokkaligas) said that they believed a little in their religion. Six students (five Brahmans and one Vokkaliga) no longer practised their religion, and five students (three Brahmans and two Vokkaligas) said they no longer believed in it. The rest of the students did not answer the question.

Like the men of this sample, the Christian women students had strong religious beliefs. The piety of Indian Christians is a matter of interest to Westerners. Only one of the twenty-one students interviewed believed only partly in her religion, and practised it partially. The others were strong adherents to their churches, whether they were Roman Catholics or Protestants, and their families showed religious unity and strength.

As in the case of the men students, most of the women spoke of family prayers at home, and of readings from the Bible. They also attended church *en famille*. Several of the girls said that the only thing that prevented their attending church was illness.

Among students from the different communities, of the five students who said they no longer believed, one thought the rituals were stupid. Another openly defied her mother. *Br. 174*: "Only my brother does the pooja in the grand manner every day at our home. I do not like keeping images and statues and dolls and elephants, and doing pooja before them. In the evening my mother lights the lamp and walks around the pooja room. This I do not like at all. I argue with her that this is a stupid custom, and that she is just being superstitious. Then she scolds me for talking irreligiously and says that it has been the custom down through the ages, and we must believe in it and follow it."

Another case shows how religious differences between student and mother often lead to conflicts, which cause some young women to conform just to avoid trouble.

Br. 190: My mother and I often have conflicts over religion. She scolds me for doing the morning poojas quickly. She is very religious, and fasts once in every fifteen days, and she wants me to do the same. I have fasted about eight times. Two of these times she forced me to. Sometimes she will scold me, saying that I will attain "punya" only if I fast. Then I try to fast a whole day, but I find it a great physical strain. Every Saturday we have special poojas in the morning which take forty-five to fifty minutes. We do not take any food before them. I do not like missing my coffee, and I feel bored by the long pooja, but Mother forces me to do it. I go to the temple on Thursdays, but my mother goes regularly on both Thursday and Saturdays and she wants me to go with her as well. When I refuse she scolds me. My mother is also fond of going to religious lectures and wants me to accompany her, but I feel very bored with these meetings and refuse to go. Then she will be very angry with me, and we argue.

Some who are braver rebel against too much religious pressure. *Ch. 188*: "My mother wants me to read a whole chapter of the Bible every day. Sometimes I read a little and then she will scold me. I find it very boring, so sometimes I give the excuse that I have no time, and do not read it. Then my mother will be furious with me. I like to watch an elderly Brahman couple next door doing poojas, especially on festival days, but my mother objects and does not even allow me to go and visit them. This has made her stricter with me about reading the Bible and going to church."

Even the students who were very religious and carried out most of the religious rituals did not appear to observe the custom of fasting as much as their mothers did. Those who said they only believed a little, or not at all, found performing poojas, visiting temples, and reading religious books all rather boring.

Both the men and the women students showed as much variation in their religious beliefs and practices as they did in other types of behaviour. The Christians showed less loss of belief than did the Hindus. This was probably because their position as a minority group is now rather precarious; formerly they had a protected position under the British, although they have had little security since Independence. Consequently, they have drawn closer together, and as religion is their main common symbol of identification, it has become the focus and strength of their unity. Moreover, as their religion is more formally organized, with functionaries who are trained to adjust to changing conditions through the establishment of new organized groups, they are better able to adapt their programmes, if not their beliefs and rituals, to changing conditions. In this way they are able to hold the allegiance of the young people more firmly.

Like all countries that have changed from a basically agricultural economy to an industrial one, India is gradually becoming more secularized. The effect of this is felt first usually by those who acquire higher education and become more urbanized. A change in overt religious behaviour, such as a decline in the strict performance of rituals, will precede a loss or change of belief. One reason for this is that many students do not feel that they have time to follow all the religious prescriptions in detail. Others come to believe that the rituals are not necessary, and do not fit in with their new concepts of life. Some students will continue to carry out the rituals because their parents put pressure on them to do so, although they may no longer believe in them.

As has been seen in connection with other changing conditions which have been explored in this study, some students have been quicker to change than have others. Many students still seem to have retained a deep belief in their religion. This may be due to the fact that their early beliefs have never been seriously challenged, as these are based on strong superstitions and fears. Another reason may be that they come from very closely knit religious families, and are more influenced by their faith than by the contradictions to their beliefs that they are encountering at college and in the outside world.

Even in a group which, like the Christian community, is highly "secularized" in some respects, religious faith may still be strong, for it may be the chief unifying and sustaining force for a minority group whose position is insecure.

As religion is one of the strong binding factors in the Hindu family, it is not surprising that it was the more independent Hindu students (in the sense that they had moved further away from a close identification with their families) who also tended to be less religious and more inclined to indiscipline at college. The Christian students did not follow this trend, for whereas most of them still held strong religious beliefs, they were not nearly as attached to their families in the sense of wanting to live with their parents or in-laws after marriage.

CONCLUSIONS

In summing up the effect of changes in caste, family, or religion on the indiscipline of the student at college, it could be said that traditional structures that have existed for centuries do not change easily or smoothly when a country becomes urbanized and industrialized. The outward symbols of caste have changed to the extent that students, as well as those in business and the professions, mix more freely and dress more alike. However, legal changes that were meant to eliminate caste privileges have sometimes had a boomerang effect and have strengthened caste bonds. Many Indians still find it easier to advance in the economic and political spheres if they try to move ahead alone. In Mysore, the division of the different communities into Forward and Backward castes has tended to encourage the solidarity of the more favoured castes, such as the Lingayats and the Vokkaligas. This division has increased the fears and anxieties of the Brahmans and Christians, who have been placed in the less favoured Forward category; but contrary to expectation, these worries have made them anxious to work hard at college, rather than release their frustrations through indiscipline which might jeopardize their education and careers. Because the influence of the joint family has also been slow to change, many students find themselves pulled in two directions. On the one hand, family ties, a sense of family responsibility, and the fear of facing an unknown world without family support, tend to keep them close to their families. On the other hand, the demands of an increasing circle of friends at college, more opportunities for leisure time, and new ideas and influences tend to supersede the influence of former close family and kin ties. This has not occurred without strain and anxiety, and it is probable that the need to release these tensions on some object outside the strict family environment has often made the college the butt of student frustrations.

Breaking away from religious observances and beliefs releases the student from one of the important traditional controls over his behaviour. Loss of religious faith in itself may not be difficult to adjust to, but when it occurs at the same time as a student loses many of his early beliefs, it may be a very upsetting experience.

4

Ambitions
and
Careers

Planning careers tends to be one of the greatest anxieties for young people in rapidly industrializing societies. The occupational structure becomes so complicated that even parents are often unable to guide their children in their choice of careers. Students typically come from the middle or upper classes where a college degree is both a prerequisite for getting a job, and an essential status symbol. In India the struggle to find employment is so intense that when it is added to middle-class ambitions one could hypothesize that the major anxieties of most male students would be found in this area.[1] Moreover, if the student belongs

1. Aileen D. Ross, *The Hindu Family in Its Urban Setting*, pp. 190-93. See also: *Report of the Study Group on Educated Unemployment*.

The Hindu, April 29, 1962. "One felt that [the students] had a pessimistic attitude to life in general. They were uncertain of their future, and they spoke with a detachment which sounded odd for young men of, say nineteen. Even students who thought they could get decent marks in the examinations spoke doubtfully about prospects of continuing their studies unless they got scholarships. They wanted to go on to some kind of a job which would fetch them some Rs.200 a month. Asked what kind of job they wanted to take up, two [said that they] favoured teaching; the others' wishes varied from an executive job in a decent firm to an upper division clerkship in a central government office. These students quipped and joked about the long queues in employment exchanges, or about reading the 'situations vacant' column the first thing in a newspaper. It was clear they were painfully aware of the long period of unemployment before they could settle down in life. 'I will be lucky if I get a job before the end of the year,' one student observed."

The Hindu, August 17, 1963. Figures given in New Delhi in August 1963 showed that there were twice as many unemployed at that date as in 1958. The figure was 708,358. However, there is a change in the type of unemployed. At that time it was stated that 90 per cent of the unemployment occurred among students who did not complete their undergraduate degrees. The rest occurred among engineers and medical students.

For many years Kerala has been one of the states with the highest number of eduto a joint family, pressures on him to get a degree that will lead to a good job may come from a wide variety of people.

Another pressure on a son may come from the rising ambitions of the family. This situation would be expected to occur as a country becomes more highly industrialized, for many new occupational opportunities arise, and the former economic specializations of the various caste groups break down. As this sample of students came mainly from the middle, or supposedly striving classes, it would be expected that they would have high ambitions. To what extent was this true? Did parents press their sons to get a good education that would give them important positions and/or good marriages? Did the students themselves want to have important careers and become prominent people; and, if so, what effect did this striving have on their behaviour as students? Or were they content to live in much the same way as their parents lived? Did students from wealthy families, or from families who could insure jobs for their sons tend to be better disciplined than those who were fearful of the future?

A study of ambitions is complicated by the fact that people from different environments have different goals. A middle-class son who aspires to be a business executive, for example, is looked on as "ambitious" by middle-class people, but it is just as likely that a village boy whose parents are illiterate has just as high ambitions in aspiring to become a clerk or a teacher. This problem was partly overcome in this study by relating the student's choice of job to his father's occupation. If he wanted a more important job, then he was considered ambitious. The desire for higher degrees, and the evidence that the student studied hard at school or college were also taken into consideration in the assessment of student ambitions.

Data from interviews showed that a college degree was of the utmost importance to the life plans of most of the men students of this sample, for a degree is a better gateway to a job in India than in most countries.

---

cated unemployed. Unemployment is considered such a serious problem that it has been at least partly responsible for the trend toward communism. Literally thousands apply when a job is offered. Industries are being established which are expected to alleviate the condition to some extent, but they are developing slowly.

Eastern Economist, March 30, 1962, p. xiii. In 1962 it was estimated that in Mysore State the following number of students were applicants on the registers of the employment exchanges: Matriculates, 29,478; Intermediate College, 2,917; Graduate students, 3,378. This makes a total of 35,773 students.

The Hindu, September 14, 1963. In the following year it was estimated that there were over 2,300 unemployed engineers in Mysore State alone.

It is essential for an adequate standard of living, and, as everyone understands the problem, there is little condemnation of students who obviously go to college in order to get jobs. The attitude of Bombay students to degrees could perhaps be generalized for all India. "Most of the students come mainly to work for a degree which will enable them to obtain a good position, and barely a handful are interested in the pursuit of knowledge for the sake of knowledge."[2]

The alternative to a degree is to go into business, if a young man has influence or connections in that field. Manual labour is out of the question, for the few who work in such occupations are regarded as failures.

The student's worries about his future are reinforced at home by the anxiety of his parents who, themselves, have had to struggle to gain an adequate livelihood, and often expect to share in the financial fate of their sons. Their eagerness to have their sons enter medicine or engineering, without considering either their personal suitability for these professions, or their desires in the matter, underlies the parents' anxiety to see their offspring in secure and remunerative occupations.

Thirty-two of the Brahman, sixteen of the Christian, nineteen of the Lingayat, and twenty-eight of the Vokkaliga male students wanted to go on to study for higher degrees. Of these ninety-five students, twenty-one wanted to get M.A.'s, thirty-two M.Sc.'s, and twenty-two, B.L.'s. Eighteen wanted other degrees, such as a Bachelor of Education. Two Brahmans and one Christian wanted to go on to get Ph.D. degrees. One of the reasons that so few students aspire to Ph.D. degrees is that these degrees do not necessarily mean a step up the occupational ladder in India, or an increase in money income, particularly if the student is studying in the humanities or social sciences. A Master's degree in these fields is enough to secure a relatively good lecturing position. Nor is a Ph.D. an entrance into the realm of research, for there is practically no emphasis on research in these fields. Thus, a Ph.D. would only mean three or four extra years at the university without much tangible profit.

A number of the wealthy students wanted to go abroad for further study. Of the remaining sixty-four male students, thirteen wanted to get jobs immediately after graduating, twenty-three were not interested in studying, and twenty-eight did not answer the question. Many were aware that a B.A. or B.Sc. did not lead to an important job. This was a matter of great concern to some of the students, for unless they could

2. *Report on a Survey . . . of the Students of the University of Bombay*, p. 50.

get higher degrees, they felt that they would have to become inspectors in banks, minor assistants in offices, or clerks—all occupations considered to be beneath the dignity of a college graduate.

Several students were planning to take two higher degrees concurrently, such as a B.L. and an M.A. This is a rather common practice for students who feel insecure about the future. They want, not so much to broaden their knowledge, as to be able to fall back on the second degree should they fail to get a job in one of the fields they have chosen. Many students take graduate correspondence courses in order to qualify in a field, or to have more credentials. On the other hand, a number who took graduate courses were thought by informants to be using this method as a means of prolonging their stay in the shelter of the university before having to face the agony of finding gainful employment and assuming financial or family responsibilities. The fate of the educated unemployed is so well known that many students who have no influence to help them get a job are afraid to face the hazardous reality of the work world. Thus, the desire to go on to study for higher degrees cannot always be assumed to be an indication of high ambition. It may, rather, be a means of whiling away time pleasantly before settling down to the responsibilities of adulthood, or it may be due to the fears of moving out into the world from the sheltered environment of the college. It can be assumed, however, that students who studied hard were ambitious to get ahead or to get a job.

About half the male students (seventy-five out of one hundred and fifty-nine) said that they had studied hard at college; the other half had not. More Brahman, Lingayat, and Vokkaliga students had studied hard, as compared with Christian students. Of the latter, only nine had really worked at college. The reasons most often given for studying hard were interest in the courses, and the desire for a good future. Other reasons were family pressures, the necessity for getting jobs, and the hope of bringing honour to the family. Those who had not studied hard —about half the students—had either found the courses boring, had other interests, been too lazy, or preferred going with friends to studying. A number of the Christian students had found that, after attending boarding schools in which there had been very strict discipline, the freedom of college had been overwhelming, and they had found it difficult to study.

Some of the students found the working conditions at college so difficult that they simply gave up. They did not belong to the 10 per cent of students who were wealthy enough to buy the "bazaar notes" that some professors had had mimeographed, and as there were not enough books in the libraries, they were unable to supplement the information given them by their lecturers, and so were too discouraged to study.

To what extent did this sample of students aspire to positions higher than those which their fathers had achieved? It is difficult to assess the prestige of different occupations accurately at a time when the whole occupational structure is changing. During the British regime the civil service had high prestige in India, and some of its positions drew very high salaries. A few Indian businessmen made large fortunes, but for the most part business incomes were not high. Business was not a traditional occupation that held much prestige, nor was it given high rating by the British. The gradual industrialization of the country is changing the attitude to business. At the same time, the Indian civil service has lost some of its prestige, and the relative levels of income between the highest officials and the businessmen in India have completely altered. Politicians, too, have risen in prestige since the Indians took over political power. Other people who formerly had great prestige, such as princes, landlords, and priests, have, on the whole, lost their top positions in this regard, and even lawyers, who were formerly held in high respect, now rate lower. Social workers and those in education have tended to decline in importance, mainly because the state has taken over the control of so much in these fields.[3]

The classification of occupations in Table I is an attempt to compare the occupations of the fathers of this sample of male students with those their sons aspire to, in terms of relative prestige.[4] No attempt was made to introduce the remunerative factor into the estimation of the prestige of the occupational structure.

The figures in Table I show that the ambitions of the sons were higher than those of their fathers, and that there was a decided trend

---

3. D. R. Gadgil, "Some Fundamental Defects of Our Present Situation," pp. 6-8.

4. The scheme of classification used by the Indian Statistical Institute in Calcutta which is patterned after the "International Standard Classification of Occupations," and which bases its classification on the type of functions performed by an individual—not merely the section of economic activity in which he is engaged—was not used in this study as it was based on eight classifications, and so was too elaborate for the size of this sample. Moreover, as this sample came from a rather small area of the total occupational structure, it seemed better to devise a scale that would give a rough suggestion of the prestige ranking of the occupations of fathers, and those chosen by the students. Advisers with a good knowledge of the prestige ranking of different occupations assisted in determining the classification.

TABLE I

OCCUPATION OF FATHERS OF MALE STUDENTS COMPARED TO
STUDENTS' DESIRE FOR JOBS AND THE JOBS THEY EXPECT TO GET

Prestige of Occupation*	Father's Occupation	Occupation that Sons want to get	Occupation that Sons expect to get
High	37	73	61
Medium	42	29	22
Low	5	12	9
Agriculture	37	9	10
Father retired or dead	25	—	—
Do not know	—	21	40
No answer	13	15	17
	159	159	159

*Occupations of high prestige; professional, administrative, high business and executive positions

Occupations of medium prestige: semi-professional, smaller business positions, clerical jobs

Occupations of low prestige: skilled, semi-skilled, or unskilled jobs

on the part of those who had been brought up in villages towards urban occupations. About one-third of the fathers whose occupations could be ascertained had had occupations of high prestige, and nearly half of the sons had aspired to these occupations. This table also shows evidence of a trend that is occurring in many countries; namely, that students with agricultural backgrounds do not want to return to the land. Although one-third of the fathers worked in agriculture, only a few of the sons wanted to continue to do so. One son felt that he might be forced to go back to the land, although he did not want to.

In spite of the belief of Gadgil that the civil service has declined in prestige as compared, say, to business, government jobs were still avidly sought after by many of the students of this sample because of their security; and because once a person is admitted, there is a good possibility of his moving up to the higher ranks.[5] Business was not chosen extensively, for it has not yet attained such high prestige in Bangalore as it has in the larger cities such as Bombay or Calcutta, and also it was

5. *Report of a Survey of Living Conditions of University Students*, pp. 6-9. A study of occupational choice among the students in Kerala showed that whereas only 18 per cent of the fathers of the student sample were in government jobs, 58 per cent of the sons wanted to enter government service. And the choices of the students in Lucknow listed government service at the top, followed by business and teaching.

not a traditional occupation for any of the students. About 10 per cent of the students wanted to become lecturers, but very few wanted to be teachers, as the salaries for teachers have declined rather sharply. Teachers and clerks were often mentioned as alternative possibilities for jobs, but to aspire to either position signified a cry of despair for most students. No one wanted to go into social service.

The confused way in which many of the students were thinking of their future careers was evident from the diverse nature of the choices when a student mentioned more than one job. For instance, one student wanted to be either a welfare officer, a teacher, or the manager of a private firm.[6] The twenty-one students who did not know what they wanted to do were either confused about job opportunities, or had not made up their minds. Some of them said they would try anything, they were so fearful of not getting a job.

New occupations are constantly created in a changing society. Students often go to college without having thought too much about the next step in their careers, for getting a degree is so important that they feel their futures are secure when they gain admission to college. A boy from a village, with no friends or influence in the city, is in a difficult position.[7] Kabir thinks that these factors makes a student's courses seem purposeless, and also gives him higher aspirations which cannot always be fulfilled.

The majority of students in secondary schools or colleges have no definite plans about their future and do not know what they would do after they have finished. Their education is largely purposeless, and because it is purposeless, it does not fit them for any gainful occupation. Large numbers flow from schools to colleges and universities simply because they cannot think about anything else to do. . . . In many cases, they are not even looking for a job, but living in the vague hope that something will turn up. What makes the situation even worse is the higher expectations aroused

6. The Christians in India seem to be facing the same problems as are people in many Western countries in recruiting people for the priesthood. Several priests thought this was because students are not now willing to devote themselves to a cause, particularly if they have ambitious parents who are also against it. Only one student, a Lingayat, wanted to become a religious leader.

7. An article in *The Hindu*, "Around the Colleges," July 8, 1963, speaks of the lack of guidance students get at college to help them plan their careers. "With a variety of occupations to choose from, the person who holds a university degree has no idea what job he should ask for. . . . In our colleges there is no agency to advise final year students on employment prospects. Students generally depend mostly on their parents' influence, and heavily on employment exchanges or newspaper advertisements."

by entry into institutions of higher learning. The students are no longer content to accept openings which might have satisfied them after they finished school.[8]

The case of a Brahman student illustrates these points.

Br. 65: When I finished high school with a first class I was confused about my next step. My parents are not educated, so they could not guide or advise me. When I saw that most of my friends were going to college, I went too. It was only later that I found the maths and physics very difficult. I took tuition and, with great difficulty, completed my intermediate, but only got very low marks. I could not secure a seat in the medical or engineering colleges, so I went on with my B.Sc. degree, even though I knew that it would not be of much use. There was no other hope for me.

Again physics and maths hampered me from doing well. I got an ordinary pass. Once again I was a discard. I went on trying to get a job. I registered my name in the regional Employment Exchange. I had no influence. My father did not know anyone who could recommend me or do anything for me. I kept quiet for a few months, but the unemployment problem haunted me like anything. Then at last I applied at an office and was selected for a clerical post. This did not satisfy me. I knew that there was no future in that job, but what could I do? I knew that my marks were very low. Then I learned that one of the colleges had opened a morning section in arts and commerce. I made up my mind to take a B.A. degree so that I could go on to an M.A. This time, although the subjects were easy, I had no time to read because of my job, so I failed. But I am sure that I will pass with merit in the end, and I want to then take my M.A. in sociology. After that I want to become a lecturer and then go on to take a Ph.D.

8. Humayun Kabir, *Education in New India*, p. 155.
The Hindu, "Around the Colleges," July 8, 1963. Even after college there are many who do not show much ambition: "A common charge against our graduates is that they have no 'mobility' and that they are 'unambitious.' About six hundred graduates were called at the Employment Exchange and told of a job in Poona, and hardly a dozen opted to go. When the need arose to fill nearly six hundred vacancies in clerical cadres in Defense Services, the entire 'live register' at the Exchange was hauled up and about eight hundred graduates were called. Only fifty opted for the medical test and only one or two got selected. . . . Unemployed engineering graduates are given a stipend of Rs.150 per month, and diploma holders Rs.100 per month, for one year if they work in some factory recognized for the purpose. Last year, nearly three hundred such stipends went by default because 'there were no applicants.' "
Another case of this uncertainty about the future occurred in Bangalore: Chanchal Sarkar, *The Unquiet Campus*, p. 8. "Of a group of M.A. (English) students in Central College, Bangalore . . . of seven students not one knew what he or she would do after passing. Pressed to express an opinion, two or three mentioned teaching, a couple agriculture and one social work. But . . . no one had applied his mind to details. Those who spoke of teaching, for instance, had not thought whether it was in school or college that they would teach, or whether they would go in for training. . . . Those who spoke of agriculture (they had lands in their villages) had not considered learning something about agriculture. Asked about their purpose in doing the M.A. in English they shifted, rather pathetically, from insisting that it was because they wanted a liberal education to admitting that it seemed to them a useless effort."

When the occupations that the students *thought* they would get are compared with those they *wanted*, the picture changes to some extent. Fewer students (sixty-one, as compared to seventy-three) thought they would get the top jobs they wanted, and twenty-two, as compared with twenty-nine thought they would get jobs of moderate prestige. About the same number thought they would go into agricultural occupations. The number of those who did not know what jobs they would get nearly doubled (forty, as compared to twenty-one).[9] This means that many students had the ambition to get better jobs than their fathers had had, but as they saw little hope of obtaining a good job, their main desire was to get any job that would give them a living salary. The general attitude of these students could be summed up in the words of two of the Brahman students who, when asked what jobs they thought they would get, said, with fear in their voices, "God knows!" and "Do I get one?"[10]

An analysis of the attitudes to jobs of the students from the four communities showed certain differences. The Christians have traditionally followed semi-professional, technical, and railway occupations; the Lingayats and Vokkaligas, agricultural occupations (very often being landlords of high prestige); and the Brahmans, those of highest prestige, namely, academic, religious, and professional kinds of work. Under the British the Brahmans entered the civil service in great numbers. On the whole they still have high aspirations, but many of them are realistic

9. Rose K. Goldsen, Morris Rosenberg, Robin M. Williams, Jr., and Edward A. Suchman, *What College Students Think*, p. 23. Only the Indian students who had a wealthy background seemed to think of the satisfaction that they would get out of their work. To many of the students a job seems to be a "necessary evil." This attitude of the Indian students contrasts with that of Goldsen's sample of American students. "They see work and a career as a means much more than a way to earn a living, much more than a necessary evil that cannot be avoided. Almost all the students expect that their work will provide perhaps not the major satisfaction in their lives, but certainly a very important source of satisfaction."

10. *Report on a Survey . . . of the Students of the University of Bombay*, pp. 44, 45. In the Bombay study 65 per cent of the students worried or were particularly anxious about their future prospects, their careers, and the prospect of unemployment. In that sample the students questioned came from professional colleges as well as the arts and sciences faculties, and so it included many ambitious young men who were anxious to build promising careers for themselves.

Goldsen, Rosenberg, *et al.*, p. 34. In Goldsen's study the majority of the American students interviewed appeared to take it for granted that they would eventually achieve high incomes, whereas this optimism was only evident in a very few Indian students of this sample. Goldsen did not believe that the optimism of the American students was unrealistic as college students are very much in demand in America today. In fact, the need for trained personnel is so great in business, as well as in professional and scientific occupations, that many business corporations send special recruiters to the college campuses to try to recruit the most promising graduates.

in recognizing the trends of the times and know that their aims are far too high. Many are desperate, trying with all their might to hold on to their slipping occupational status, but with little belief in miracles. More Brahman students showed anxiety about their jobs and futures than did interviewees from any other group, and they told of more cases of discrimination against their fathers, brothers, or relatives in regard to jobs or promotions than did students from the other three communities. Seventeen of them had no idea what jobs they would be able to get. They were well aware of the intense anti-Brahman movement and of its decreasing political power in Mysore State. They knew there would be few influential friends or caste members to assist them in getting higher positions.

The Christians, long an unpopular minority group in India, have also learned to be realistic about their position. The Christian students of this sample aimed at the more sheltered jobs, such as technical work, or positions in the armed services, or the railways, where they would be, to some extent, free from discrimination. As they are a weak minority group in Mysore, with little political power, and have never held influential positions, they are not as great a threat to the rising castes as are the Brahmans. Since many of the Christians are highly skilled technically, jobs of a technical sort are still open to them. Moreover, since their close association with Western traditions has made them less resistant to manual labour, they are more willing to learn technical skills on the job than are most high and medium caste Indians. The Christian students also tended to want to follow in their fathers' occupational footsteps. In this way they would have someone ahead who could be of assistance, and would also learn the necessary steps for admittance or advancement more easily. They were surer of what they wanted to do than any other group. Great pressure had been put on most of them by their families to study; and the parents had also given them more guidance, probably because they were fully aware of possible economic discrimination effected by their religion.

The occupational ambitions of the Lingayat and Vokkaliga students tended to be more alike. Many of them had rural backgrounds, and this had prevented them from being fully aware of occupational opportunities in the city. Some who came from wealthy families living on large plantations wanted either to return to that way of life or to go into "big business." Some from more modest backgrounds were ambitious to return to be head of their village. Both the Lingayats and the Vokkaligas are now somewhat protected by political power and so feel that they have influence at their disposal when they graduate. Many of them have the choice of returning to their land if all else fails. Only a few were worried about their futures. These students tended to come from poor rural families and believed that they would have no help from relatives, or from their community. Obviously some of them did not "know the ropes" for getting ahead.

The ambitions of the students from the different castes and religions thus show the influence of the position of each group. The Brahmans and Christians have been longer exposed to Western influences, and so have higher aspirations than have students from the other two groups. On the other hand, they seem to understand the drawbacks of their positions as Forward communities, and so are realistic about their futures. The Lingayat and Vokkaliga students tended either to feel secure about their futures, or else to be confused; those who were confused came from poor village families from whom they had had little guidance.

AMBITIONS OF PARENTS AND STUDENTS

Having discussed the desire of students to study for higher degrees, the extent to which they supported these desires with hard work, and the aspirations of the students in terms of future occupations, we can now analyze the extent to which parents were ambitious for their sons, and to which sons had similar aspirations to do well or to get ahead.

There may be many reasons for parents showing a great interest in their son's education: it may be due to poverty and the desperate need of the family for a higher income; or to the fear that the caste or religious background of the student may hinder his getting a job; or to the desire of parents who come from a "rising" caste to have their son move into an occupation of higher prestige.

The term "ambition" in this study will therefore be used in a broad sense, not only to describe the desires of students to get ahead, and of their parents to see them get ahead, but also to refer to pressures on sons by their parents and/or relatives to work hard at college.

Ambitions are rarely based on one clear goal. Rather, they incorporate a variety of desires. The stated purpose of a student, "to be a doctor," may not be wholly due to his desire to be a professional man, but may include some other goal that can only be achieved through that occupation. A Brahman student, for example, wanted to get a good job in order to help his brothers who had financed his education. Another student wanted to become a prominent man, in order to prove to his relatives that he was capable of that achievement. Still another wanted to get a technical job, for if he became a clerk, his "intellect would die."

Table II shows the different strengths of the ambitions of fathers and sons. The criteria used to measure ambitions were the pressure put on sons, or encouragement given them by fathers in school and at college, the extent to which sons had worked hard at their studies, and the students' own statements about their future careers.

TABLE II

AMBITIONS OF PARENTS AND MALE STUDENTS

	HIGH		MODERATE		LOW	
	Parents	*Students*	*Parents*	*Students*	*Parents*	*Students*
Brahman	22	24	21	16	10	14
Christian	14	11	13	9	1	8
Lingayat	9	14	11	6	6	6
Vokkaliga	11	5	14	21	11	10
	56	54	59	52	28	38

Total number whose ambitions could be ascertained:
Parents: 143
Sons: 144

This table by no means tells the whole story, for siblings, grand-parents, uncles, aunts, or other relatives often urged the students to study hard and get ahead. Even neighbours sometimes added to the feeling of pressure of a student by insisting on knowing his marks at school and college, partly, no doubt, due to the fear that he would outdo their own children, but also because they desired to use him as a standard by which to judge their own children's progress. However, as the father is usually the person most concerned with his children's future, it can be assumed that his influence is the most important in shaping their attitudes. A number of teachers believed that many parents are not really interested in having their children gain knowledge at school, but are more con-cerned about their passing the examinations. The worst thing that could happen to such children was having to face their parents' anger when they had not done well. There were many cases of pupils who signed their own report cards so that they would not have to show them to their parents. A large number of the students of this sample told of the punishments they had received when they did not do well at school. Typical kinds of punishment, and their effects on pupils and students have been described in another study.[11]

An analysis will first be made of the reasons for the different ambitions of the total sample of students, in order to show the extent to which these came from feelings of economic insecurity, social conscience, etc. Then the four communities will be treated separately in order to try to see whether there were differences in the ambitions of fathers and sons in each group.

The reasons for the high ambitions of some of the students seemed to fall roughly into four categories. The first group of students felt that they must work hard and get ahead because of a deep-seated anxiety about the future: "It is the only way for a poor Brahman to get ahead." Their families were not influential enough to help them get jobs, and the Brahman and Christian students felt that their caste and/or religious background were against them.

Members of the second group were motivated to work hard because of a strong sense of family obligation. They identified themselves strongly with their families and wanted to do well in order to be of assistance to them, more than for personal reasons. Some of these students were eldest sons, which is a position of great responsibility in the Indian family. It is their obligation to see that younger brothers are educated and settled in jobs, and that their sisters are married. This may entail helping to provide large dowries for future husbands. The eldest son has a particularly heavy load to bear if his father is dead. A number of students fell into this category.

Some of the students in this group came from poor families. Often, a son might be the only financial hope of the family, and sometimes he might have been "backed" as the son who would be most likely to benefit from a college education. This, in turn, would help him to become a major support of the family. Such students were deeply disturbed by their families' financial problems. They had brothers to educate, sisters to marry, and cousins or relatives to help. Some of them felt a great burden of gratitude to relatives who had financed their education. A Christian student was particularly worried because his father had sacrificed a great deal to send him to college, and the family had pinned all their hopes on his being successful enough in his studies to get a good

11. Ross, *The Hindu Family in Its Urban Setting*, pp. 121-28.

job. A few of these students were concerned about their own future careers as well as about their contribution to the family.

The students who fell into the third category were mainly ambitious for their own sakes, but their aims were different. The largest number showed ambition in the usual sense of this word; that is, they were concerned about their own fame and fortune. They wanted interesting jobs with good pay. A Brahman student, for example, wanted to go into private practice in medicine because he would not be hampered by government rules, would not need influence or protection to get ahead, and so could make a very good name for himself. A Christian student felt that he was one of the privileged few, as he was the only one in his family with a college education. This had made him feel that he must work hard to live up to his exceptional opportunities. Another Christian wanted to continue in a branch of engineering where he would have little competition, and so could get to the top easily. Of the Vokkaligas, one wanted to return to become a leader in the city: "I want to shine by myself, by my own efforts." Still another wanted to work hard to become a Sanskrit scholar so that he could feel equal to, or better than the Brahmans. One wanted to become a political leader.

Other students had a very different attitude. Some came from wealthy families where their parents had been indulgent. They were mainly concerned with having a good time, both in the present and in the future. They were not interested in their studies and never worked hard. They spent most of their time roaming about with friends, or going to the movies. Some of them wanted to go abroad to study and enjoy themselves. Others, in spite of their lack of application to their studies, wanted high positions so that they would have lots of money, own cars, and be looked up to by everyone. "I don't want to remain a nobody." These students were carefree, and assumed that their fortunes would just fall into their laps. One hoped that the girl he married would raise his status, as he felt that he had no time to study or work himself.

The ambitions of a few Brahmans in this category were high, but such students had quite different goals. All they wanted to do was to "study and learn." This, to them, was the "good life." They had confidence in their ability to achieve what they considered to be "good and proud lives."

The ambitions of the final group were oriented toward a mission in life. They spoke of the ideal of service. Three of the Christian students wanted to serve the nation: "To me, life is a mission. I do not want to waste any time." Another had decided to be a teacher, as he thought this was the best way of carrying out his obligation to his country. Finally, a Lingayat student who had grown up in a religious atmosphere was so influenced by it that he wanted to become a Sanyasi, even though his family strongly objected to this idea.

> *Li. 107*: I have spent a good part of my life in the Mutt, and I have developed an immense liking for my religion and my Mutt. I have always aspired to become the religious head, preaching my religion and converting people to my faith, and so enabling them to lead a happy, contented life. My father argues that, as there is plenty of property, I have nothing to worry about in the future, and I should get married and live happily looking after our property. He doesn't like my being a Sanyasi, which means "losing a son." He is so persistent and sometimes so logical that he sows doubt in my mind, and this disturbs me very much.
>
> My brothers and sister think that a Sanyasi has no respect or prestige today, so they want me to give up this mad idea and decide to marry. This disturbs me, too. Personally, I see great scope for serving society as a religious head.

This small sample suggests that religion is the main influence which gives students a sense of obligation extending beyond their own concerns, and those of their families and relatives, to the wider world.

To what extent did the ambitions of the students of the four communities differ? To what degree were their ambitions supported by their parents or other family members, and what effect did this have on the students' attitude to college? Table II sums up the numbers of fathers and sons who were found to have high, moderate, or low ambitions.

Brahmans

Roughly the same number of Brahman parents and sons had high ambitions, but it was not always the same parents and sons. Of the twenty-two parents who showed keen interest in their sons' education and/or future, only thirteen of the sons seemed to feel the same keenness to get ahead, whereas eight sons had high ambitions when the parents' ambitions were low.

Interest of the parents who were deeply concerned with the future of their sons usually began when the boys were in school. Fathers warned or encouraged their sons to get good marks and distinction, or punished or "abused" them if they did not.

Br. 102: My father is very anxious for me to get a first class, so I study hard. If I go home late in the evening the first thing my father or mother says is, "If you loaf around with friends you won't pass your examinations, and what will happen to you? Do you think you can get a job if you don't pass with credit? Don't expect any money from us if you fail. You will have to look after yourself; you can't expect us to support you." My parents always punished us whenever we did not study.

On the other hand, members of the family can reinforce the student's ambitions by supporting and encouraging him.

Br. 11: My two brothers took an interest in my education and helped me financially to go to college. They still encourage and help me. My brothers are very anxious for me to complete my degree so that I will get a job and a good place in society. They put some pressure on me to study, for if I finish early I can help my family.

Encouragement from members of the family is not always altruistic, as the success of each member reflects on the whole family. In seven cases, pressure had been put on sons to become engineers, for engineering is one of the most coveted and remunerative jobs in India today. In some cases the parents were bitterly disappointed when their sons did not do well enough to get seats in engineering colleges.

The sons whose parents did not support their high ambitions had a particularly difficult time finishing college.[12]

Br. 14: My parents did not want me to go to college, because my brothers had all stopped studying after high school. Father thought my brothers might revolt against him if he allowed me to. He wanted me to get a job, and was very disappointed when I went to college. He is not interested in my work there, or in my future plans. I can only continue at college because I have never failed, and getting distinction in my examinations had given me a freeship. I work hard, both at college and at home. I have no other distractions as I have very few friends. I can't make friends, because I haven't any money to treat them with, or enough money to go with them, and also because I am orthodox.

This person was one of the "non-participating" students discussed in Chapter 6. He was mainly interested in his studies and his professors. Being on his own, with opposition at home, he had no time or inclination for indiscipline.

12. *Report on a Survey . . . of the Students of the University of Bombay*, p. 45. "The 49 per cent who feel frustrated by the thwarting of their ambitions feel it all the more because an understanding parent would have easily solved the difficulty. In most cases the reason stated is 'elders do not agree with me,' 'no encouragement from home' . . . 'uneducated family background,' 'strict and conservative parents,' etc."

The case of another Brahman student also illustrates the importance of family support, particularly in a situation where the brothers have been successful. *Br. 13*: "My main ambition is to get a Master's degree in science, so that I will get a good position. My mother, brothers, and uncle all took a keen interest in my studies. They want me to succeed because they have all got on well in life." This interviewee was also one of the "non-participating" students. He, too, mentioned his interest in college and his antipathy towards the unruly students.

In another case the son had to contend with the opposition of his uncle in addition to that of his father because of his desire to go to college.

> *Br. 75*: My father ran a general shop and my uncle was his partner. I had to help in the shop when I was studying at high school. I failed continuously because my whole time was spent in the shop and I had no time to read. Then my father, who was very worried about me, and disgusted with my repeated failures, made me give up my education, and work all the time in the shop. I was very sorry, and hated the shop, but Father was adamant. I had to work all day in the shop, receiving kicks and blows from both my father and uncle. My position grew worse each day. I was always worried about my future. I did not want to be a businessman, but wanted to be educated and to lead an independent life as a government servant. Finally my uncle allowed me to go back to high school, but I had to continue to work in the shop as well.

In still another case the whole family punished a student for failing an examination. *Br. 61*: "The whole family felt my failure deeply. My brother is harsh with me, and my grandmother bangs me. I feel that failure is my fate, and that I cannot overcome it."

Six of the students with moderate ambitions had parents who were very anxious that they should do well at college. Five of these boys had failed one or more examinations. Eight of the other Brahman students who had moderate ambitions at college had parents who showed about the same amount of interest in their work. The parents of both of the remaining two students had taken very little interest in their education.

Fourteen of the Brahman students, but only ten of the Brahman parents, had low ambitions. Again there was a difference in the ambitions of some of the sons and parents, although five of the sons whose parents had shown very little or no interest in their education, had low ambitions. But three of the sons who had very little ambition had parents who showed such great interest in their studies that they were often punished for not doing well at school. These three students also had pressure put on them to study by brothers and/or grandparents. The six remaining sons who displayed little ambition had parents who showed only moderate interest in their school work. Four of these boys were punished for not doing well, and three failed in college, one many times.

Christian Students

In the Christian families of this sample, fourteen parents had high ambitions for their sons, but only eleven sons had the same aspirations. Thirteen parents and nine sons had moderate ambitions, and only one parent lacked an interest in his son's future, in comparison with eight sons who had low ambitions.

Several of the parents had high ambitions for their sons and wanted them to become great men. Other parents who had done well themselves expected their sons to succeed also. Pressure in these cases thus came from family tradition and precedent. *Ch. 134*: "I come from a very well-educated and highly-placed family. My grandfather went to Oxford. Later he was the Vice-Chancellor of a university. All my uncles have gone abroad to study and have returned to big government positions. My father is a doctor." In another case the mother had always wanted the son to be a high government official like his cousins, and the pressure on the son to study came as a result of the family's poverty. Everyone knew that he must continue to get a freeship if he was to finish college: "I was always forced to be good and studious." It may be significant that such students all experienced a great deal of anxiety about their futures.

Pressure on students to do well sometimes came from the fact that close friends of the family had become well qualified, and held good positions. Meanwhile, there existed the ever-present spectre of the "educated unemployed." "There are so many graduates in India that you must be a double graduate to get ahead."

Often parents put pressure on their sons, either in the form of punishment (sometimes beginning in a severe way at school), or by constant advice "not to fritter away their time with friends," or by encouragement.

Three of the Christian students were the first in their family, or in their community, to get a degree, so all eyes were on them, and their successes or failures were watched avidly.[13] In five cases it was the mother, and in four others, the father who was the most anxious for the son to get a good degree. In three others, it was the grandfather, and in five cases, friends, who were particularly anxious for the student to succeed. Only one of the Christian parents was not interested in his son's education, and seemed not to care about his future, but eight Christian students had little inclination to study or get ahead. Three of these students had parents who were highly ambitious for them, and the others had parents who were moderately ambitious. Of these students one found the life at college so free after boarding-school, where he was forced to work hard, that he spent his time enjoying himself. Another had got in with friends who were happy-go-lucky, so that in spite of his mother's scoldings, he did not work hard. Still another was very lazy and hated studying. He knew that his college fees were a financial strain for his father, but in spite of this, and in spite of his father's anger, he allowed his friends to entice him away from his studies. Three of the Christian students who had moderate ambitions had parents with high ambitions. Two of these had been punished for not working harder.

The parents of the remaining students with moderate ambitions were not interested in their children's education. The Christian students would perhaps be expected to have the highest ambitions. They have been closer to the Western way of life, and their parents are, on the whole, more highly educated than those of the other communities of this sample. Also, the Christians are members of a minority that feels discriminated against, and they would feel the need to get ahead. However, it may be that just because the ambitions of their parents were high, many of them felt failures at not having been able to get seats in engineering or medical colleges. Many of them had worked hard at college until they passed the P.U.C. examination that determines entrance into professional colleges, and when they failed to get seats, became despondent. In other words, they seem to have given up and have spent their time getting what enjoyment they could out of college. This could account for the eight Christian students with low ambitions, in contrast to only one father with low ambitions for his children.

13. A head waiter at one of the Bangalore hotels was sending his children to a private Roman Catholic school. Another waiter from the same hotel was putting his son through college. Both were Christians. Cases of this sort would not be unusual on the North American continent, but it is very rare for men in their position in India to be able to afford private or higher education for their children.

Lingayat Students

The attitude of the Lingayat students was different from that of the Christians in that more of the students had high ambitions than had the parents. Nine parents had high ambitions, as compared with thirteen sons. However, more of the parents had moderate ambitions than had their sons, and the same number of each had low ambitions. Two of the Lingayat students were the first members of their families to get college degrees. They were both anxious not to disappoint their parents. In six cases, both the sons and the parents had high ambitions. In four of these, relatives and friends had reinforced the parents' high ambitions for their sons. In one case the parents, who came from a village, had low ambitions and did not understand the value of education. Thus, although their son was very ambitious, the father wanted him to stop college because of the expense. On the other hand, one son wanted to give up his education and return to his village, while his father wanted him to go on and achieve a high position. *Li. 83:* "After I finish my B.A. I want to go back to the village to do agriculture, but my father wants me to become an officer or an advocate. He hates my returning to the village. According to him, village life is not suitable for an educated person. I don't agree with him. I am disgusted with studying, but Father insists that I go on. What can I do? I am homesick for the village and my family."

Of the students with low ambitions, one spent all his time at the movies, or going for walks with friends. Another had no interest in his studies, but wanted to go into business where he could be independent. Still another wanted to go on studying merely because it was such a carefree life. He did not want to settle down, but to "wander about, and always be with his friends."

Vokkaliga Students

As the Vokkaligas are a "rising" caste and now have a good deal of political power, one might expect the fathers in this group to be ambitious for their sons. This was true of the sample studied. More of the Vokkaliga parents had high ambitions for their sons than had Vokkaliga students for themselves, but approximately the same number had low ambitions. On the other hand, a good many of the students came from villages, and their parents were not highly educated themselves. This might counteract middle-class aspirations.

Uncles, brothers, grandparents, siblings, and even aunts often urged

178

the students to study hard or get ahead, as in the other communities. In one case it was the uncle who insisted that his nephew continue his education after high school. The boy came from a hard-working family, and his father and grandfather had both punished him harshly for neglecting his studies, or cutting classes while at college.

In one case in which the father was highly ambitious for his son to "become a great patriot and work for India," the son's ambition was simply to get a degree. He was not concerned with doing well or with becoming a great person. In another case in which the parents were deeply concerned about their son's future, the mother wept when the son failed, and the father continually showed his anxiety about his progress. Another example reveals that a student, who was himself ambitious, got support from his uncle and brothers. *Vo. 60*: "I often get letters of advice from my family about my education and conduct. I am told to work hard, as I come from a humble and poor family, and so cannot afford to neglect my studies. They want me to become an officer of very high rank and then support the family well." In one case the parents' low ambition for their son resulted from the fact that the father believed a college education would spoil his son. However, the son was ambitious and insisted on going against his father's wishes.

The first son to be educated in the family, if the younger one, is often the butt of the jealousy of older brothers, and even of cousins. They tend to resent his education, even when the parents may be very happy to have a son at college. This occurred in several cases, and was a matter of great anxiety for the student.

Once the son has been to the city to college for a few years he often develops an aversion to returning to the village, or to the joint family. In one case the Vokkaliga student did not want to return to his village after graduation, as his brothers objected to everything he did, and the villagers were very narrow-minded. They would watch all his movements, and he would not be able to behave as freely as he had in the city.

In one case a student failed because of his anxieties over family problems. He had studied hard, but was too worried to concentrate.

The students who had low ambitions gave the same reasons for these attitudes as did students of other communities; they had no interest in their studies, or they preferred amusing themselves in the company of friends. One student explained: "I go through the ordeal just to get a degree."

This analysis of the ambitions of the parents and students of this sample shows so many variations that it is impossible to draw any clear conclusions. In each of the four communities, some of the students and their parents seem to be equally ambitious for their sons to get ahead, but in other cases the parents had high ambitions for their sons when they were only moderately, or not at all keen to improve their position. In still others it was the student who was anxious to get ahead—sometimes in spite of strong opposition from relatives and parents.

Although the figures are small, they show that the Brahman and Christian parents had, on the whole, higher ambitions than did the Lingayat and Vokkaliga parents. About half of the parents of the first two groups were highly ambitious for their sons, whereas only about a third of the parents in the last two groups fell into this category.

The scope of this study did not make it possible to analyze just why there was often a difference in the ambitions of parents, as compared to those of the sons, but it was evident from the data that a student could be made deeply anxious, should he desire to study and get ahead while lacking the support of his parents or relatives. On the other hand, a student who had no inclination to study, or had other personal reasons for not wanting to go to college, could be harrassed by very ambitious families.

Sometimes these anxieties were tolerable, motivated the student to work hard, and so helped to keep him from indulging in indiscipline, but in other cases the family standards were so high, or the future so bleak, that the students simply "gave up" and spent their time at college enjoying themselves as best they could. The way in which ambitions combine with other family factors to encourage students to be indisciplined will be summarized in Chapter 6.

AMBITIONS OF WOMEN STUDENTS

The traditional career of Indian women, as in all societies, has been marriage and motherhood. To what extent has this pattern changed in recent years? In most countries both single and married women of the middle and upper classes are now entering the work world in increasing numbers. Is this due to financial necessity, or are women beginning to acquire ambitions for "careers" in business, the professions, and personal services? If so, what effect is this having on their behaviour as students? How does it affect their attitudes toward college? Is the student attending college in order to equip herself for a career? What strains occur when the age-old traditional role of women is upset by a woman's alternate conception of herself as a career woman?

The same criteria used for the men students of this sample were used to try to answer these questions; namely, the interest of the women students in higher degrees, their seriousness, as shown by whether they had studied hard or not, and finally, the ambitions their parents had had for them and the aspirations they themselves had as regards careers.

Data from the interviews with this sample of women students showed that they went to college for two main reasons: to increase their marriage chances, and to relieve boredom, for they seldom have any specific interests at home to help them pass the time now that they marry at a later age. In a few cases the girls went to college because their parents or relatives wanted well-educated daughters, and hoped that they would go on to interesting careers. This latter reason will probably become more important as more middle- and upper-class families see it as a way of increasing the family income. Only a small proportion of the students were themselves seriously interested in careers. Sixty-one, or about two-thirds of the ninety-one girl students said they wanted to study for higher degrees. Only one girl, a Brahman, wanted to get a Ph.D. Forty-two wanted to take an M.A. or M.Sc. Another Brahman and a Christian wanted to become doctors.

However, in view of their remarks about their lack of interest in their courses it would seem likely that many of the students answered this question without serious thought on the matter. One reason that some parents do not want their daughters to take higher degrees is that this tends to make it more difficult to find them husbands. It is not considered correct for a girl to marry a boy who has not an equivalent, or higher degree, and this, of course, limits the choice of men.

Twenty-four of the students were not interested in doing graduate work, did not like studying, or were planning to be married after they got their B.A. degrees. Six students did not answer the questions.

In comparison to the men students, about fifty per cent of whom had studied hard at college, only about a third of the girl students said they had done the same (thirty-three out of ninety-one). These figures seem appropriate in view of the fact that, whereas there was no doubt that the men students had to get jobs after graduating, most of the women students were not planning to work for very long, so that it did not matter whether they got high standing in their courses or not. One lecturer who had lectured for ten years said she had never had a girl in one of her courses who was a serious student. She believed that even students who went in for medicine tended to do so because of the glamour and sense of adventure, rather than because they regarded it as a serious career.

Reasons given by women students for not studying hard were much the same as those given by the men students. They were not interested in the courses, were bored, did not think it worth the trouble, were too lazy, or wanted to have a good time. Most were satisfied just to pass. A few said they preferred to work at extracurricular activities and games, and felt that, as they could pass without studying hard, they simply did not need to study.

The students' lack of interest in their courses is borne out by the observations of their lecturers. The general impression of those who were questioned on this matter was that the large majority of girls had no idea of what they wanted to get out of college, except that they felt it might help them to get married. One informant, who was one of the first women to study at a college in Bangalore, said that when she was at college the courses were the girls' main interest, but that now girls do not seem as interested in their work as in their saris, and in the fashions of the day. Her impression was that girls now go to college to have a good time.[14]

The girls tended to take courses in subjects with which they had been familiar before going to college. If they had taken chemistry or mathematics at high school, for example, they would take them again at college. They might, on the other hand, take science rather than arts courses, as a knowledge of geography, mathematics, or chemistry would give them more chances of getting teaching positions when they graduated. A few of the more serious-minded girls took physics, or honour courses. These are thought of as "tough" courses, which will lead to higher degrees. There seems to be little experimenting as yet in new subjects, except for home science, and this is a subject which the girls and their families both consider useful for marriage, rather than for a career.[15]

14. The interest in fashion, and the emphasis on fashion and dress make it very difficult for some of the poorer girl students who cannot afford to compete. They often try to borrow saris and jewellery so that they will look as well dressed as the other girls. One or two colleges have tried to wipe out these invidious distinctions by insisting on a uniform sari. After a period of revolt the students finally accepted this change in dress.

15. Goldsen, Rosenberg et al., p. 57. Even girls in the Western countries which have encouraged higher education and jobs for women for a longer period of time still tend to think of preparing for careers only if they do not marry. However, they are more likely to want to work after college and before they marry, and an increasing number are plan-

Daughters may acquire the idea of going to college or of having careers from many sources, but in India the parents' attitude will probably have more influence on the daughters' ambitions than it does on girls in Western countries because of the girls' closer contact with, and attachment to their families. The parents of this sample of students varied considerably, as far as their interest in their daughters' education was concerned. At one end of the scale were parents who were completely against giving their daughters a college education; at the other, were a few parents who had high ambitions for their daughters, and whose interest in their children's studies began when the girls first went to school. These parents had usually sent their daughters to private schools, provided they were able to afford the fees. In Bangalore, these schools are usually run by Christians and have English as the medium of instruction. The parents were very anxious that their daughters should know English thoroughly, and also wanted them to go on to college. A few had promised that they would send them abroad to study, after they got their degrees.

Many parents are so anxious about the future of their children, both sons and daughters, that they put great pressure on them to study hard at school, and children who do not obey may be severely punished. Only a few of the girl students of this sample, however, said that they had been punished when they had not studied at school. The form the punishment took was mainly scolding.

Forty-five of the women students had been encouraged to go to college. In thirty-two of these cases both parents had been ambitious about their daughters' future. In eleven cases the father was the one who had encouraged his daughter, and in two other cases it was the mother.[16] In one case, although the wife, a college graduate, was keenly interested

16. *Report on a Survey . . . of the Students of the University of Bombay*, p. 36. The findings of this study support those of the Survey of Bombay students in that "The sustaining influence goading or encouraging them on towards the attainment of a goal, a university degree, is the parent, in most cases the father, in some cases both the parents, or the relatives of the student."
In the Bombay Study 83 per cent of the students said that their parents, or elders took an interest in their studies.

ning to work after marriage. But not many enter college with a sense of dedication to a particular profession. "A dedicated career girl is a deviant; in a real sense she is unwilling to conform to her sex-role as American society defines it. For professional work among women in this country is viewed as an interlude, at best a part-time excursion away from full-time family life—the family life which the coeds yearn for, impatiently look forward to . . . and define as largely monotony, tedium and routine. . . . It is this basic contradiction which makes it difficult for college women to come to terms with themselves."

in seeing that the daughters were well educated, the father was angry whenever he had to pay their fees: "Why should you girls go to college? What's the use of it?" He was also against the older sister working, until he realized how useful and important her salary was in helping the family finances. The mothers who lacked interest in the education of their daughters generally felt that the girls should not be educated because higher education was not a necessary adjunct to their marriages. Some parents do not see the point of paying for extra education that the girl will never use. The fact that fathers appear to be more anxious than mothers to educate their daughters is due perhaps to their more realistic approach to a girl's future. They have been exposed to the changing times more than the mothers, have seen girls working outside the home, and so are more used to the idea.

Sometimes the daughter was encouraged because there were no sons in the family, so the parents ambitions settled upon them; or a brother's career influenced his sister, and she wanted to follow in his path. *Br. 219*: "My brother is abroad working on his Ph.D. From what I hear, he is doing fascinating work. It has attracted me so much that now I have taken my brother's work as an ideal to be achieved. It is my ambition to do research, and my parents are very enthusiastic about my plans."

Parents who are not well off are likely to concentrate on one child in the family, as they cannot hope to finance the higher education of all their children. The wealthier parents, and those who are highly educated are apt to be more liberal in their views of women and careers, but also more realistic about the importance of their aiming at careers. This attitude was seen in an extreme form in one of the Christian families, where it was "one of Father's dreams to see all his children graduate." When the daughter failed her matriculation, she wanted to stop studying, but her father would not hear of it. In another case, parents continually exerted great pressure upon the children to get college degrees.

Ch. 170: I grew up in an atmosphere where my father kept saying that he wished all his children to be highly qualified persons. My father wants me to continue my studies and get an M.A., and then try for a scholarship and go abroad, but I do not think that I am so very clever. At first I was not even interested in getting a B.A., but my father kept saying—generally at the dinner table—that I would feel inferior later on in life if I did not have a degree. I also knew that girls of my age from respectable families, and of average intelligence, always take their degrees. I did not wish to be left out, neither did I want others to think me unintelligent, so I came to college for a degree.

Pressure on the girl is even stronger when all the relatives join in, as in the following case: *Ch. 186*: "My family expects me to get a first class in my B.Sc., and then do my M.Sc. Since all my family and relatives expect me to get a first class, I study hard. Sometimes I worry whether I will be able to get one; it will be disgraceful if I do not."

Nine grandparents, fourteen brothers, and four sisters of this sample had encouraged the girls to go to college. Relatives were influential in eight cases. The reverse can be true. In several cases relatives were thought to be jealous of the girls' education, as they kept telling the parents that it was a waste of money to educate their daughters.

Relatives quite often seem to resist the new trend toward higher education for women, for they feel that the girls should get married instead. Sometimes the whole family may be against it. *Br. 212*: "I do not get any encouragement from my home. I get a lot of discouragement just because I am studying; they do not even talk to me."

A few of the girls were courageous enough to defy their elders who were against higher education for women. *Li. 176*: "My eldest uncle is very much against my going to college. He wants me to stop studying and get married right away. We have many arguments about it. He does not see the need for my getting a degree. I am the first girl among all our relatives to study for a degree, and my uncle resents this very much. He has brought two proposals for me, but I have refused them, as I want to marry his younger brother, my second uncle, later on."

Several of the girls were not allowed to go on to higher education, because their community would be against it. In some sub-castes it is still thought to be "too fashionable" for a girl, and some members are jealous that a girl should get higher degrees when they have not been able to help their own sons attain them. Very occasionally a friend was mentioned as being the one who had influenced the girl to go ahead.

Parents may encourage high ambitions in their daughters, but not allow them to fulfill the desires that may be created at college.

Vo. 185: My grandfather and my father's elder brother are not very well educated, but my grandfather has great ambition to see all his grandchildren highly qualified and foreign-returned. My father's elder brother has three sons and two daughters. One son got a scholarship for a postgraduate degree in London. The other four children were sent by my grandfather for post-graduate degrees abroad. But he does not like the girls to work. Now my cousins are married to men who are less educated than themselves, and are staying at home. My grandfather has promised to send me to America after my M.Sc. They all encourage me to try for an M.Sc. and then go abroad, but in our family no one will allow me to work afterwards.

Twenty-four of the girl students had no ambition to study further. None of these liked studying. One preferred to read detective books. Several of these girls wanted to learn dancing, music, and needlework, or do housework and cooking, in view of the fact that they were going to get married. One was so keen to become a professional dancer that she said she would rather stay unmarried than let her art and ambition stagnate if her future husband would not allow her to perform in public. An exceptional case was that of the student who had been encouraged by her brothers to learn to fly, and her ambition was to become a perfect flyer, rather than to get a degree. *Br. 199*: "I will make good use of my flying. I prefer dying the death of a hero to dying a peaceful death like any other person. Crashing in a plane and dying is more worthy, for one may die any day and it is much better to die when one is serving the world."

Still another of these students, being the eldest of the family, had too much work to do at home to think of taking further studies. She had to look after the younger children, help her mother cook, and do all the shopping, in addition to looking after her relatives. One girl had found college so disappointing that her ambition to become a doctor had declined since she had been at college, even though her two brothers gave her every encouragement to carry out her plan.

The future of girls who plan careers is often just as insecure as is that of the boys. In one case the father wanted his daughter to be a doctor, but because she thought it took too long, and because she might not have been able to get financial assistance from the government she took a B.A. instead. She decided that if she could get into a professional college after that she would take her M.A.; otherwise she planned to get her B.T. and become a teacher.

The difficulties faced by an ambitious girl in search of a career are illustrated by the case of this Christian student. She got a full freeship for college and first wanted to be a chartered accountant, but she could not get a seat in the college. Then she wanted to go into engineering. But she explained, "The local college wanted Rs.7,000 as a donation, which we could not afford. Oh God! I have so many ambitions, but there are no means of achieving them."

This sample of students could probably be duplicated from among any group of college women around the world. A few have been motivated to go on to carve out careers for themselves and so study hard; but the great majority are rather indifferent to the knowledge and skills they can learn at college. It is probable that in India the latter still constitute a larger proportion of the women students than in the more highly industrialized countries, as higher education and professional careers are still a relatively new trend. It is also probable that on the whole there is still much more resistance to higher education for women. Many Indians still see it as a useless luxury, as it is not expected to be an asset to a married woman, and marriage is still their chief goal. Mothers, too, do not see it as an assistance in running a home. Relatives and members of the same caste may be quite against it. They oppose it in the first place because of its novelty, and in the second because the money spent on a girl's education might perhaps be spent more usefully on assisting their own sons to get higher education. In the Western world a college education for middle- and upper-class women is now considered to be almost a "natural" step after school. Western parents are also aware that eligible husbands may be found through co-education, whereas the Indian parent is afraid that co-education may possibly end in a dreaded "love" marriage, and in any case, as they are responsible for finding the girl a husband, they feel they do not get any assistance in this matter from her college participation.

It is one thing for a student to say that she would like to work after she graduates, and quite another matter for her to do so.

The trend toward women working outside the home in India has been accelerated by the new job opportunities opened up by industrialization, particularly in the white-collar categories of employment. The Five Year Plans of the Indian government have also publicized the growing need for trained and professional workers in many fields, and this certainty of work has probably encouraged many women to train for these occupations. It is not uncommon to see statistics of this sort in the Indian newspapers and journals.

According to the Planning Commission . . . the country will need, by the end of the Third Plan, more than three lakhs of women doctors, thirty-six thousand nurses, eighty-one thousand, five hundred midwives, four hundred pharmacists, 1.5 lakh of social workers and over 1.5 lakh of women workers in small scale industries for various Plan projects. How can they be found, educated, and trained within this period without sufficient financial allotment? (*Deccan Herald*, Editorial, September 7, 1961.)

The challenge of these openings does not seem to have seeped down to this sample of college students.[17] Although sixty-three of the ninety-one girls interviewed said that they wanted to work after college, the majority of them were aiming at white-collar jobs. Thirty-six wanted to become teachers, clerks, secretaries, typists, salesgirls, or telephone operators. Eleven more wanted to take the easy professional path for a girl with an M.A., and become lecturers, usually until they married. The remaining sixteen students were particularly ambitious. One wanted to be a lawyer, one a physicist, one a child psychologist, one a political scientist, and one a spiritual leader. Two of them wished to become doctors and another two to become engineers. Seven wanted to go into research.[18] One of the girls who wanted to be an engineer was influenced by the fact that a great many of the men in her family were engineers. Another girl thought that if her husband and in-laws did not like her, or she did not fit in with them, she would be able to get a job. She was one of the few women of this sample to show a desire to be independent. Her attitude was influenced by the fact that she had found her home life very dull.

The women students seemed much less ambitious about the type of work they wanted to do than were the men students. Another way in which they differed from the men students was that they were not nearly as unsure about getting the jobs they wanted as were the boys. Forty-nine of the girl students had no doubts about getting the jobs they preferred.

If this sample of students follows the pattern of other graduates in India, no matter what the students say about *wanting* to work, it is

17. Ross, *The Hindu Family in Its Urban Setting*, pp. 197-205.
18. Goldsen, Rosenberg *et al.*, p. 49. "The occupations women choose to go into are quite different from those chosen by the men. They overwhelmingly select the traditional 'women's occupations.' Of all the men we polled, about half desired to enter engineering, medicine, business or law; but less than one-tenth of the women chose any of these occupations. Conversely, thirty-seven per cent of the women we polled selected teaching, social work, secretarial work, art or journalism and drama, compared with about one-seventh of the men.

"The values that women seek to gratify in their occupational life are quite different from those that appeal to the men. Relatively speaking, the women stress the value of working with people; and they are much less likely to emphasize the reward values of occupational life."

likely that not many of them will, in fact, end up by working; or if they do, it will not be in jobs that are on a level with their intellectual ability and/or training. Several lecturers, and the principal of a women's college were very upset at the disinclination of women students to take jobs after graduating in fields which were open to them, and which badly needed workers. At one college specializing in home science only forty-two girls out of one hundred and seventy-two who graduated between 1956-1961 had worked, and some of them for only a relatively short period of time. Eighteen of these girls had taught in high schools, fifteen had lectured in colleges, and one had become a lawyer; but four had become clerks or secretaries. Only eight had worked after marriage.[19]

> *Principal of Home Science College*: Most of our students do simply nothing after they graduate. It is true that all the home science positions are filled in Bangalore, but there are plenty of opportunities for our graduates in the country. High schools have started giving courses in home science, and have to take untrained teachers in this subject. The salaries are good, too: Rs.150 per month.
>
> But parents simply won't let their daughters go to the villages or towns to work. They are afraid they won't get husbands for them, or that they will fall in love and marry outside their caste. They are even afraid of their going to other cities to work. There was a good job open in home science in Mysore City, but the parents would not let their daughter take it, even though she could have lived safely in a hostel. It isn't the girls who are at fault; many of them would be willing, and many are very bright, but the parents intervene.

The fact that it is difficult for women to live alone in strange villages, towns, or cities increases the problems of supplying the smaller cities and towns with the doctors, nurses, and teachers they so urgently need. The Principal of the Home Science College previously mentioned was discouraged about the situation, as she knew of the great need in India for specialists. Nor would the parents of trained students listen to the advice of their children, once the latter had returned home. This is a common occurrence in countries where young people have tried to introduce into their homes new health or nutrition measures learned at school or college. In this sense their education in practical matters seems to be wasted.

19. These figures were taken from the college files. They are more disturbing when broken down into three-year periods, for whereas thirty-seven out of seventy-four graduates had taken jobs from 1955-58, only ten single girls out of eighty-nine graduates had taken jobs from 1959-61.

Fewer parents showed an interest in their daughters' getting jobs, as compared with the number of parents who wanted their daughters to get degrees. However, a good job is now beginning to be recognized as an asset, for the daughter can help with the family income before she is married. Some parents are even willing to sacrifice their daughters for their sons. *Ch. 188*: "My family expects me to work soon after I leave college, and to help them financially until I get married. I want to do my M.Sc., as I can get a . . . better paid job with one, but my parents object. They want me to earn as soon as I finish my degree. My second sister was also very keen to do her M.Sc., but they have forced her to work. My parents are interested in giving their sons a very high education."

Kannan mentions a case in which the father had not allowed his daughters to marry because their salaries would be lost to him. In still another case, he said, the parents wanted their daughter to remain a spinster and earn for them. Later, when she found that all the good proposals for marriage were turned down by her parents, she insisted on marrying.[20]

The antipathy of the parents to their daughters' working, which is the orthodox attitude in India, was not confined to any one communty, although the majority of the Christian parents took it for granted that their daughters would work, at least before marriage. In one case the parents expected their daughter to work for about three or five years after graduation to help finance their new home, whereas parents in five Brahman, one Lingayat, and one Vokkaliga family had not progressed from the traditional idea that a girl's work was an insult to her parents, the implication being that they could not support her, and therefore she must help them out financially.

In the case of one Brahman, one Lingayat, and three Vokkaliga students, it was relatives, or other members of their respective castes, who objected to their working. Relatives may also oppose a woman's working if she only receives a small salary, particularly if her family is wealthy enough to support her without her having to work. In fact, financial necessity is one of the major criteria permitting women to work, and if there is no economic need, the middle classes see no reason for women to have jobs. When a woman begins to work, her relatives and friends insist on knowing her salary. In one case they were "incensed" at the "undignified" situation of a woman graduate who had

20. C. T. Kannan, "Intercaste Marriage in Bombay," p. 65.

to work for a low salary, although she had had no previous experience in her field.

One Brahman student stood up for her right to work. Her family wanted her to get married immediately after college, as no woman in their family had ever worked, but she argued that she was only seventeen years old and did not want to marry until she was twenty-two or twenty-three. Finally, she persuaded them to let her teach. Another Brahman student was allowed to teach Sanskrit, as long as she remained in Bangalore and lived at home.

Students who do not work after graduating seldom have enough to occupy them at home and are usually bored, for their social life has not expanded sufficiently to meet the new leisure time of women who now marry at a later age. Several girls had wanted to become doctors, but their families could not afford the training. In one case a student was anxious to become a lecturer, but she thought that she would probably have to take a job as a clerk or saleswoman in order to help finance her younger sister's graduate work.

One of the problems of enticing qualified graduates to work in many of the developing countries is that many occupations have not yet acquired any prestigious woman models. A girl who seeks to enter a new type of work must pioneer to establish the occupation as a suitable one for women, and must also be able to assure herself and others that women are capable of undertaking such an endeavour. The main problem of recruiting nurses in India lies in the fact that nursing is still thought of as "unclean" work, unfit for decent women. No local equivalent to Florence Nightingale has arisen to help define the profession as one of such a high order of devotion and self-sacrifice that it deserves a position of prestige. The attitude to it at present is illustrated by the case of a Brahman girl whose family disowned her when she trained as a nurse after her wealthy husband had died.

The same thing applies to the field of social work. Gandhi has to some extent popularized it among some students in India, but there is a lack of prestigious models for women in this field as well. Only a few of the upper-class women do voluntary work, and although giving to charity is part of the Hindu religious philosophy, only a small number of the Western type of organized philanthropic money-raising campaigns are as yet held in the larger cities. Middle-class incomes are so low in India that people cannot afford to give much, and as personal responsibility still rests largely on a kinship, rather than a civic basis, and the philanthropic pattern is not yet integrated with the other structures so that it is an adjunct or a necessity to a career, pressures to contribute to outside agencies have not yet fully developed. The beginning of such activity is found in such service clubs as the Rotarians, but until the large corporations become involved in such a way that raising money becomes an important aspect of business careers as well as a means of attaining social prestige for women, giving will not become highly organized, and social work will not attain the high prestige it has in other countries.

The same lack of women models also exists in the business world. Few women have "made the grade" in such a way as to give young girls courage, or to motivate them to seek high business positions. Moreover, a girl may be socially isolated should she work in a bank or business concern, for the social segregation of the sexes is still carried over into the office. Most of the girls who work in offices have few friendly contacts with the male staff. They do their work and go home, having had little of the chit-chat, banter, or gossip that lighten the routine of office work in countries where the sexes mix more freely. Even if there are other women in the office they may belong to other castes or communities, and so have relatively little in common.

With the prospect of merely filling in time before marriage, possibly bored with her work, with no means of getting into contact with the grapevine, and with few models of other women to encourage her to get ahead, the Indian girl is generally not concerned with advancement. Moreover, her early training has not helped her to acquire the independence, initiative, and self-confidence that are essential for attaining the higher positions in the work world.[21]

Marriage, however, is still the main obstacle to both college degrees and work. Whereas seventy-one of the ninety-one women students interviewed said that they wanted to work after college, only thirty-one

21. *The Hindu*, February 15, 1962. "In a preponderantly male set-up, the initiative of women even in the highest levels is naturally restrained. Temperamentally too, they might appear to lack robust self-confidence, but the real truth is that they would not like to take the risk of earning disapproval for anything they might happen to do. They are very good at the meticulous carrying out of instructions, and given proper encouragement they show up exceedingly well. In higher levels of administration the qualities of clear thinking, quick decision after sizing up a situation, courageous expression of views, and a drive to get things done quickly and firmly are absolutely required, and mere show of authority does not take one far. All these qualities are developed only by proper training and guidance by senior officers—whether men or women. . . . In the case of women one has to be careful to see that they do not develop a fear complex or worse still they do not prefer the line of least resistance."

wanted to work after marriage. The opposition of families, relatives, and prospective husbands is the main obstacle, but in any case, most women are not yet interested in careers.[22]

Pressure for them to work, however, is increasing because of declining middle-class incomes. Pressure on daughters to prepare themselves for work after college is also increasing because of the growing realization that, in some communities where there is a lack of suitable husbands, marriage is not as inevitable for women as it used to be. A Brahman student was planning to take post-graduate courses and then work, *if* she did not marry. Five of the students said their parents did not want them to marry.

CONCLUSIONS

As a society becomes more highly industrialized, talent and skill rather than nepotism become the criteria for job-selection. This is a gradual transition which depends on changes in the obligations to kith and kin, and on increasing aspirations for a higher standard of living, more power, and more recognition. During the transition the older customary occupations will give way to new. In India there are many signs that the caste system is slowly giving way to an open-class society. This encourages vertical mobility, and so college degrees become increasingly important as gateways to careers, and more and more pressure is put on students, both by parents and by lecturers, to study hard and get high grades. Some of the main problems that Indian students face in finding satisfactory careers are the struggle to finance higher education, burdensome family financial responsibilities, the confusion about a choice of career, the spectre of the "educated unemployed," the lack of influential relatives to help them get jobs, and the disadvantages of belonging to a group designated as a Forward community. On the other hand, students who come from wealthy families, who can count on nepotism, or who belong to a Backward community, will tend to enjoy themselves at college rather than taking it as a serious part of their career. Greater tensions would be expected if both parents are highly ambitious, and the sons are not; or if sons are highly motivated, but get little or no encouragement or support for their ambitions from their parents.

22. Goldsen, Rosenberg *et al.*, p. 47. Even in the United States where women have more opportunities and incentives to remain single, it is stated that "for most of the women, family life decidedly takes preference over working at a career. Our data indicates that just about every college girl wants to marry and have children, and that she fully expects to do so. . . ."

As the need for skilled and professional workers increases, and as the family faces more economic insecurity, more women are drawn into the labour market. This causes a profound change in the traditional role of women. At first they are willing to accept the less skilled positions, but they, too, gradually become more ambitious and want the type of training and education that will permit them to enter the more interesting and remunerative jobs. Marriage, however, remains the main goal of women. Parents, relatives, and the great majority of the young women themselves prefer it to careers, but they recognize that a college degree is becoming an increasingly important acquisition for middle and upper-class Indian girls, as it greatly increases their chances for marriage. Some families may become so dependent on a daughter's contribution to the family income that they will postpone her marriage—perhaps indefinitely.

The students who will work hardest at college are those who have a strong sense of family responsibility, those who are deeply anxious about the future (particularly if they are the eldest or only sons), those who come from poor families that have struggled with poverty, or those who are personally ambitious. A few will be deeply interested in knowledge for its own sake, or will feel they have some mission to serve society. It is unlikely that such students would be indisciplined, for they have a purpose in life and would want to succeed, rather than waste time in revolt. Economic insecurity and pressures from parents and others, then, do not necessarily lead to indiscipline. It was precisely those students who were anxious about their futures who worked harder at college and did not waste their time on agitation or protest.

5

Social Life
and
Marriage

The idea of a satisfactory social life, or of the pleasurable use of leisure time outside the family, has not yet become part of the thinking of most male Indian students, although many of them are gradually becoming accustomed to movies, cafés, and other types of amusement. Many of their families have moved recently from villages where there were neither planned activities, nor organized youth groups, and where leisure time was spent mainly in chatting and gossiping with members of the family, relatives, or friends. In the city, however, there are not as many relatives to visit or chat with, and the interests of the different family members become more diversified. Thus, students tend to be bored, unless they can be with their friends.

Sarkar warns that the body as well as the mind must be "adequately engaged" to prevent restlessness at the student age.[1] The Indian student has a great deal of leisure time on his hands, for the educational system does not force him to work hard during the college year, and as the Indian economy does not provide part-time jobs for young people, he has little to do during vacations. Consequently there is absolutely nothing for many students to do during the holidays but loaf. They can no longer trick their parents into giving them money for some hypothetical college need, and many parents cannot afford to give it for pleasure. Thus, students may not have enough pocket money to permit them to make use of commercial entertainment. They are separated from each

1. Chanchal Sarkar, *The Unquiet Campus*, p. 22.

other, too, in summer, and are not organized, so they cannot even indulge in group indiscipline. Sunday is a particularly dull day for many
students.

Leisure time hangs so heavily on the hands of many of the male
students that they often attend meetings because they have nothing else
to do. A meeting at least fills in time and is more interesting than doing
nothing. At one university the author was surprised to find a packed
hall, with students standing outside listening through the doors and
windows, for a meeting on "Education in Canada," which was called
hurriedly, and took place after the last lecture before the Christmas
holidays. In Canada one would have expected a handful—if that—of
students at such a meeting, at such a time.

> While most of our universities and colleges provide facilities for games
> and extracurricular activities of various kinds, . . . a great many of our
> students do not in fact have wide and healthy interests in physical and
> cultural activities. The proportion of students who play any games is
> extremely small, and participation of students in intellectual or artistic
> activities is also very slight.[2]

Some of the associations to which men students belong are the
Y.M.C.A. and the Y.M. Indian Association. The Catholic students have
different organized groups. Public entertainment has increased markedly in the last few years in Bangalore. There are now six or more concerts
a year of classical European music, and several amateur dramatic groups.
The radio broadcasts several hours of European music, jazz, rock-and-
roll, and semi-classical music. Records are becoming increasingly fashionable, as in the West, and those of a popular artist are bought out
immediately. But on the whole there is a lack of interesting activities for
many young men who have finished college and have not yet got an
occupation.

> *Informant*: After the examinations the wealthier students go and visit
> their relatives, or have other things to do, but boys without any pocket
> money or jobs simply have nothing to do, so they hang around the colleges.
> The professors say "hello" enthusiastically, but they have no time for
> them, and don't want them around, and the boys still at college don't
> want them around either. So they have nowhere to go. There is a terrible
> let-down after the last few hectic months of parties and examinations.
> They simply have *nothing* to do.

2. *Report on the Problem of Student Indiscipline.*

Most of the things that the students would like to do, such as travelling and taking part in cultural and intellectual activities, are far beyond their means. There are few organized activities for young people outside the colleges. Organized youth tours, consisting of about thirty students with a chaperoning teacher, are increasing, but again it is a question of money, and as one student says, "We stay glued to this place." Thus, time often hangs heavily on the hands of students during the vacation. Some occupy themselves with informal visiting, and roaming about the city. A student will call on a friend, and the two will move on to the next friend, and gradually a group will get together. A student without friends during the vacations has only "lonely pleasures, with nothing to do but think of his future and daydream." Part of the students' dilemma results from their training. They have always been dependent on others for guidance and direction, and they do not know how to fill in their time when they are left to their own devices.

Listening to radio programmes is a source of amusement and relaxation for those who can afford radios. Some students will spend hours listening to jazz. Those who do not have radios often congregate in crowds outside hotels or restaurants with public radios, to listen to an important event, such as a cricket match. Bicycling is another form of amusement. Students are often seen moving along the streets on their bicycles, three abreast, laughing, and chatting. Bicycles are now made in India, and bicycle taxes have been reduced by one rupee so that they are cheap enough to have become the "poor man's conveyance." Families approve of their sons having bicycles, as these can be used by the different family members, and the student can also assist by carrying messages or parcels. It has been estimated that nearly every home in Bangalore now has a bicycle.

If students live in rented rooms they have more freedom, for they have a place in which to entertain their friends. They will often convene in the rooms of those who have radios. It is more difficult for students who live at home to entertain their friends in the way they would like, particularly if their parents are very orthodox. They may not have separate rooms, may not be able to talk or use the radio freely, and probably have the constant feeling that their parents are supervising their behaviour.

Most student social activity takes place in the corridors, compounds, and lounges of the colleges. It is here that firm friendships are made. As most homes function with a minimum of furniture, and Indian students are used to squatting rather than sitting, the lack of equipment and furniture in many of the colleges does not hamper their social interaction. At the same time, most of the colleges are overcrowded and noisy. There are few adjacent snack bars or soda fountains where they can gather. In addition to this, students often lack pocket money, which limits the use of eating places for social purposes. For the poor students, "there is nothing to do but study in their leisure time."

When asked how they spent their leisure time, several of the men students mentioned two or more activities. Eighty-eight said that they took part in such group activities as games, cultural activities, clubs, or associations. Eighty-four more said that they spent their leisure time on such individual activities as reading, studying, and hobbies. Ninety-one went alone or with friends to the movies, took walks, loafed, or listened to music. Sixty-nine chatted with friends, six went with girls, and forty-eight merely said that they spent their time with friends.

Practically no students mentioned recreation with their families. Almost all the cultural activities mentioned took place at college, and these included dramas, debates, and literary meetings. Interest in games did not always mean that the student participated in them; he might just be an on-looker. Cricket was the favourite sport, but a few played tennis and badminton, table tennis, football, or basketball.

Those who spent a lot of time reading usually read magazines, detective stories, or novels. A few read scientific magazines. Hobbies included photography, drawing, collecting stamps, and making model aeroplanes. A few Brahman students spent their leisure time in political organizations. One or two others read Sanskrit, went for picnics, teased girls, visited relatives, went to the temple, or did social service. Ten students seemed to spend most of their leisure time helping with home duties.[3]

Although thirty-nine of the women students said that they spent their leisure time in a satisfactory way, fifty said that they did not. Twenty-five of the Brahman and fifteen of the Christian students, that is, well over half of the students in each group, found their leisure-time activities unsatisfactory.

The women students suggested a number of improvements, with a view to making their leisure time more pleasant. In the first place, they wanted fewer rules and restrictions at home, in the hostel, and in their

3. For an account of the social life of a sample of people in Bangalore, see: Aileen D. Ross, *The Hindu Family in Its Urban Setting*, pp. 236-45.

social activities. They also wanted to be allowed to go out more often with friends, and to have the opportunity to express their own ideas. They wanted their elders to be more broad-minded and less critical. They explained that their relatives often inhibited their freedom by objecting to the students' swimming in a pool, even when wearing saris, or by not allowing them to go for walks alone, without a brother or older person accompanying them.

In the second place, the students suggested more diversions. Twenty-six wanted to see their friends more often, have more parties at home, go on more excursions with their families or with other students, mix with more people, go to the movies more often, and travel. Seventeen suggested that they would like better facilities for entertainment, such as clubs or associations, where they could enjoy music, take part in dramas, and play more games.[4] Eight of the students wanted to have more friends among boys and to have the opportunity to become better acquainted with them. They wished to attend co-educational colleges. Forty students were content with their leisure-time activities.

For the girls, reading was the most favoured way of spending leisure time, followed by listening to the radio, embroidering, and knitting. Chatting and visiting friends were the next important leisure-time activities. Some girls sang, or played a musical instrument, and a few enjoyed games; some visited their relatives. Other popular activities were gardening, photography, writing, walking, and going to the movies. Eighteen girls had to spend much of their time at home doing housework, or washing and ironing clothes. Poverty is a factor that prevents some women students from having many social activities. One girl said that, because she had to wear artificial silk saris or imitation jewellery, she felt so inferior she refused to go to weddings or parties. Other students came from such poor households that their leisure time at home was spent in doing housework. *Br. 212:* "There is practically no social life in our home. I go back from college, and immediately start cooking and cleaning. I sometimes wait for my brothers to eat until 10:00 p.m.; then I serve their food, listening to their sarcastic remarks. I am not

4. There is not a great deal of variety in the entertainment offered in women's clubs. As women have never had to take the initiative in starting new ventures in the family, they do not know how to develop new interests. Some would like to do social work, but have little idea of how to go about it. Young married women have the same problem. One Christian spoke of the difficulty of getting anything of interest to do outside her home. She had tried church work, but found that the type of work, such as embroidery, did not interest her for long. There are more opportunities for educated young women in the cities, but the social life is very dull for them in small towns and villages.

allowed to go to my friends' homes. I very rarely see a movie. I would be happier if at least I was allowed to stay for the functions at college, but my father and brother are very narrow-minded and will not allow me to go to them."

The social life of women students is also hampered by the fact that they have little freedom to move outside their homes unescorted. If there is a celebration at college a group of girls will go together to a hotel for coffee afterwards, but then go right back home. In comparison to this lack of freedom, boys may talk or walk together anywhere; they may go for long bicycle rides together, or sit in parks, or even on the curb of the road, and talk for hours. Most of them are also quite free to go to hotels or movies, as long as they have the money to do so.

FRIENDSHIPS

One of the recent effects of urbanization upon Indian students is that peers are becoming increasingly important, both as companions and as guides. Friendships among men students are usually very strong in India, for in many cases, when students move away from their family and caste traditions, they find little understanding at home for their own problems of transition. This is especially true if parents are illiterate, or nearly so, or if students come from villages, and have had no opportunity to know the conditions of city or town life. *Li. 108*: "I discuss all my problems with my friends, and they discuss theirs with me. Since my people at home are not educated, I cannot share my feelings with them, and I cannot discuss anything intellectual with them. I feel they cannot understand me at all, so it is my friends who are very important, and I feel lost without them. They are not merely a means of spending one's time pleasantly; they are more than that."

Even those students in this sample who were well off, and had well-educated parents, were often *very* dependent on their friends. Although their relationships with their families were affectionate, they were not necessarily companionable. The father-son relationship is still typically one of authority, and the son seldom thinks of discussing his personal problems with his father. Nor have they many interests in common. The father is not expected to play the "friendly" or "companionship" role that he is in North America. The relationship of the student with his mother is usually very close, and he may often go to her with his financial and other practical problems. However, he does not necessarily feel that he needs to tell her how he is going to spend his money, or discuss his personal problems with her, so he keeps much of his behaviour a secret from his parents. When his friends come to the house they talk of their classes, or of politics, never of their private problems, for they do not want to talk about these matters in front of their elders.

The male student's relationship with his sister is usually close and warm. He sees his role as her protector, and she reciprocates by looking after him at home. She serves him coffee and food when he comes in, even late at night. However, brothers and sisters have few interests in common outside the home, and so there is little to talk about. Even brothers do not share their problems unless they are much the same age. They may discuss sports, or shout over politics, but will probably have few mutual friends.[5] The student's peers, therefore, are his *real* intimates. Together, students talk endlessly of their interests, going over and over the same subject. It is to his friends, too, that a student goes for help. Some of the students said that they would be more obedient and satisfied if their parents allowed them to mix more freely with their friends, or entertain them at home. Friends were the most enjoyable part of college life for a number of the students. Many cut classes solely to enjoy their friends' company.

The students who were working, as well as studying, seldom had much time for friends, or perhaps had friends only where they worked. Being older than the other students, they found the people with whom they worked more congenial.

No matter what problems the men students have in making friends, the women students have even more difficulties. No studies have yet been made of the extent to which Indian girls have been moving away from the primary contacts of the family to contacts with their peers. Girls who live in villages may have had more opportunities and freedom for making friends because of the relative closeness of their homes to those of their friends, but those living in cities have often been hampered by living far away from their friends. Young girls are not usually allowed to travel far alone, and it is harmful to their reputation to be seen out alone at night. Generally, they do not have as much pocket money as their brothers.

It seemed clear that most of the women students of this study depended on their girl friends, and to a few women these friends were very important. Sometimes they had met them at college, and there

5. For a fuller description of the sentimental attachments among the different members of the Hindu family, see: Ross, *The Hindu Family in Its Urban Setting*, Chapter V: "The Substructure of Sentiments."

was great distress at the thought that they would soon be separated. Sixty-seven of the girls said they had many friends, as compared with fifteen who had either no friends, or only a few. However, further interviewing showed that many of these friends were rather casual acquaintances, and the girls usually had only a few close or intimate friends. The latter served the function, as with the men students, of forming an important in-group, and gave the girls sympathy, reassurance, and some feeling of security. Their friendships were more likely to follow the North American pattern, where girls usually move in cliques of two or three, rather than belonging to groups as large as do boys. Only two girls said that they went with a gang or crowd of girls.

Twenty-three of the students (ten Brahmans, five Lingayats, four Vokkaligas, and four Christians) visited their friends freely, and invited them to their own homes. Three girls were prevented from visiting friends, and their friends from visiting them, because they lived so far apart. Two others were too poor to invite their friends home. Fourteen had acquaintances or close friendships with girls from other communities or castes. Most of these girls visited each others' homes, although sometimes visits were restricted to times of feasts and festivals. This information suggests that college may be one of the very few places in which women can meet people from other communities, and thus it may serve to break down the traditional close confinement of women to the companionship of women of their own caste or religion.

Eight of the girls were allowed to go to the movies with friends, but the others only went with their relatives. The number of movies they saw varied from one or two a week, to one every six months. Attending movies depends on a proper escort and money. That it is an important factor to most college girls is evident from their conversation when they get together. The girls' mannerisms and dress, and perhaps their changing attitudes to men, are often reflections of what they see on the screen. A few students felt deprived because they were not allowed to attend movies.

Mutual lending and borrowing is a sign of close friendship. Books and notes, and even saris, trinkets, and (occasionally) money were borrowed or lent by women friends. As with the men, solace was another of the main functions of their friendships. One student said that her friends were her only comfort in Bangalore.

Ch. 214: I discuss all my problems with one of my friends. She, too, tells me all her problems. I can trust her. I go to her room whenever we have a free hour. I think a close friend is an asset, for I do not know what I would have done without her. I tell her all the things that happen at home, and the days when I am depressed I go and stay in her room for hours.

My friend also belongs to a very orthodox family. She, too, has her own problems regarding the narrow-mindedness and conservatism of her parents, but she escapes this somewhat because she lives in the hostel.

Another role that friends fulfill is that of offering practical assistance. One group of friends had a common purse. Each girl put in what she could and the money was used at the college canteen, and for movies. Friendship also provides relaxation, particularly for students who live in hostels and do not have a great many things to do aside from studying.

Several of the women students were lone wolves who found the trivial gossip of the other students distasteful, and were more interested in their own hobbies. Some of these girls were too shy to make friends and felt inferior whenever they had to talk or mix with other girls. Others simply did not like being with girls.

Perhaps the most important factor that prevents Indian girls from making friendships as close as those formed by girls in the Western countries is the fact that the majority of them still find most of their companionship in their homes, particularly if they come from a joint family. They therefore may not feel the need for the friendship or support of their peers. However, when they move into a new college environment, they are often separated from their families and relatives. The women students discover that they must find new groups who can share their problems and guide them through novel experiences; this security they may find among peers who are going through the same period of transition. The intimacy of the college environment keeps the girls together for four years, which is a long enough period for them to build up close relationships. Students who reside in the college hostels have an even greater need for making friends, and more opportunity for doing so.

The college environment, though, does not wholly account for the differences that the women of this sample showed in their amount of leisure time and in their number of friends; the relative broadmindedness of parents or relatives, and their wealth or poverty, seemed to be more important in determining these differences.

To return to the subject of student friendships in general, the function of the peer in guiding students through their new experiences was evident from the way in which some of the men students spoke of their friends as "a source of inspiration," or told of their helpfulness, even though they might be too poor to help financially. One spoke of his friends as being his "mind and soul." Another said that he could not stand being without his friends. Some students found that their friends were more important to them than were their families. This attitude raised problems when families would not allow their sons to entertain their friends at home. The traditional visiting pattern is among relatives, who are extended limitless hospitality. Many of the students' families have not yet adjusted to the idea of entertaining their sons' friends, particularly if the latter are from different castes, or from different religious backgrounds.

The Christian students felt particularly close to their friends. If this attitude represents a general trend in their community, it supports other findings in this study which show that the Christian community has gone further than the other three communities toward an acceptance of an urban and industrial way of life. The Christian students seem to be more independent of their families, and more reliant on peers. A number of them said that they would do anything for their friends, and the friends would do anything for them. One said, "Friends are all I have." They spent as much time as possible with friends, got advice from them, had no secrets from them, and were close enough to know "everything" about them. Being with friends was the most enjoyable thing they did. On the whole, the Christian families seemed to encourage their sons' friends, and to invite them to their homes more than did the parents of other communities. The Brahman and Christian students had more friendships outside their own community than did the Lingayats or the Vokkaligas.

Reciprocation seems essential in these friendships. To keep friends one must return, in some way, what is given. The most obvious way is through entertaining, either by inviting friends to one's home, or by taking them out and treating them. Several students said that their inability to reciprocate in some tangible way prevented them from having friends, or made them unwilling to accept friendships on the basis of always being the recipient.

Li. 103: My social life is not at all happy, for I have no amenities. I very often feel lonely and find it difficult to live in one room. I have no house of my own and so I cannot entertain my friends, because I cannot invite them here. I do not normally go to their houses for parties. I do not have enough money at present to go out on excursions, or to go sightseeing or to do other things with them.

Of the male students in this sample, eight did not get any pocket money, and twenty-nine only got from Rs.1 to Rs.10 a month. This meant that, as some had to pay their bus fares, they did not have anything, or had very little for coffee, movies, or their own personal needs. It was almost impossible for them to treat friends, or share in the entertainment of their friends if it cost money. Forty-three of the students got from Rs.11 to Rs.20 per month, thirty-four from Rs.21 to Rs.30, thirteen from Rs.31 to Rs.50, and twenty-four received over Rs.50. Some who came from wealthy families could get additional money if they presented a good enough reason, and some from the poorer families could trick their parents into giving them money for such college expenses as text-books, and then use the money for amusement. However, in most of these families there was simply no extra money to spare, even for genuine necessities. The remarks of a Lingayat student show how poverty curtailed his social life.

> *Li. 108*: As I come from a poor family and it is absolutely essential to have money for entertainment, I cannot expect to have a good social life. I have several friends who are also poor like me. I cannot make friends with students who are from rich families, for it always turns out that either they do not like my friendship, because I happen to be the son of a poor police constable, or they show pity towards me. I don't like either to be pitied or be in the company of those who do not want me.
>
> Generally I go with friends for a walk, and very rarely I go to the movies, for I do not like to be the guest of other people all the time. I have never thought of taking girls out or making friends with them. This is simply because of poverty, and because I come from a very low social background. Poverty is a barrier to all my social life.

Most of the students' pocket money came from parents, but sometimes brothers would give it, or, very occasionally, a relative. Nineteen of the students earned what pocket money they had after contributing to the family income from their earnings.

On the whole the women students did not receive as much pocket money as did the men; nor did they expect to. Eleven did not receive any. Twenty-eight received up to ten rupees a month, which was just enough for bus fares. The families of some girls were so poor that the students had to walk quite a distance to college as they could not afford the fares. Thirteen of the girls got Rs.11 to Rs.20, eleven got Rs.21 to Rs.30, and two received from Rs.31 to Rs.50. No woman student received more than fifty rupees, whereas twenty-four of the men students received over that amount. As girls are not allowed as much freedom as men, they have not as many ways of spending money. Most of them spent it on clothes, trinkets, and novels, rather than on restaurants, coffee, or movies. Parents usually paid their daughters' movie expenses, unless the girls went secretly with their friends. Only one girl, a Christian, earned her own pocket money. The others received it, like the boys, from parents or brothers.

The men students suffered from the problem of having to borrow money from friends when they could not pay their way; this caused a great deal of embarrassment and hindered them from going with friends as often as they would have wished.

BOYS AND GIRLS

To what extent are mechanisms arising to meet the new conditions caused by the rising age of marriage, the greater increase in sex stimulation through the mass media, and the greater and freer contact of boys and girls at college? To what extent are the sex mores altering so that boys *desire* freer mixing? If the mores are changing, what are the main difficulties that boys and girls find in getting to know each other? What obstacles do they meet because of the traditional attitudes of their parents, their relatives, and the public?

Urbanization and industrialization, with their accompanying changes in the economic roles of the two sexes, and the increase in formal education, have brought young men and women together in new situations in India, where it is no longer possible to maintain the traditional strong sex taboos. The emphasis on sex in both Indian and Western movies, as well as in books, magazines, and advertising, continually presents new patterns of sexual behaviour. College students are probably more influenced by these media than are any of the other young Indians, as students have more leisure time than those who are working. The cinema is the students' chief form of entertainment and recreation, and although a student may at first recoil from the freer sex relations they see portrayed in Western countries, they are undoubtedly stirred by what they see. Informants believed that a subtle presentation of sex in Indian movies was increasing.

In India the social segregation of boys and girls, and of men and women, has been so complete for so many centuries that few Indians yet understand or accept the idea of "friendship" between the two sexes. In most middle-class homes in Bangalore the women still remain quite apart when the man of the house is entertaining male guests, and usually only relatives visit each other as couples. Thus, friendship between college men and women is quite beyond the Indian parents' comprehension; they cannot conceive of boys and girls going together as companionably as boys do with boys or girls with girls. The picture of friendship they see in American or English movies, or read about in books, seems to them always to be of a pronounced sexual nature, and they firmly believe that this type of relationship has only one aim— immoral behaviour.

The opposition of parents can be better understood by Westerners if it is remembered that Hindus have seldom seen their parents, grandparents, or their own generation engaged in mixed friendship groups. Thus, as a woman's chastity is her chief attribute, they tend to see the closer social contacts of young men and women as transgressing one of their most cherished values. They see few or no reasons to encourage mixing and many reasons to discourage it.

The strictness of the social segregation of young people varies in different parts of India. More contacts occur in the larger northern cities, and fewer in Bangalore which, although a city of over one million people, is somewhat isolated from the main modern currents. Still fewer contacts occur in Kerala in South India. Social segregation also varies in different communities. Young Anglo-Indians move more freely and easily together than any other group. Marastrian young people also mix to some extent, and certain more urbane Christians. In families belonging to the diplomatic service and the armed forces, the two sexes tend to have more contact. Muslims, and certain castes such as the Marwaris, are probably the most highly segregated.

The anonymity of the large city, and the fact that it provides many places where young men and women can meet secretly, make it a more likely place for new friendships or sex experimentation to take place. Moreover, many urban families are somewhat uprooted from their traditional homes and customs, and so are readier to accept change. In Bangalore, however, the number of cinemas, parks, or hotels where it is possible for a young man to entertain a girl are so limited that it is very difficult for a couple to escape unobserved, particularly as it is still such a novelty to see single men and women together in public. The best district in which to escape the attention of family, relatives, or neighbours is the fashionable Cantonment area, but the attractions are very costly, and few students can afford them.

There is a considerable difference between the social life of students who spend their leisure time in the "Cantonment" in Bangalore, and that of people who go to the "City." The Cantonment area was planned by the British and still retains an English flavour in its architecture and merchandise. Symbols of its past are seen in the Anglican Cathedral. Cubbon Park flanks one side, its main entrance presided over by an imposing statue of Queen Victoria. A statue of King Edward dominates the formal gardens. On the other side of the broad Maidan are the barracks and the Presbyterian Church of St. Andrew. The new Mahatma Gandhi Memorial, a recent addition which takes the form of a small garden surrounding a statue to the hero, is on the Maidan. The main fashionable street, formerly South Parade and now called Mahatma Gandhi Road, is flanked on one side by the most expensive shops, the fashionable restaurants, and the English-speaking cinemas. It is *the* fashionable street. Every evening from six to eight, and on Sunday afternoons, it is crowded with many young men of college age, sauntering along in couples, or in larger groups. They chat eagerly, watch the girls, and, if they have the money, go into a hotel to linger over a cup of coffee. The boys who frequent this area are more sophisticated, and come from wealthier families. Thus, their parents are probably more lenient about their mixing with girls. At any rate, it is in this area of the city that they become accustomed to the idea of boys and girls mixing socially. Outside this small area boys cannot take girls out publicly. This, then, is the area of "emancipation." It is also the area around which many of the better-off Anglo-Indians live, and they help to give it a Western atmosphere with their Western dress.

In spite of the traditional opposition to the mixing of the sexes, there is no doubt that the barriers separating them have been lowered to some extent in recent years. This is due largely to higher education. Many of the students of this sample felt that they could now at least smile at a girl, or even talk to her without their intentions being misunderstood. This could not have happened at the time of my last study in 1955.

The increase in the number of students of both sexes attending college, and the increase in co-education has made the college and university the most likely place for meeting the other sex. Formerly, family and religious festivals were almost the only occasions on which boys and girls could even see each other.

However, even at co-educational colleges many difficulties arise regarding the meeting of boys and girls, and many more if they take the adventurous step to dating. Most co-educational colleges have some mixed extracurricular activities. Girls debate against boys, and sit on committees with them, but on the whole only a few girls participate in this new type of behaviour, and so the contacts between boys and girls are mainly restricted to watching each other, smiling, or, for the bolder, wishing the other good-day, or saying a few hurried words in the college corridors.

In one co-educational college the boys have their classes in the morning, and the girls have theirs in the afternoon. At college functions the traditional pattern of the girls sitting on one side of the hall and the boys on the other is followed. They enter and leave the college by different doors. The Principal, being apprehensive of trouble or of complaints from parents, tries his best to keep them apart, and even watches his male and female lecturers carefully. Some colleges are co-educational in name only. The girls have separate classes and rarely even speak to a boy.

On the whole, then, there are, as yet, very few places where young men and women can meet naturally and without suspicion. Very few parents encouraged or allowed the sons and daughters of this sample to entertain the opposite sex in their homes, in spite of the fact that a number of the male students said that their social life would never be satisfactory until they had more freedom in this respect. Christian parents were an exception; most of them allowed their teenage children to invite their friends home, and encouraged their sons to go to mixed parties and even to dances, although they did not always wish to have them date individually.

The Roman Catholic Church in Bangalore supervises a mixed social club for college students and organizes conferences in different parts of India where male and female students dine at the same table, and share recreation and work as fully as they would in a Western country. The Hindu students, however, had no such assistance or guidance in helping them to adjust to this new relationship. Their parents were seldom helpful, and most students who were bothered by this new problem would not dare to discuss it with them. This often led to a good deal of secrecy in regard to taking girls out, or even speaking to them.

One hundred and twenty-one of the 159 male students interviewed desired a closer relationship with girls, but 112 of these students thought that their parents would, or might oppose it. The greatest opposition came from the Vokkaliga parents.

The students felt that not only would their parents be disappointed and heartbroken if they went with girls, but that they would also thoroughly misunderstand their intentions, and so lose faith in them or treat them badly. Moreover, the family would get a bad name. Orthodox parents were thought to be the biggest obstacle. Broadminded or educated parents, who were "good sports," were less likely to object.

The dilemma of students who want girl friends can be seen from this interview. *Li. 62:* "At present I have no girl friends at college whom I can take out. There are only a few whom I can smile at. Some girls near my home often come to my house to borrow books or other things. My parents do not object to them, but if I took out girls whom they didn't know, they would certainly bang me like anything. I am very keen to talk to and go with girls, but what can I do?"

Opinions varied as to whether many boys and girls went out secretly. Of the sample, only four boys admitted having done so: one Brahman, two Lingayats, and one Vokkaliga. There is some indication that a good deal of the secret dating that goes on is between boys and girls of different castes.

The strictness of parents sometimes forces a girl to have secret meetings with boys. *Ch. 249:* "What is mainly wrong with our boys and girls is that they always try to meet each other without their parents' knowledge. Most of the girls today sneak out mainly because of curiosity, and moreover, if you are told not to do a thing, you will want to do it more. I feel that too many restrictions spoil everything. I go with boys, and I feel there is nothing wrong in doing so."

Relatives, too, were thought of as being opponents to dating or mixing, and as being dangerous, for they were often eager bearers of tales. The great majority of both men and women students were sure that their relatives would object to a girl and boy even speaking to each other in public. In a few cases the parents allowed their daughters to see boys, even though a relative was against it.

On the other hand, students thought of their friends as being more of a help in this situation than a hindrance. Only forty-one of the men students believed that their friends would be against their going with girls. Some felt their friends would object because of moral scruples. Others thought that going with girls would provoke jealousy among their friends. This might result in spitefulness and in a type of teasing which they were not willing to face. Girl students also had to run the gauntlet of their friends' teasing, and possible jealousy. *Br. 217*: "I have a few boy friends. I go out with them to have a cup of coffee, or I go out to movies or evening walks with them. At such times some of my girl friends see me with them. Later, they tease me and tell me in a sneering way that they saw me with a boy the other day. This is the only difficulty I encounter when I go out with boys."

One boy who was successful with girls was dubbed "Romeo King" by his jealous friends. On the other hand, some of the Christian students looked upon boys who dated as heroes. These boys were the centre of attention, and would be constantly asked for introductions to girls by their less fortunate friends.

Another deterrent to the students' participation in this new behaviour was that elusive entity known as "public opinion." Many of the boys were afraid of the consequences of being seen talking to girls because of what "people would say," or because people might carry tales: "Everyone would hate me." Public opinion was particularly dreaded by the students who lived in villages. Their chief fears were that their actions would be misunderstood, that they would be thought immoral, and that their own characters, as well as those of the girls, would be ruined. A number who did not believe in closer contacts said that these were contrary to Hindu practices and teaching and believed that they would lead to such regrettable things as love marriages, pregnancy, etc. The feeling that a girl who went with men would fall into complete moral degradation was expressed by one student who said that such a girl would become "a pot touched by a dog." Another said: "Going with one of those girls from an undignified family is like throwing a stone into a pool of dirty stagnant water, and getting spots from it on ones' clothes." It is this intense feeling about the chastity of women which makes the movement to freer social contacts so repulsive to many of the students.

Another factor that tends to curb the potential rebelliousness of both boys and girls in this respect is that, as they have never learned the social graces attendant on mixed social intercourse, they do not know the appropriate behaviour. Many of the male students said they were too shy to go with girls, and stated that they "dared not face them," or even go near them. *Br. 93*: "I have tried for a long time to get a girl friend, but can't. I muster up courage, but it disappears when I find myself face to face with them. I don't know what to say." The Vokkaliga students in particular, coming from villages, faced with the new sophistication of urban life, and seeing educated girls for the first time, find it difficult to know how to behave. Their cruder rural manners do not increase their chances with the fair sex, who think them insulting.

Lack of pocket money is an inhibiting factor. Also, the family may have such a low income that the home is not considered a good enough place in which to entertain girls, for it is usually the more sophisticated girls from the wealthier families who are willing to date. One student felt that he could not go out with girls because his clothes were not good enough. He also felt that as his home was small and lacked furniture, he did not want to ask girls to it.

Another reason that still keeps boys from trying to go with girls is that they might incur a great deal of responsibility if they should date them for if a boy is seen often with a girl, it is assumed that he is going to marry her. On the other hand, being seen with him will ruin *her* reputation, and so he will feel forced to marry her, as no one else will.

Forty-six men students (ten Brahmans, ten Christians, nine Lingayats, and seventeen Vokkaligas) said that they definitely did not want to take girls out. It is impossible to say how much they were drawn to the idea, despite their strong denials.

> *Informant*: The boys will say that they don't want to go with girls, but they will often stand for a long time, just watching them leave their houses, or coming back from college. They are too shy to talk to them, but they get *furious* if they see them talking with another student! They get jealous if they see them getting attention from anyone else. I think a lot of them would go with them if they could.

Not one Christian student, however, thought that mixing was immoral, and the attitude of these students to girls seemed more relaxed. They were not too emotionally eager to take them out, nor were they morally disturbed over the issue. Their problems in this regard were more due to shyness, lack of confidence in themselves, or lack of money: "Girls are too expensive." Some thought the only way to cure the unnatural relationships now existing, and to stop the teasing and harrying of girls, was to encourage boys and girls to mix more, as this would remove the strangeness and mystery which now provoked the boys' behaviour.

Whereas every Christian student questioned thought that boys and girls should mix more, only thirteen Brahmans, nine Lingayats, and thirteen Vokkaligas agreed with this. However, even those boys who said they took girls out were so aware of the hazards and possible consequences that they were not willing for their own sisters to go with boys.

Most of the Christian students also said they were against teasing or ragging girls. This may be due to the fact that the Christian community is a small world, and any boy who makes himself unpleasant will soon be known to all; or because the boys have more chances of meeting Christian girls, and so do not face the problem of finding ways to see them. However, it may also be due to the fact that there are fewer restrictions in their relations. Some of them spoke of knowing or even dating a number of girls, but never of hooting or jeering at them, or making fun of them. They spoke of teasing as "indecent." In contrast to this, one described the behaviour of some Hindu students who were unable to meet or go with girls. *Ch. 146*: "The boys in my hostel are crazy about girls; they rag and tease them because they have no opportunities to meet them. Boys who know girls usually behave well. We know many girls; we visit their houses and we don't make fun of them, and don't hoot or jeer at them."

It seemed that the Vokkaliga students teased the women students more than did members of the other communities.

Girls constituted one of the main subjects of conversation among the men students. This would be an expected pattern in Western countries, but it can be assumed that girls did not feature in male conversation in India until they became a matter of concern. In other words, young men and women are now aware of each other in a way that was not usual even a decade ago.

In view of the strong opposition from parents, relatives, and neighbours, which students expect if they go out with girls, it was not surprising to find that only twenty-eight students (eight Brahmans, twelve Christians, four Lingayats, and four Vokkaligas) said that they took girls out. Seventeen more (nine Brahmans, three Christians, three Lingayats, and two Vokkaligas) said they would like to date; and thirteen (four Brahmans, one Christian, three Lingayats, and five Vokkaligas) were hopeful of doing so in the future. Thus a little under half of the one hundred and fifty-nine men students in the sample (fifty-eight) took girls out, or were anxious to date. Eleven more said that they talked to girls.

If we subtract the Christian students from this total of fifty-eight (for their mores are more lenient in this regard), then we could say that only forty-two of the remaining one hundred and twenty-eight students, or roughly one-third, had rebelled or wanted to rebel, against the traditional mores.

Although the male student would undoubtedly suffer from the anger or outrage of his parents if he paid attention to the opposite sex—one student said that he would be put out of the house if he were caught—it is on the girl that the heaviest penalty falls. Even smiling at boys, or greeting them may mark a girl as a "bad" woman, and if she is seen at the movies or at a restaurant with a boy, her reputation may be so ruined that her parents will find it impossible to find her a husband. Even her sister may be penalized by her conduct, as it indicates that there is "bad blood" in the family, and so it may be difficult for both of them to find husbands.

The consequences of challenging the traditional norms, then, are so drastic that it is little wonder that most girls are still reluctant to respond to the boys' advances. Nor have they lost their traditional fear of men, and this fear makes it even more difficult for boys to date. *Vo. 239*: "I do not go with boys and I do not like the idea of going with them. I do not even speak to them; my mother would never forgive me if I did. I never even think of them. I am scared of boys; I am sure that I would not be able to go with them freely."

Those who have been more exposed to modern forces, however, like the boys, are beginning to want to mix socially with them. The main reasons given by the women students against mixing were similar to those of the men. They did not think it suited the Indian way of life and believed the old traditions were better. An additional reason was that the boys themselves would have a low opinion of them if they did go out with them, and would think of them as poor marriage risks, for if a girl behaved like that *before* marriage, she could hardly be trusted after marriage. For this reason the girls who are known to go out with boys, or try to attract them, are called "flirts," and have a bad reputation with the more orthodox students. *Vo. 66*: "I don't like the modern college girls who always go after boys and attract them by their dress. They are shameless and arrogant Amazons who entice and spoil boys. They are responsible for their downfall."

It can be seen that underlying all these opinions is the idea that mixing is immoral. That boys and girls would misbehave if they mixed too freely, even in clubs or associations, or if they got to know each other too well are prevalent ideas. It is thought that too much sudden freedom could create havoc. Some of the girls said that such freedom would probably be enjoyable at first, but that it always led to trouble. One girl stated: "When they are let loose they really go crazy." Implicit, too, in their dislike of mixing was the fear that it would end in a "tragic" intercaste or love marriage. However, this seemed to be an attractive notion to some girls, and they thought that college might be the means of getting them "an adventurous intercaste marriage." Like many of the men students, they had simply no conception that the relationship between boys and girls could be one of companionship, but thought of it in purely sexual terms. A few students had changed from the traditional point of view enough to feel that it was not a crime to go out with boys, although they personally did not want to. *Br. 197*: "I have never felt the urge to have any male company. Even when I meet my father's friends I feel embarrassed, and it is difficult to speak to them. I even dislike the idea of mixed colleges."

The sixty-five women students who thought that it was acceptable for boys and girls to mix more freely (thirty-five Brahmans, seventeen Christians, four Lingayats, and nine Vokkaligas) varied in their ideas of the degree to which this companionship should occur. Some thought that it was acceptable as long as the girl did not go out alone with a boy, but felt that the two should not mix to the extent to which they did in Western countries: "Let the East be the East and the West the West." Still others said that mixing would bring about a natural relationship, and so help to eliminate the usual self-consciousness and shyness. Several found boys more interesting than girls, for they did not want to talk about fashions and saris all the time, or waste their time gossiping.

A few students did not go out with boys, but were allowed to entertain them in their homes, carefully chaperoned by mothers or aunts, or the whole family. More often, however, it was the brothers' friends whom the girls met at home. Occasionally a girl would be allowed to go with her brother and his friends to the movies, or to a café, or friends of the family would bring their sons to the house and she would meet them, again supervised by the family. On the whole, however, the girls of this sample seemed to have met very few young men, even in these supervised ways.[6] This is evident from the experience of a Brahman student. *Br. 164*: "I would like to have more opportunities to meet boys. I know very few besides my cousins. I am not allowed to talk even with the brothers of my girl friends. Our relatives, and the other members of the community are very orthodox."

Some more liberally-minded parents do not mind their daughters stopping in the street for a few minutes to talk to boys they know well, or they might even allow the boys to escort the daughters to a public exhibition; but they would be shocked if the girls went to cafés or movies with boys. Most of the girls said that even though they knew their brothers' friends well, they were so shy that when they met them on the street they would merely "wish" them, and move on without stopping to talk.

The majority of the men and women students who favoured more mixing felt that the occasions on which it was appropriate for them to meet were college functions, such as model assemblies and debates, or when doing social work. A few thought that it would be all right for them to join mixed clubs or play games together, or act in dramas. Fewer still thought that they should go to parties together, and only two or three said they should meet at dances. Public lectures or religious excursions were accepted by a few. Women students in particular seemed to feel that they would be safer and more at ease in mixed groups than alone with a boy.

There are still many problems, however, for those who try to organize mixed meetings. On one occasion, at a meeting of a Christian organization for young men and women, a new rector who did not know that the boys and the girls had mixed well together in the past, separated them in the hall. This caused so much trouble (the boys even threw

6. Even among adults it is almost impossible for men and women who are not related to mix socially. A middle-aged lecturer said that he could not possibly take a female member of the staff out for dinner or coffee, unless he did so secretly, as it would cause a great scandal. Parents are sometimes so disturbed at the thought of their daughters going out with boys that they go to the principal of the college to ask him to see that it does not happen.

It is difficult to get any information on prostitution in India except in some of the largest cities such as Bombay. Around 1955 there was a good deal of open soliciting in the more fashionable areas of Bangalore. Both men and women are now prosecuted if caught, and thus open soliciting has been cut down, but may exist in the more remote "red light" districts. There is, as yet, no sign of the "call girl" phenomenon.

banana peels and other things at the girls) that the programme could not be carried out.[7] In another instance it was the student who tried to organize a mixed association who got into trouble.

> *Informant*: I got some American students to help me start a mixed association at college. We had a big opening meeting, with fifty-six students, six of whom were girls. They all came from the wealthier classes, and were beautiful and quite modern. Our opening meeting was a great success. We had a big buffet tea and everyone mixed well, but the students who did not belong kept peeping in the windows; they were furious about it. They grew to hate me.
>
> We had other meetings, but the university began to get anonymous letters protesting about our association. They said, "What do you mean by allowing girls to go out in public like this? Our girls should stay in their homes. A girl should not be made vice-president and make a public speech; it is not right. Young men and women should not go on picnics or out together."
>
> Finally we had to stop, because we were afraid that the reputation of the girls would be ruined. My parents continued to get anonymous letters about me for some time after that, telling of all the terrible things I was supposed to have done.

The extent to which changing sex experiences are affecting student indiscipline is symbolized by the existence of the "Roadside Romeos," or "Eve-chasers"—students who spend a lot of time teasing girls in various ways. It signifies one of the ways in which the tensions of a changing society are released, and it could not have arisen unless a significant number of young men had been aroused sexually, without adequate new ways of satisfying their new desires.

Up to the time of this study these were the only names that had arisen spontaneously to describe a new type of deviant group behaviour in India. There was no equivalent to the "beatniks," or even to the "angry young men." This suggests that the increasing strain in the relationships between the sexes was felt more than the stresses promoted by other aspects of change. This does not mean, however, that many young men are not disillusioned, discouraged, and frustrated with the slow rate at which conditions are improving in India.

Though student indiscipline has occasionally assumed serious proportions, the more extreme forms of youthful rebellion, violence, or of juvenile

7. Sarkar, p. 12. This has been noted by Sarkar: "In Mysore and Hyderabad I was told that, at public performances and programmes, if girls happened to take part it was almost impossible to restrain the boys from rowdyism."

delinquency, have not manifested themselves in the disturbing scale and volume which plague Western societies. Nevertheless, there undeniably exists a widespread feeling of frustration, cynicism, and insecurity.[8]

At the time of this study, young Indian men still had enough visible evils to fight within their country—major problems such as poverty, casteism, and corruption—to have the hope of building an ideal India without having to face the sense of emptiness which afflicts so many young people in the affluent societies.

There also seems to have been very little increase in the adolescent crime rate in India over the past few years. A development that might turn into the equivalent of the English "teddy boys" is appearing in some parts of India, where students and adolescent boys have begun to wear drain-pipe, skin-tight pants with a three-button, tight coat. Some of the braver, or angrier, also wear their hair standing straight up on their heads. In Lucknow some young men wear bush coats, with sexy designs or the faces of cinema stars painted on them. However, not many young men can afford the luxury of wearing distinctive clothes.

The slowness of the rise in distinct deviant types of behaviour is put down by several writers to the fact that India is still close to her past, and also to the fact that Hindu ideals, as well as the Hindu way of life, are still highly influential, even with the intellectuals.

> Most intellectuals in underdeveloped countries are not "cut off" from their own culture. . . . They live in the midst of it, their wives and mothers are its constant representatives in their midst, they retain close contact with their families, which are normally steeped in traditional beliefs and practices. The possession of a modern culture does remove them, to some extent, from the culture of their ancestors, but much of the latter remains and lives on in them.[9]

There is some indication, however, that "angry young men" are appearing in India. One writer speaks of "the emergence of a genera- tion of bitter men who present the logical positivist view of science, literature, arts, politics." He says: "Their vigour and anger are over- whelming. . . . They do not have 'beatnik' costumes, they have the material comforts like others, and may be in the same age group. They have their own world, with places to go and things to do. They are

8. Editorial in the *Deccan Herald*, Bangalore, September 20, 1961.
9. Edward Shils, "The Intellectual in the Political Development of the New States," p. 349.

sore about everything—the commercialization of literature and art, current politics, etc."[10]

An Australian journalist thought that he, too, detected an emerging group of "angry young men": "Indian intellectuals have a very low opinion of their country. A Westerner who talked only to Indian intellectuals might well feel that there was no hope for the country at all, for a more hopeless, ruthless, disillusioned group it would be hard to find. Some have taken off into sterile abstractions, some have taken to the bottle, or spend much time telling you how modern India is. . . . Most intellectuals are quite out of sympathy with the fuzzy prohibitionistic puritanism of the Babu politicians who are so prevalent in congress."[11]

Maude seems to have been in touch with some rather embittered regional journalists who have low incomes and little scope for exercising their initiative, as they write for a relatively small world. This attitude is probably not true of the leading journalists, nor of the population as a whole, as a comparatively small proportion of the population is westernized.

Most of the girl-baiting in Bangalore is done on a group basis, although it is probably not highly organized. Several young men may come across a lone girl, or several girls together, and begin to tease them. This may lead to physical harm.[12] Sometimes three or four students may set out with the intention of indulging in their favourite pastime. They will surround the girls, calling them names and ridiculing them. The girls' ultimate defence is to threaten the boys with their sandals, but this is often a signal to the boys for renewed attacks. A girl riding a bicycle may be surrounded by boys on bicycles; this has been known to have caused accidents. Most of the more energetic baiting takes place in the vicinity of the colleges. The boys may sit on the college compound walls, shouting out rude remarks to the girls, or, if it is a co-educational college, they may form two lines through which

10. "Bitter Generation," *Illustrated Weekly of India*, August 6, 1961.

11. Angus Maude writing in *The Hindu*, November 7, 1961.

12. D. P. Mukerji, *The Problems of Indian Youth*, p. 7. "More criminal than these murders is the display of hooliganism against girl students. It makes one's blood boil to see bruises, as I have seen, on young girls' heads and arms made by hockey sticks."

Mrs. Vijayalakshmi Pandit (quoted in *The Hindu*, July 25, 1963): "When I read in newspapers that girls are molested or teased in the streets of a city like Poona even during daytime, I hang down my head in shame. . . . [This shows] how backward we are, and with what indifference we tolerate such disgraceful misconduct on the part of irresponsible youths."

girl students must run the gauntlet on their way to classes. Some of the rather crude remarks are made by the men students who come from villages where they are accustomed to talking in this way to the village girls. The city girls are insulted by it. Policemen have been posted outside the gates of the largest women's college in Bangalore, and the "Roadside Romeos" are often warned, or picked up on charges and fined. Some girls like the teasing, and an increase in provocative dress, with saris being worn more tightly, may show a desire for attention. However, most of the women students dislike and fear being teased. Girls often arrive at college crying, when they have been the subject of attention. The antics of these young men have become so well known that they are often referred to in the press. An article in the *Deccan Herald* of March 25, 1962, also spoke of the increase in such surreptitious acts as nudging the women in the cinemas, or in restaurants and exhibitions. Boys are often warned or picked up on this charge and occasionally they are fined. In another letter to the Editor of a local newspaper the acts of the young boys were also thought of as being due partly to the fact that the women did not know how to protect themselves from them.

> The nefarious activities of the "Roadside Romeos" are indirectly encouraged by the "extra feminism" of our girls, which is socially mistaken for maidenly coyness and womanly grace. It is high time that our girls forsook their shyness and lack of self-confidence, and like their Western sisters, boldly retaliated, which should not be so difficult during daytime on city roads. It is not the fear of punishment but the liability to be detected that deters the criminal. . . .

Another indication of the way in which young men do not know how to behave themselves when they are near women appeared in the case of an affair held at a women's college, to which many of the men students went and where they made a tremendous row. They even gathered around the girls' dressing room, until finally it had to be changed. The students' behaviour, and the problem of the perverts who gather around the women's colleges, make it impossible for these institutions to hold college functions in the evening, as the girls may be bothered.

Occasionally one girl is singled out for attention. This happened to the first girl to enter a commerce course in one of the Bangalore colleges.

> *Informant*: She is the only girl in a class of forty to fifty boys, and they tease her ummercifully. Her father has tried to intervene, and now they

throw paper balls and other things at him when he rides past on his bike. Once the girl got so furious with them that she threw her sandal at them. This only made matters worse. Her father is desperate and doesn't know what to do. He wants to go to the police about it, but that would only encourage the boys. The girl is in a very bad state; she can't sleep at night and is terrified to go to her class.

Another typical tale came from one of the wardens of a girl's college who had had a very distressing time one evening when she was shepherding the girls back from one of the parks. They were surrounded by a crowd of students who kept shouting and pushing them until they at last attained the shelter of the college compound.

These illustrations show that the behaviour of the "Roadside Romeos" is completely contrary to the traditional Hindu treatement of, and attitude toward, women. The higher castes, in particular, honour the modesty, chastity, and meekness of women above all other things and would protect them in public to the end.

In the traditional Hindu society, sex urges were satisfied by early marriages, and as friendship or companionship were not necessary between boys and girls, or men and women, they were not part of a boy's needs or experience. When the sex urges are so channelled, frustration due to separation does not arise. It is only when alternate possibilities are introduced, which cannot be satisfied in a socially acceptable manner, and no new patterns have arisen to help adjustment to the new needs that sex may become an individual or group problem. In stressing this point, Shils says:

> When the age of marriage was earlier, the young Indian male was able to have sexual intercourse under conditions provided by convention and custom. The Indian student nowadays has no opportunity for legitimate sexual intercourse; his own residential conditions and the security control exercised over young women in college block his way, even *if* he wishes to have it illegitimately. Furthermore, he has nearly as little opportunity for the erotic gratifications of holding hands, caresses, kissing, or the mere presence of young women. Young Indian women are still carefully guarded by their parents and wardens; and, although the sons are permitted sufficient freedom to be able to prowl about, and, in the titillating atmosphere of the big city, even to whistle at girls, the young women are kept under lock and key. They are too shy; and, even if they were not, the young men are too uncertain of themselves. . . . The sexual dispositions are certainly alive, but they must work in a "sexual vacuum." There are no objects to which they can attach themselves. There is a little homosexuality, but probably not very much. There are no "girl friends," and,

221

unlike the case of their coevals of 50 years ago, there is no wife to whom to feel the pressure of obligation, if not, at first, of affection. There is so little to bind the youth into a pleasing or compelling routine.[13]

An analysis of the backgrounds of the "Roadside Romeos" would probably show that the main source of the frustration of these young men lies in their inability to find some outlet or satisfaction for their newly aroused sexual impulses, and it is quite possible that although their behaviour represents the extreme expression of frustrated, newly awakened emotions, many other young men, and some young women are beginning to feel the tensions engendered by deep emotions with which they cannot deal in a satisfactory way. College is one of the few places where they can be near the opposite sex and (as little mixing is allowed) be tantalized by each other's presence.

MARRIAGE

Marriage is one of the most crucial problems for a society, as well as for its individual members, for it determines not only whether the family will continue in its traditional way, but also whether certain other important social systems, such as religion or caste, will continue. Should many people decide to marry people from other religions or castes, the social barriers will gradually weaken. Other changes in marriage patterns, such as the age at which marriage takes place, will inevitably have repercussions throughout the structure of the society.

As marriage is still considered to be a woman's main goal in India, and as it is one of the parents' chief responsibilities to see that their daughters are satisfactory married, the women students were interviewed intensively on this subject. It was thought that the anxiety engendered by the parents' growing problem of finding suitable mates for their children might be passed on to their daughters, and increase their anxieties; and these anxieties might also be released in the college setting. Moreover, as the age of marriage has risen in India, it is usually at the college age that parents begin to search for husbands for their daughters.

Goode believes that family patterns in India have not changed as rapidly in the last decade as have those of China or Japan, although they have changed more rapidly than have those of the Western countries. He attributes this to the slow rate of industrialization and urbanization which, in turn, have been retarded by the rigidity of the caste

13. Edward Shils, "Indian Students," pp. 10, 11.

system, the persistence of the joint family, the character of the Hindu religion, and India's long period of political and economic dependence.[14] However, there have been changes in many aspects of the family in India, and these have led to strains and conflicts among the different family members.

Marriage is one of the areas in which change is particularly noticeable. In the first place, it has become more difficult for the urban upper- and middle-caste parents to find suitable partners for their sons and daughters. This situation is the result of a number of reasons. Moving to the city prevents many families from having close contacts with suitable husbands in the same sub-caste, on the other hand there may be a disproportionate number of women in the sub-caste, or another problem might be that horoscopes do not tally.

If it is difficult to marry off one daughter successfully, it is still more difficult to get suitable husbands for a number of daughters. Several of the girls of this sample were not worrying about their own marriages, but about those of their older sisters, for their parents were having great difficulty in arranging their marriages and had not had time to think of their younger daughters. *Br. 174*: "My third sister has a very difficult horoscope to match. My parents have been trying to get her married for the last four years, and are now seriously worried about it. Two proposals came for my fourth sister but my parents do not want to get her married before the third sister, and so she may not get a husband." In this case the problem was related to the rigid Hindu custom that daughters must be married in order of birth. Thus, a younger sister is very seldom married until her older sisters have husbands. It is therefore a tragedy for a girl to have an older sister who is not appealing or in some way cannot attract a husband. One of the students had been sent to college because her two older sisters were still at home, unmarried. This meant that she was technically not "at home," and so the stigma of having more than two marriageable daughters in the house at the same time was removed. She believed that her only chance

---

14. William J. Goode, *World Revolution and Family Patterns,* pp. 204-6.

George A. Theodorson, "Romanticism and Motivation to Marry in the United States, Singapore, Burma, and India." According to Theodorson, the data collected for this study show that the Singapore Chinese students were closest to the romantic attitudes to marriage of the American students. The Burmese students came next. The Indian attitudes were the most contractualistic. "The data also support Parsons and Waller and Hill's hypothesis that romanticism functions to maintain high motivation to marry, with the decline of traditional sources of motivation. The data suggest that contractualism when combined with the rejection of traditional norms may be less functional than romanticism in maintaining high motivation to marry."

of marrying was to get a job where she would find a man who would fall in love with her, as her parents were having such a difficult time providing husbands for her sisters.

Girls who have had a college education are usually able to make better marriages than those who have gone only as far as high school. This is one of the main reasons that middle-class parents send their daughters to college, but it is always a gamble. Several girls said that the main worry of their parents was that they might not be able to get husbands with an equal amount of education. This is sometimes a particularly difficult problem for a daughter who must marry within her own sub-caste or religion if there are not many highly educated prospective husbands. This problem is so universal that in several families brothers were against their sisters taking graduate degrees, as it would be so difficult to find them husbands with comparable education. The only other factor that can compete with the desire for equal educational qualifications is great wealth. On the other hand, girls from the lower castes have more chances of good marriages if they do *not* have college educations, for there is a larger proportion of uneducated men in these castes. This problem of marriage and education is not as great in villages, for the young men are not interested in educated wives. In fact many novels in the regional languages tend to depict girls who go to college as "immoral," for mixing with men means to the villager that the students are having "affairs."

The Christian parents of this sample seemed especially anxious to have their daughters marry educated men. This desire was so strong that it sometimes overcame their antipathy to their daughter marrying outside their religion. Informants said that, as there are not enough educated Protestant boys in some areas of India, Protestant girls are marrying educated Hindus or Muslims. Roman Catholic parents will sometimes allow their daughter to marry someone from another religion if he will turn Catholic.

In the second place, as the cost of educating a daughter is related to the cost of marrying one, marriages are becoming an increasingly heavy financial burden. Dowries are still a very important part of the marriage transaction in most castes, in spite of the fact that the dowry system has been meeting growing resistance and was officially abolished in May 1960.

In November, 1955, the Indian Institute of Public Opinion asked a sample of over eleven hundred respondents whether they approved of the dowry system, and whether they thought it should be abolished. Sixty-five per cent said that they did not approve of the dowry system, and the same proportion said that it should be abolished. As might be expected, *females* show less approval of the dowry system than males (seventy-six per cent do *not* approve of it as against sixty per cent of the males); after all it is the dowry that often becomes a barrier to their marriage.[15]

The cost of the dowry is one of the most persistent worries of parents, particularly if they are not well off, or if they have a number of daughters to marry. *Li. 171*: "My parents have not started any marriage negotiations, because I am young and can work for a few years. They are worried that suitable boys will want dowries, which will be a burden on them."

From the point of view of the bridegroom, a dowry is the only means by which his father can get back the money he has spent to educate his sons, and to pay the dowries of his own daughters. He may have borrowed money to do this and so gone into debt. Even Christian parents often have to provide large dowries. *Ch. 248*: "My parents, especially my mother, are terribly worried about getting me a good bridegroom. In our community we have to give a big dowry to get a good and educated bridegroom. Normally the price depends on the profession of a bridegroom, his family and his wealth."

The abolition of the dowry system by law can hardly be enforced if conditions remain that make it useful. Even newspaper advertisements for marriage still mention it occasionally.

All these problems tend to produce the result that there is always a shadow over the house, when the daughters come to the marriageable age, until their marriages are arranged.

Another important change which affects many of the relationships within the family is that educated women now tend to marry at twenty years of age or later.[16] This is a tremendous change from child marriage. One of the main factors causing this trend is the growing desire of parents to have their daughters educated in order to obtain more suitable husbands, or else to assist them to get jobs.[17] This difference in

15. Goode, p. 218. For an account of attitudes to dowries in the sample of people from Bangalore, see: Ross, *The Hindu Family in Its Urban Setting*, pp. 260-64.

16. Ross, pp. 232-36. The Indian Census figures tend to hide some of the meaningful trends in changing marriage patterns, as they are heavily weighted by the rural characteristics of four-fifths of the Indian population.

17. *Census of India*, 1950, Vol. XIV, Part 1, pp. 107, 108.

Goode, p. 236, "The increasing political and occupational participation of women in Indian life, and the demand for educated wives, will continue to raise the age of marriage in the cities. Rural areas will probably change slowly, following the lead of the cities."

the age of marriage of the educated girl can be seen to be a disruptive factor in the traditional family scene, for the bride will enter her husband's home at an age when her character is more formed, and when she has a stronger attachment to her own family. This, in turn, will make it more difficult for her to give her complete allegiance to her new kin. The fact that her education may be much higher than that of her mother-in-law adds to the difficulties of her acceptance of the submissive role that the mother-in-law expects.[18]

Another change resulting from the trend toward later marriages is that the daughter now has more distinct opinions about it. It follows from this that the modern girl often wants more influence in the choice of her husband. "More influence," however, still meant to this sample of students only the final say in regard to the man whom their parents had selected. Very few girls want to arrange their marriages completely on their own, but this in itself is a great change. A number of the girls of this sample said that they had not consented to marry the first man that their parents had selected, and so they were given a second or a third choice.

Girls in Northern India seem to have greater freedom of choice than those in the South; the more urbanized Hindu, Christian, and Anglo-Indian daughters are freer than are girls who belong to castes living in villages, although the extent to which their choice is really "free" should not be exaggerated. Freedom of choice in marriage only works in a society if the people who marry are old enough to be able to make suitable choices, and the society supplies mechanisms through which the young men and women are able to meet and come to know each other

18. Aileen D. Ross, *The Hindu Family in Its Urban Setting*, p. 246. "Child marriage meant that the bride learned to fit into the ways of the new household and carry on its traditions to a much greater extent than girls who marry at a later age, for the child bride changed her environment before she had become too strongly attached to her parents and family, and before she was too deeply immersed in family customs to be able to change to those of the new home. As she was in a subordinate position to her husband and in-laws, she had to fit into the new pattern, with no chance of asserting her own individuality."

A.P.B., p. 59. "The age of marriage is increasing because a boy who is not following his particular caste occupation is not sure what kind of job he will be able to get when he finishes his education. For this reason he will probably want to wait until he has found a job offering some economic security before he marries. On the other hand, the father of the girl will not want his daughter to marry a boy whose economic prospects . . . are uncertain, and so he will tend not to get his daughter married so soon. In earlier times, when the son went into the family occupation, these uncertainties did not arise. With the age of marriage rising for these reasons there comes the problem of older brides finding it more difficult to adjust to new and strange ways of doing things within the close confines of a joint family."

in a way that will enable them to select suitable partners. This has not yet happened in India.

> Although the parents need not fear the caste group so much as formerly, and the young men and women can at least sometimes establish an economic base independently, in fact their social relations are so structured that they have little opportunity to mix in an equalitarian way with a wide range of people of similar tastes and education. . . . Since these questions tap only a very general sentiment in favor of freedom, and do not pose even hypothetical reality conditions, we must suppose that the active sentiment in favor of freedom of choice is still fairly low, and the reality of its expression most minimal.[19]

Another change that is appearing is the desire for the girl to get to know the boy better after the engagement ceremony and before the marriage. Some of the girls of this sample said that this would not be allowed in their communities. However, one of the Vokkaliga students was allowed to write letters to her fiancé and to go out with him in the evenings, apparently unaccompanied. In another case a girl was allowed to go out with her fiancé as long as she was accompanied by the parents.

Still another trend may be seen in certain novels which tell of the girls' concern about the way they are inspected by their prospective in-laws before they are married. The following excerpt from a short story suggests that some girls are beginning to rebel against this custom.

> I am sick of all this but I have to go through this again and again to please mother. . . . These grooms-to-be come to our place as though I were something being sold in the market to approve and buy. This will be the last interview. I will never again be a party to this showpiece business. I wonder what demands this fellow has in store. Twenty thousand rupees? A foreign trip? Admission to an English college?[20]

Girls always know when marriage negotiations are being carried on by their parents, for the houses are often so crowded that the parents' conversation can be overheard. Thus the boy's family and relatives will be discussed openly. The parents will try to see that the daughter does not marry an eldest son, because he has the responsibility of the family

---

19. Goode, p. 217. A change from the system of arranged marriages to freedom of choice can not come about until many of the related family and social patterns have changed. The tragedy of girls who are ahead of their time in wanting full freedom of choice has already been shown in another study.

20. *Deccan Herald*, September 1961, Srikantha: *No Tremors!* This is a short story about a girl who is being inspected by her future bridegroom.

on his hands. Nor would they choose a boy who has several sisters to marry, or brothers to educate, for these will add to his financial responsibilities. The families of twenty-eight of the women students had already started negotiations for their marriages. Four other girls were already engaged.

To what extent did the students themselves worry about their marriages? Did their slowly dawning awareness of the growing problems of obtaining a husband, and/or their own gradually awakening desires augment their restlessness, as in the case of the "Roadside Romeos"? As far as marriage was concerned, the usual diversity of views was shown by the sample. Some girls said that they had not yet thought about their marriages, and their seeming disinterest was supported by the topics of their conversation with their girl friends, which seldom included discussions of boys. Some definitely had confidence that their parents would find suitable husbands for them. In this respect, Indian girls are at an advantage, as compared with their Western counterparts; for the chief problem of the latter at the college age is to find a husband, supposedly on their own, at the same time that they are acquiring a college degree. Others had seen the problems their parents had encountered in trying to get husbands for sisters and were definitely aware of the difficulties ahead.

A number of the students worried that their dark complexions or their personal appearance would prevent their getting husbands. Others tried to console themselves by saying that they knew that their skin was very dark, but beauty was of little importance in a wife.[21] The personal appearance of their husbands was important to a very few, although two girls mentioned that they would like their husbands to be tall. Several wanted their husbands to be well educated, but only seven mentioned good jobs and wealth. A number also wanted their future husbands to be sociable, and to have a good character. Three were afraid that they might get narrow-minded husbands. These girls were

21. Colour of skin is an important attribute in marriage among middle-class Indians. The desire for a bride or a groom with a "fair complexion" is often mentioned in marriage advertisements. Even babies are judged in terms of the colour of their skins, and there will be an unfavourable reaction to a dark baby. Children pick this up, and may, at an early age, refer to some one as "ugly" if their skin is dark. In one case a brother felt a very strong responsibility for getting his sister married, as up to that date the family had been unable to get her a bridegroom because of her dark complexion. Several others spoke of the difficulties of marrying girls with dark complexions. One mother was worried about marrying her daughter because she felt that her face looked "old" for her age. This made the girl very worried about her looks; she was afraid that her husband would not like her appearance, or would find her uninteresting. Other informants thought that this attitude to colour was changing.

228

better educated and more modern than most of the men of their communities and would have problems finding equally modern husbands.

In summing up, it is difficult to know whether the fears of girls in regard to their marriages are increasing or not. However, a good number of girls from this sample had seen, at close hand, the problems of getting good husbands; and as these problems are increasing, it is to be presumed that the number of girls who are afraid either that they will not be able to marry, or that they will not get a suitable man, is increasing.

There is no word for "spinster" in the Kannada language, but women still feel it to be a great indignity not to be married. One said, "People laugh at unmarried girls. They are shown little respect as they grow older." More than this, in some communities it is taken for granted that women are leading "wicked" lives if they do not marry. Several of the women lecturers said they found it very difficult to be reconciled to their single status.

In spite of the disapproving attitude of Indians toward the single woman, eleven students said that they did not want to marry. Two of them were very religious and wanted to dedicate their lives to being spiritual leaders. Two others seemed to have some antipathy to marriage and declared that they would only marry as a duty, if their parents insisted. Still another of the eleven cherished her independence too much to marry. *Br. 217*: "I prefer to remain single. I do not want to get married. As an unmarried woman I would not like to live with my brothers, but would like to stay with my parents as long as I can afford to. Once I come to know I can no longer be with them, I want to set up a separate establishment for myself. I want to take a job and be financially independent permanently, but my parents don't like the idea."

A few of the other girls seemed to feel such a deep responsibility toward their families that they wanted to spend their lives supporting or looking after family members. One of them wanted to devote herself to educating her brothers. Another was an only child and felt it to be her duty to live on with her parents and support them. One case showed the change in expectations of some parents who now want their daughters to help finance the family. *Vo. 180*: "As I am the eldest in my family, my parents expect me to work and help them financially. I may have to work until my brother finishes his engineering course. I do not wish to get married at all. I would like to get some nice job and go on working."

A few of the girls also expressed an antipathy to marriage. They said that they wanted to work if they were not "forced" to marry. Several others wanted to wait some years before they married. Three others were more worried about getting seats for their Master's degree than about their marriages. After obtaining degrees they wanted to work for some time, and so marriage was too far away to be a problem.

The responsibility of brothers for the marriage of their sisters seems, on the whole, to be as strong as ever, particularly if these young men are the eldest or only sons. In one case the brother quarrelled with his parents, and went to the extreme of leaving home, which he thought might persuade them not to marry his sister to the man they had chosen. However, the parents were afraid not to accept the offer because there was a scarcity of bridegrooms in the village. So the girl was married to the boy and has led a very unhappy life ever since.

Many brothers feel their responsibility so deeply that they consider they must marry their sisters off before they themselves get married. *Br. 11*: "Many relatives visit our house to negotiate for the marriage of my brothers, but my family wants to marry off my sisters first. One sister is ready for marriage; she is a teacher and helps the family financially. The other sister is studying and also getting ready for marriage, and so we are searching for two bridegrooms. I must help get them married after I have finished my education, for I see how hard my brothers are struggling to get bridegrooms for them, and I must help them."

CONCLUSION

The traditional joint family provided its members with a large enough group of people to make it a satisfactory recreational unit. The move to the city cuts many families off from relatives, and the diversification of family interests that arises in urban centres impels the different family members to seek friendships outside the family circle. The gradual rise of many interest groups, and of organized entertainment also draws young people outside the family for their recreation. This tends to strengthen their relations with their peers, and to draw them away from their families. However, the problem of the Indian student in finding a satisfactory way to pass leisure time is augmented by the fact that Indian cities, by and large, have not yet adjusted to the new needs of youth, and so there are not many planned recreational activities, opportunities for sport, or organized youth groups. Another problem is that most families cannot afford to give the student enough pocket money to allow him to use the facilities that exist. A third problem is that the new ways of spending leisure time are often frowned on by parents or relatives. This is particularly true for young Indian women, as it is not yet customary to permit them the freedom to take advantage of commercial or organized recreation.

Movement to the city, and away from relatives, and the new separation of family members will make young people increasingly dependent on their peers, who will be able to give the guidance and information for the transitional period that the family may not be able to provide. In fact, friends may become so important in helping a student find a new identity that students may come to depend on them more than on their families. At college the students' friends may often come from different communities, and thus they may be the main means through which barriers between the different castes, sub-castes, and religions are gradually undermined. However, lack of pocket money may hamper the student in making friendships, for friendship is based essentially on a system of practical and "psychological" reciprocation.

The friendships a student makes at college may be all-important in leading him into indiscipline, or helping him to avoid it. Many of the students of this sample mentioned cutting class to be with their friends, for example, or because their friends enticed them away "to have a good time." The growing importance of the influence of peer groups, as societies became modernized, is well documented in sociological literature.

Friends may also support a student in his defiance of college authority or of his family, and so give him the courage to stand against them when he would not dare to do so on his own. They may also support, or even enforce, his indiscipline in the class-room. Friendships may therefore be regarded as being possibly one of the most important factors in determining a student's behaviour while at college.

The growing uncertainty of the relationship between the sexes in India seems to be another very important factor in determining whether students will release their frustrations in some sort of indiscipline, for college may be one of the few places where young men and women meet, or are near enough to be tantalized by each others' presence. It also presents one of the few situations in which the newly-aroused emotions of the young men can be released in a tangible way against the women with whom they cannot have normal contacts. Thus, they may tease them, or give way to more violent behaviour, such as attacking womens' hostels when they are aroused to collective action. Because they have greater freedom to roam about the city and attend movies and other types of entertainment, men students will be probably more upset by the changes in the sex mores than will the women students. The latter are still strongly protected by their families. Their lack of pocket money, and the fact that they are not permitted to move about freely, or spend much time with friends limit their exposure to the new trends in the relations of the sexes.

Freer mixing and personal choice in marriage are impeded, as few new mechanisms, such as "dating," or mixed formal organizations, have yet been accepted by the public in such a way that men and women students can meet each other in a more natural way and so test each other's personalities.

6

Participants
and
Non-Participants

The preceding chapters have shown that there are many factors in the lives of Indian students today which could lead to tensions and frustrations, and these, in turn, could easily be released in some sort of aggressive behaviour. Some of the students' problems have been described in the foregoing analysis of the effects of college conditions, of family, caste, and religious backgrounds, of ambitions, and of the social life of this sample of students. Some of these tensions and frustrations are found in societies in which the students do not take part in protest movements and rowdy demonstrations. Certainly not all Indian students take part in agitations; on the other hand, many are forced to do so by their colleagues. What peculiar combinations of structurally conducive factors tend to move some Indian students into action?

An attempt will now be made to assess the relative importance of these factors by analyzing how they affected one group of students who took part in the Youth Festival strike in Mysore State, and another group that remained aloof. The numbers of these groups are so small that all they can do is to serve as a guide for future research.

The Youth Festival strike may not be considered the best example to choose, as it was a relatively spontaneous demonstration undertaken for a rather glamorous cause, and it attracted, perhaps, a certain type of student. However, just because there was little pressure on the students to join, and because the action of the police, particularly in killing one student, provided another incentive to rouse students to action, it is perhaps a better example than the 1962 and 1963 strikes in Mysore, which were more carefully organized, had strong leadership, and lasted long enough for a great deal of pressure to be put on those students who did not want to demonstrate. In other words, many students left their classes because they did not dare refuse—not for the structurally conducive reasons that are being examined.

In order to try to find out why some students took part in demonstrations and others did not, the sample of students was classified into "Participants" and "Non-participants" on the basis of three variables: studying hard, cutting classes, and having taken part in the 1959 Youth Festival strike. Twenty-three of the male students (seven Brahmans, five Christians, two Lingayats, and nine Vokkaligas) were found to have studied only at the time of examinations, to have cut classes as often as they could—one had not attended a single class all year—and to have taken part in the Youth Festival strike. These students were labelled "Participants." Thirty-seven others (eighteen Brahmans, three Christians, nine Lingayats, and seven Vokkaligas) fulfilled the requirements of having studied hard, of never having cut classes, and of not having participated in the strike. They were called the "Non-participants."

Ten of the women students (six Brahmans, three Christians, and one Lingayat) were found to fit into the Participant category, and fifteen of them (seven Brahmans, four Christians, one Lingayat, and three Vokkaligas) were found to be Non-participants. It is to be noted that both Participants and Non-participants came from all four communities in the case of men students, and that the only exception to this trend, as far as the women students were concerned, was that no Vokkaligas had participated in the Youth Festival strike. The reasons the men students gave for joining in the Youth Festival strike showed some of the basic differences between the Participants and Non-participants. Only three of the Participants said that they had joined because the decision of the Youth Festival authorities was unjust; nine others joined because they wanted holidays or fun, or because their friends had urged them to. One did so out of curiosity. Two others played peripheral parts: one took part only in the first demonstrations, and the other joined only in the throwing of stones.

Twenty-four of the Non-participants, however, did not join the Youth Festival strike because they were not interested. Three refused to take part because they did not believe that the students were justified; four were away from Bangalore; one said he was afraid. Three students did not join, because their fathers would not have allowed them to do so. "Father would have killed me," one student said.

An analysis of the various characteristics of the two groups shows that, although the sample is very small, there are some distinct differences between them. In the first place, the male Participants came from families with higher incomes than those of the Non-participants. The average family income of the former was Rs.434. The range of their incomes was from Rs.100 to Rs.8,000 per month. If the one family that received 8,000 rupees per month were to be eliminated, the range would be then from Rs.100 to Rs.1,500. On the other hand, the average income of the families of Non-participants was Rs.198 per month. The range of their incomes was from Rs.50 to Rs.550. Only two families received over Rs.500.

The questions which were meant to bring out the sense of family obligation and identity of the students are not completely reliable, as most Hindus accept the fact of family responsibility so automatically that they tend to react at once in terms of their training. Moreover, it is one thing to project one's behaviour into the future, and quite another to accept one's responsibilities when a situation is actually experienced. However, all that could be done was to enquire into the interviewees' opinions of what they *would* do in a certain situation. About an equal proportion of the Participants and Non-participants—nine of the former and five of the latter—did not want to live with their families after marriage. Five of the Non-participants and four of the Participants were undecided. However, the difference in their feelings toward their families was more clearly evident in their answers about feelings of obligation. Only two of the Participants had a strong feeling of responsibility toward their families, as compared with thirty-one of the Non-participants.

In their relationships with their families, the Participants also showed less agreement. Fifteen of the twenty-three said that they had had either a few, or a considerable number of conflicts or arguments with their families; three had had minor conflicts. On the other hand, only twelve of the Non-participants had had conflicts of one type or another with their families.

On the whole, religion was not as important to the Participants as it was to the Non-participants. This is another traditional area of behaviour that is expected to have a place of paramount importance in the lives of all Hindus. Two of the Participants still believed implicitly in their religion, and scrupulously followed the traditional rituals, whereas five did so only partially. Three had no interest at all in religion. On the other hand, twenty-seven of the Non-participants still believed in and practised their religion; three did so in part, and only two did not believe or practise.

The attitude toward college of these two different groups of students also showed some degree of variation. None of the Participants placed their courses or studies at the top of their list of preferences, although one said that he appreciated some of his lecturers. Ten of them liked their friends and the freedom of the college life better than anything else at college. One said that he liked "everything." Seven favoured sports and games. On the other hand, twenty-six of the Non-participants liked their studies and courses more than anything else. Six liked their friends most of all, and ten liked "everything." Only one said that he did not like anything at all at college. The Non-participants appeared on the whole to be much more interested in their courses, and this attitude was supported by the fact that they had not cut classes.

The Participants disliked, more than anything else, the dullness, strictness, and lack of freedom of college life. Two of them disliked the students who were rowdy, or who teased girls, and a few were against the unsympathetic administration. The dislikes of twelve of the Non-participants were centred around the mischievous and defiant behaviour of other students. Four complained of the library, and of other college facilities. Three thought there was too much freedom at the university, and six disliked their lecturers. It is significant that these last six students mentioned lecturers, and not courses.

The fathers' ambitions for their sons seemed to be somewhat similar for the two groups. Eight of the parents of Non-participants and five of the parents of Participants had high ambitions for their sons. Eighteen of the parents of the former and ten of the parents of the latter had medium ambitions. Six of the parents of the Non-participants and seven of the parents of the Participants had low ambitions. However, this situation is reversed when we look at the ambitions of the students themselves. Twenty-five of the Non-participants and only one of the Participants had high ambitions. Twelve of the former and six of the latter had medium ambitions; one of the Non-participants had low ambitions, but sixteen of the Participants fell into this category.

In considering the interest the parents had taken in their sons, as compared with their ambitions for them, we again see that the Non-participants had had more support from their parents. Fourteen of their parents had had a high interest in their sons' work, whereas only five of the Participants' parents had been concerned. Twenty of the parents of the Non-participants had had a medium interest in their sons' work, as compared with eleven of the Participants' parents. Six of the parents of the Non-participants had had very little interest in the studies and careers of their sons, in contrast to seven of the parents of Participants.

Another revealing factor that suggests a difference in the attitudes to college of the two groups was that whereas the Non-participants had never cut classes, all the Participants had. Nine of them cut classes because of boredom, six to go to the movies, six to be with friends, and two to take part in sports.

Again there is some difference when the worries and anxieties of the students are considered. Eleven of the Participants did not seem to worry about anything in particular, and eleven worried only occasionally. Six of these were concerned about jobs or about their futures. Only one worried "often." Thus, about half the students said they had very few or no anxieties, and were carefree about their studies and about life in general. Of the Non-participants, however, twenty-five out of the thirty-seven worried, many of them "often." Only twelve rarely or never worried. Of those who seemed particularly troubled, five were anxious about jobs and the future, and nine had financial problems. Five of these students did not have enough money to feed themselves properly, to see their friends, or to lead a satisfactory social life. Twenty-four of the twenty-five students who often worried had family problems. Some of these problems concerned heavy financial responsibilities, such as having to support parents, or, as eldest sons, feeling the responsibility of having to help finance their brothers' education, and the education and/or dowries of their sisters. Their anxieties might also be related to their efforts to achieve more freedom from family controls.

Since ten of them were eldest sons, they held the major position of responsibility among the siblings. In four of these cases the father was dead, which meant that the oldest son was responsible for the welfare and financial support of the whole family. The fathers of six others were dead also, and this would add to their burden of getting degrees and jobs in order to help support the family. In three other cases the students were only sons, so that family responsibility would fall largely on them. Thus, nineteen out of the thirty-seven would be expected to bear heavier family responsibility than would the average student. These duties would include the support of their mothers, the education of younger brothers and possibly sisters, and the arrangement of marriages for their sisters. A smaller proportion of the Participants shared similar characteristics in that seven of them were eldest sons, two were only sons, and the fathers of two others were dead.

Sixteen of the Non-participants said that their social life was satisfactory, whereas twelve stated that it was not. Seven revealed that they were only partly content with their social life. Most of these students seemed to be in need of more money to enable them to go out with their friends and to take part in sports and other entertainments. Thirteen of the Participants were content with their social life; four were not. The remaining six said that they would be happier if they were allowed to entertain their friends at home and go more freely with girls.

Only two of the Non-participants had any interest in girls, but nineteen of the twenty-three Participants had had major or minor problems concerning girls.

This small sample suggests that students who tend to participate in, or to spark student indiscipline, do so to escape boredom, and to have fun and excitement. They are the students whose futures are more secure. They tend to come from families who have no trouble in financing their education, and who have enough influence to see that they have jobs when they graduate. Most of them have little or no interest in their studies, or in any particular subject. They will probably be among the students who have become more independent and have, to some extent, moved away from their families. The comparative freedom of college life may be so intoxicating for them, after the strict family controls to which they have been accustomed, that they may be led easily into demonstrations or protest activity. They have also had enough freedom and pocket money to begin to explore the possibility of breaking through the rigid barriers of sex segregation. Once this has happened, sexual attraction may intensify their frustrations and add to the need for releasing them in some way; for even though they may be able to date secretly, there are not yet enough opportunities for them to explore this realm thoroughly.

An informant who has lectured for many years, and who has shown discerning insight into the personalities of his different students, expressed other lecturers' opinions about indisciplined students in this way.

Many of the men students who come from wealthy families have as little interest in their studies as do students in similar economic positions elsewhere. They drift into college and go through the process of attending their classes. Their only aim is to secure a degree in one way or another— but with the least effort. They have absolutely no interest in their courses, nor any inclination to become interested in them. These students like attending college, as it gives them the opportunity of making friends, spending their time as they like, and making mischief. They are also attracted by the extracurricular activities, but tend to play a passive role, for their main aim is not to enjoy such college entertainments as dramas or debates, but to use them as a means for creating disorder and confusion.

These students can disregard work at college because they have some sort of security. They know that they will be able to get out of any jam they get into. They are protected by their family and caste backgrounds. A degree is not necessarily an important bread-ticket for them, and so failure is of no consequence—it arouses neither guilt, nor shame, nor regret.

These students lack any sense of purpose, and there is no hope of arousing the desire to strive for an ideal, for the college environment does not stimulate either. There is a void or vacuum in their outlook and attitudes. Many of them are dull, uninteresting, and monotonously unambitious.

One of these students discussed the matter from his own point of view.

Vo. 32: I don't like the mistaken idea that some professors and students have of our group. We are all in the same class; we are sports, well built, and talkative. We all sit together in one place, chatting in a lively way. We do it to pass the time even though we know it is wrong. Even at college functions our group sits together in the back benches. Whenever our group appears, the students and the staff look at us. The way they do it, and their comments about us, just make us bolder.

Many of the lecturers' and other people's remarks make some of the girls think badly of us. This makes us do even more things. Sometimes we tease the girls on their way to college or to college functions. This is not with any bad intention, but merely for excitement. We are really a most harmless group, although in the eyes of others, we seem very dangerous.

I am disappointed in college because, even though there are a number of activities that interest us, whatever we do is misunderstood.

The fact that a smaller number of women fitted into the Participant and Non-participant categories made it more difficult to assess their backgrounds. However, an examination of the differences that were apparent showed the same trends emerging as had appeared in the case of the male students.[1]

The average income of the families of the ten Participants was Rs.347, whereas that of the fifteen Non-participants was Rs.200. None of the incomes of this latter group were over Rs.400. However, three of the families of the Participants had incomes over that amount. One family had an income of Rs.500, another had an income of Rs.600, and a third family received Rs.1,000. The Participants came from larger families and were younger. Not one of them was the eldest in the family; one was second, one was third, and six were sixth, or younger. One was the ninth child in the family. Five of the Non-participants were the eldest in their families; four were sixth or younger among the children. Therefore, they were presumably more responsible, as the eldest daughters have positions of responsibility in the home.

The Participants' sense of responsibility to and identification with their families was not as great as was that of the Non-participants. Only three of the former said that they wanted to take complete responsibility for their parents, and six said they would be only partly responsible for them. On the other hand, ten of the Non-participants wanted to take over complete responsibility, two wanted some responsibility, and the remaining three did not feel they would need to look after their parents. More Non-participants (eleven, as compared to four) than Participants (four out of eight) wanted to live with their in-laws after marriage.

None of the Non-participants had quarrelled much, or had disagreements with their families; eight had had minor disagreements, or a few conflicts. However, four of the Participants had had many quarrels and disagreements, and the remainder had had "some," or a few. This might indicate that the girls who did not get on well at home were more independent. This, in turn, might be part of the explanation of their taking part in behaviour that was deviant to their expected roles.

The Participants showed less interest in religion than did the Non-participants. Six of them believed in it, two believed to some extent,

1. Of the total sample of women students, sixteen had taken part in the strike, and two more said they would have if they had not been ill. Four did so out of sympathy for the strikers, three for fun, and three because they were forced to by their friends. Of those who did not take part, twelve said that they did not think strikes were justified. Eight others refused to join in, either because they did not want to, or because they did not like strikes. Five others did not take part because they were afraid of being hurt. Sixteen girls remained at home because their parents, uncles, or brothers insisted that they do so.

and one had no belief. On the other hand, thirteen of the Non-participants believed completely, and two believed partly.

Their attitudes to college also showed the same trends as had those of the male students. The Non-participants liked their courses and lecturers best, and five of them did not dislike "anything" at college, whereas the Participants liked their friends best, and only three liked their courses and lecturers. On the other hand, three others disliked their courses and lecturers more than anything else.

A slightly larger proportion of the Participants felt that girls and boys should mix more socially, and more of the Non-participants said that their parents or relatives would oppose their going with boys. This might be taken to support the greater independence of the Participants.

Seven of the Non-participants found their social life to be satisfactory, three regarded it as being only fairly satisfactory, and five felt it was not satisfactory at all. On the other hand, only one Participant was satisfied, and two found their social life only partly satisfactory. The others said that it was not satisfactory. These small figures suggest that the Participants had stronger personalities, or else had been permitted more independence by their parents, for they had dared challenge the family by disagreeing or quarelling more often with them than had the Non-participants. Moreover, they held positions of less responsibility in the home, felt less responsibility for the family, and did not have as close an identification with it. Nor did they seem to desire as close a relationship with their future in-laws. They showed less interest in religion, came from wealthier families, and were more oriented toward their friends.

Relatively more independence seems to be one of the most prominent characteristics of both men and women Participants. Either this makes them less willing to fit into college discipline, or else the strain of achieving independence in such a closely structured society is so great that they tend to release their tensions in indisciplined activity. It also seems probable that having learned how to withstand the authority of their families, they are more prepared to challenge the discipline of college life.

Young people who simply "give up" constitute another group of students who will be likely to indulge in indiscipline. The individuals are often unable to cope with heavy family pressure on them to study and succeed. The more they fail examinations, or fail to get high marks, the more "punishment" they receive—perhaps from the whole joint

241

family. This pressure is particularly difficult for the student who is below average in intelligence. Finally, their only escape may be to release their frustrations and anxieties on the easiest target—the college.

Those who fail to get the recognition they desire may also become indisciplined in order to attract attention. Since few wealthy students have shown leadership qualities in Bangalore, they are not often elected to the few executive positions in the different campus organizations, and may not have the ability to shine at sports. This tends to increase their frustrations, and leads them to indiscipline. Some may find that being unruly is the only way in which they can achieve recognition from their fellow students.

An examination of this small sample of students suggests that, contrary to expectation, frustrating conditions at college or at home and/or insecurity about the future do not necessarily lead to student indiscipline. These factors may, in fact, have quite the opposite effect. They may make the students work harder and avoid trouble in order to gain the security they desire. However, once indiscipline has been organized, and the safety of numbers is clearly seen, then the demonstrations and even the violence may attract them, for these constitute a safe way of relieving some of their frustrations. In countries where there are few opportunities for dealing with the problems engendered by rapid change, college indiscipline may be a blessing in disguise, and may prevent much of the personal maladjustment to which students are particularly prone in the modern world.

Finally, there are the "born" leaders, who tend to confine their indiscipline to the organized forms of protest. They are necessarily a small group in any college; some of them may be aspiring to leadership positions in political parties or in the community. They are usually good students, and have taken leading parts in such serious types of extracurricular activities as debates. They are highly ambitious, and many of them feel that the way to success is through advertising their qualifications publicly. The easiest way to do this is to prove themselves by leading student demonstrations.[2]

2. *Report of the University Grants Commission*, p. 17. "In nearly every instance of large-scale disorder in the universities it has been found that a few individuals have played leading parts, and these individuals figure repeatedly in troubled situations of that kind . . . the large majority of our students take a healthy and sane view of life and work in the university, and do not support rowdyism."
E. Wight Bakke, "Students on the March," pp. 202-4. Bakke remarked on the same phenomenon among the students in Mexico and Colombia, where "professional" students take four or five degrees in different faculties in order to be able to retain their student

In Bangalore these leaders are often students at the Law College. They may have been president of the Student Union, which is an excellent training ground for those who are politically ambitious.[3] Di Bona says that in any student agitation the most important student is the union president, for he is the only elected person in the university who is *ex officio* spokesman for the whole student body. This office, Di Bona believes, has changed from being that of a chairman of debating societies to a position of great importance. The union president is the leader of a large student body which can be easily roused to action. If the president thinks fit, he can call a strike, and decide when it should end. Di Bona's suggestion that such leaders tend to have great verbal ability seems to be true in the case of the leaders of the Mysore demonstrations described in Chapter 1. "Veritable torrents of words flow easily from their lips on even the most inconsequential occasions. They can move a disinterested and largely apathetic crowd into a cohesive group of dedicated supporters who will implicitly follow directions. This charismatic quality which converts mobs into movements is what makes the student leader both feared and admired by university and governmental authorities."[4]

Not enough of these leaders were interviewed in the sample of two hundred and fifty students to obtain much information on their backgrounds, but approximately a dozen were interviewed about their participation in strikes. They showed that they had exceptional leadership qualities. They knew the appropriate tactics for action, and revealed a wide appreciation of how to interpret the demonstrations to the public so that they would win their favour. Among them were the students

---

3. M. N. Chitra, "Case Studies in Students in Turmoil," p. 39.
4. Joseph Di Bona, "Indiscipline and Student Leadership in an Indian University," pp. 313-15.

---

status. In their case it was to carry on political work that they had been especially trained for. About the importance of leadership, Bakke notes, "The group activity of students is seldom the result of a simultaneous concensus on objectives. Even if a latent concensus is present, the spark of leadership is normally necessary to set action ablaze. Action is promoted by activists whose personal, but not necessarily selfish purposes can be served by enlisting their fellows in a collective endeavour. . . . [There is] the possibility that such activity will attract the attention of political leaders, and become a prelude to a political career. . . . It is therefore not surprising that ambitious young men believe that a reputation as a student 'politico' is one of the major contributions which university experience can make to a successful career.

In Mexico and Colombia nearly every political leader of importance was a student leader, "for the system feeds on itself, university life now attracts those with political ambitions and '*for this purpose*.' "

imbued with an almost evangelical fervour, who believed absolutely in the cause of the moment, and who were able to enlist many students through their devotion and enthusiasm.[5] Not enough studies have been done on the leading activists in the North American universities, but many of them seem to exhibit the same belief in and devotion to their causes.

In this chapter it has been suggested that there are three types of students who tend to participate in formal or informal indiscipline at the Indian colleges. The first type, students who are protected by the wealth or influence of their families, are able to dawdle their way through college and indulge in pastimes that they consider to be more interesting than class work. These students are the most numerous. The second type, students who are overwhelmed by family and other pressures and so become defeated, probably form a rather small percentage of the total student body, as do students of the third type; namely, the professional students who form the main leadership core of the agitations.

Since these data were analyzed, other writers have provided much more elaborate typologies of present-day students.[6] And the activists have become more numerous and effective in many countries. They are the catalysts of student frustrations, and some of them doubtless have the same skills of leadership, and the same charisma as had the leaders of the Mysore strikes.[7] The sense of guilt and responsibility felt by many North American students when they find that their countries are not living up to the ideals they were brought up to believe in may, indeed, have been a contributing factor in persuading many students to

5. Rivalries, of course, appear among these leaders. In the 1963-64 strike in Mysore, one of the leading students, a Lingayat whom the other leaders believed wanted to gain approval of the pro-government politicians, was openly hostile to the demonstrations. He tried to state his views at one of the public meetings and became so unpopular that one day the students threatened to lynch him. The Principal of his college had to protect him by taking him into his office. The Action Committee again showed their wisdom by sending students to protect him on his way home, and by placing a guard at his house until the end of the strike.

6. See; Richard E. Peterson. "The Student Left in American Higher Education," pp. 299-303. Peterson suggests that there are eight fairly distinct types of students: vocationalists, professionalists, collegiates, ritualists, academics, intellectuals, left-activists and hippies.

7. *Ibid.*, p. 304. In this article Peterson sums up the results of nine studies of the characteristics of student leftists on American campuses.

action. But other motivations such as the desire for student power must not be overlooked, and the analysis of the leaders of the Mysore strike in this study, seen in the light of these newer developments, would certainly have used this concept to explain much of their behaviour.[8] Not enough information is available about recent student demonstrations and their leadership in India to be able to say to what extent the concept of student power has influenced the thinking and action of the newer activists; or to predict to what degree they have been influenced by the thinking of the New Left, which may be developing in that country.

The hippie phenomenon has also arisen since these data were gathered. It has given us the clearest example of the extent to which some of the young generation has completely rejected the value system of their society. Because the hippies tend to drop out of the educational system at the high school level, there have not been many studies of these young people; however, a study of this group would enable us to analyze more accurately the basic factors that produce the extremely different types of behaviour among the new generation.

8. The term "student power" was coined by the Students for a Democratic Society (SDS) soon after the slogan "black power" appeared.

7

Summary
and
Conclusions

In the Introduction to this study it was suggested that the reasons given by the students for their demonstrations could be roughly classified under the headings of political protest, economic insecurity, educational reform, "causes," and fun. However, as the stated purposes of student activity have been so diversified, even within one college or university, it is clear that the reasons given by the students have not completely accounted for their participation in these demonstrations. Although it may be quite true that some students are bitterly opposed to the war in Vietnam, or are passionately concerned with civil rights in the United States, or are upset by the inadequacies of their educational experiences, we have yet to discover why so many students do *not* participate in the demonstrations, or why they want to rebel against the university authorities.

Students of collective behaviour and social movements tell us that a complex of factors must impinge upon an individual before he is motivated to move into collective action. The "issue" that sets off the action is only the spark that first ignites and then helps to channel into some form of protest the underlying anxieties and frustrations that are the real reason for the person's desire to release his pent-up feelings.

This point is supported by the fact that students in any one college or university do not always demonstrate for the same objectives, particularly over a long period of time.

Former periods of student unrest seem easy to explain. They arose due to some clear-cut crisis or situation in the students' country; they were of a temporary nature, and subsided after the crisis had been solved. They were usually prompted by some incidents or conditions outside the university.[1] The recent student unrest is strikingly different in that it is almost a universal phenomenon, and that students in different countries may agitate over the same issue, such as the war in Vietnam. In some countries this unrest has been going on for over a decade, and in most countries it appears to be becoming better organized. The leaders are using progressively skillful tactics. This wave of world-wide restlessness is too recent for us, as yet, to fully understand. "So far the message is coming in loud, but not clear."[2] But we do know that there has never been such a large proportion, or so large a number of students involved in public demonstrations as there has been in recent years.

The task of this study has been to examine closely the case histories of a sample of Indian students to determine the accuracy of the reasons they have given for their demonstrations, and to scan the literature to find out if a deeper analysis of this new phenomenon will help us answer three important questions. Why do young men and women who have been brought up in very different family and college situations, in countries thousands of miles apart, tend to take part in some-

1. New data being produced by historians and other scholars show that there has been a greater amount of student unrest and rebellion in the past than was formerly supposed. It occurred mainly in times of political crises.

See: *Daedalus*, Vol. 97, Winter 1968, for descriptions of early risings in such countries as Turkey, North Africa, Japan, and England, where a student riot broke out in Oxford in 1354.

Clifford Lord speaks of the waves of protest and deviant behaviour among students on this continent in the nineteenth century: "There have been attempts to peg this [present unrest] to the latest of a long series of identifiable student generations. The 'lost' generation of raccoon coats and hip flasks of the '20's; the 'red and pinko' generation of activist social protests of the '30's; the mature, dead serious, hell-bent-for-leather G.I.'s of blessed memory of the later '40's and early '50's; the 'beat' generation of recent years, and those who played it cool, man, cool. But today's undergraduate body is drawn too broadly from the lively American people to yield to such pigeon-holing. It is as difficult to categorize this student generation as it is to categorize the American public from which it springs and of which it is a vital part. . . . It is a new generation." ("Hurrah for Revolution," p. 3.)

2. "Campus '65: The College Generation Looks at Itself and the World Around It," p. 43.

what similar rebellious behaviour? Why is this behaviour occurring at this particular moment in history? Is this behaviour a passing phase, or are there signs that the present organized forms of action will progress to the stage at which they will become accepted, institutionalized structures in their respective countries?

Some of the points that are made in these conclusions are well supported by comparative studies; others are more or less in the nature of assumptions, in that they are not as yet supported by research. Still others are mere speculations, drawn from inferences from the popular press and/or the observations of the author. These speculations are tentative and do not pretend to cover all the complex personality factors that contribute to present-day student behaviour.[3]

To understand the recent student unrest, all areas of the student's life *qua* students must be explored. The student does not live in a vacuum, but is influenced by the total environment in which he lives; thus, it is necessary to understand the major social changes that are affecting his society, to comprehend his relationships with the groups to which he belongs, such as his family, racial, ethnic or religious groups, and to note his particular social class or caste position.

One of the major developments that is affecting the lives of students in the more industrialized countries, and one which is beginning to appear in the underdeveloped countries, is the new Youth Culture. It has been defined as a "semi-autonomous and relatively unregulated youth grouping."[4] Many societies in the past have had somewhat distinct youth groupings, but these have been integrated into the social structure in such a way as to form an accepted part of the process of socialization. The modern Youth Culture, however, differs markedly from these, in that it has been slow to gain recognition as a new structural element, and various aspects of it have been treated often as deviant behaviour, which has been dealt with by suppressive measures or ridicule. However, the Youth Culture is becoming a permanent aspect of our modern society and is gradually being recognized as such.

A Youth Culture tends to arise in modern societies in which the

3. Other writers have attempted to classify the causes of the new wave of restlessness. In speaking of Indian students Di Bona organizes his ideas under the headings of economic, psychological-social and political causes. See: Joseph Di Bona, "Indiscipline and Student Leadership in an Indian University."

Bakke goes in for a much more elaborate classification. See: E. Wight Bakke, "Roots and Soil of Student Activism."

4. S. N. Eisenstadt, "Archetypal Patterns of Youth," p. 307.

family has lost some if its importance as a socializing agency.[5] Industrialization means an increase in specialization, not only in the world of work, but also in such agencies serving children as youth organizations, Sunday Schools, sports clubs, and summer camps. These agencies tend to accentuate age groupings, and to separate children from their parents. This tendency to take control and guidance away from parents is seen also in the growth in importance of the educational system. The school now monopolizes an increasing amount of the child's time because of the expansion of education and training, and because of an increase in extracurricular activities.[6]

A separate Youth Culture is also reinforced and set apart by the gradual development of legal measures to protect the welfare of children and young people, and to control their activities—particularly those of an anti-social nature.[7] Once the formation of a separate Youth Culture is well under way, the commercial world further helps to segregate the young people from their elders by catering to them through radio and TV shows, advertisements, sports and science-fiction magazines, and popular music.[8] Affluent conditions in many of the highly industrialized countries also have given more freedom to young people, for many of them can now afford motor bikes, cars, or scooters. This freedom enables the youths to escape supervision and to enjoy what they consider to be "fun" in an anonymous environment. In India the bicycle serves much the same purpose.

Although the Youth Culture is by no means a distinctive entity apart from the society in which it exists, it has become increasingly important to the young people, as "most of the important interactions [of young people] take place within the adolescent society. There are only a few threads of connection with the outside adult society."[9] The fundamental nature of this separation of young people into a sub-culture of their own is evident from the fact that this phenomenon is not confined to any particular nation or social class, but is found in all highly industrialized countries.[10] Separate Youth Cultures do not seem to have arisen as

5. *Ibid.*, pp. 30, 307. See also: David Matza, "Position and Behaviour Patterns of Youth," pp. 198, 199.

6. James S. Coleman, *The Adolescent Society*, pp. 3, 4.

7. David Matza, "Position and Behaviour Patterns of Youth," p. 193

8. Arturo F. Gonzalez, "The Moppet Market," p. 40. See also: David Gottlieb and Charles E. Ramsey, *The American Adolescent*, pp. 33-39.

9. Coleman, p. 3.

10. Matza, pp. 198, 199. See also: Oswald Bell, "The Future of Scouting in Europe," pp. 2-5.

yet in the developing countries; even so, the students in these countries, through living in hostels and acquiring new knowledge and ways of behaving, are becoming more and more separated from their families. This separation occurs particularly when their parents are illiterate or poorly educated, or live in villages. This factor of separation, and, as yet, other unknown factors, contribute to their feeling of insecurity, and to their uncertainty of their roles in society.[11] Some writers have referred to the students' position as a "marginal" one in that they are not considered wholly as either adults or children.[12]

An increase in crime and restlessness among young people in most countries, and many of the frustrations felt by the college students are being caused by these feelings of insecurity. The fact that there is a similarity of trends in all urban-industrial societies means that students all over the world are experiencing the same upsetting results of social change, so that many of them are just as insecure as their less-educated peers in the middle classes.[13] However, students who rebel have an advantage over the non-student members of the Youth Culture because they are treated with leniency by society. This is due to the fact that the role of the student is a transitional one, and the students have a specially privileged position in that they are potential members of the élite. Many of them are protected from the harsh treatment given to rebellious non-students, for they belong to families who have enough prestige and power to protect them. Thus they are in the advantageous position of being able to release their frustrations without incurring severe penalties.

Another effect of the new Youth Culture is that, as young people are separated from their parents and the values they represent, they tend to resent parental authority. This attitude is carried over to their relations with all adults. Even if they go to a university where there is the fullest academic freedom, the most up-to-date facilities, and close relationships between staff and students there "is an inherent tendency for students to take a critical attitude towards the *status quo*. This critical attitude is the product of a tradition of criticism and alienation, and of the rebellious attitude of youth toward their elders in modern society."[14]

11. Matza, p. 57. See also: Kingsley Davis, "Adolescence and Social Structure," p. 42.

12. David Sarnoff, quoted in Matza, p. 195. See also: David Gottlieb, "Youth Subculture: Variations on a General Theme," p. 28

13. See: T. R. Fyvel, *The Insecure Offenders.*

14. Seymour Martin Lipset, "University Students and Politics in Underdeveloped Countries," p. 51.

Still another effect is that, to the extent that students move away from the influence and protection of their families, they will come to rely more and more on their peers. As the gulf widens between parents and students, the students feel that their elders cannot possibly understand them or their problems.[15] This may cause them to seek new identifications in campus organizations, for they may find in them "a kind of replacement for the collectivity they have just left . . . particularly in movements that have a sense of commitment, purpose, and high intimacy."[16] These movements may give them a new purpose in life, as they have for many Indian students who have felt alienated from the rest of their society.[17] The same feeling of alienation underlies the phrase, "I am going away to find myself!" used by many students on Canadian campuses. This expression was used so often a few winters ago on one Canadian campus that it became a campus joke, but it summarizes the confusion of many students about their role in society. Many writers have said that the alienation of the younger generation is a product of the conflicting values and demands which many of them are facing. Others have spoken of the *anomie* that an individual may suffer when "[His] personality is not stably organized about a coherent system of values, goals, and expectations."[18] This *anomie* occurs when the mores of a society are so vague that they cannot act as guides for behaviour. Modernization tends to produce forces that undermine the stable value systems of a society to such an extent that there is a good deal of confusion until new patterns develop that are appropriate for the new situations.

> . . . one of the most conspicuous features of the present situation lies in the extent to which patterns of orientation which the individual can be expected to take completely for granted have disappeared. The complexity of the influences which impinge upon him have increased enormously; in many or most situations the society does not provide him with only one socially sanctioned definition of the situation and approved pattern of behaviour, but with a considerable number of possible alternatives, the order of preference between which is by no means clear.[19]

15. Bell, pp. 2-5. T. C. N. Gibbens, "Teenage Riots Round the World," p. 12.
16. Frank Pinner, quoted in Seymour Martin Lipset, "Students and Politics in Comparative Perspective," p. 7.
17. M. S. Gore, "The Crisis in University Education," p. 349. Lipset and Seabury say much the same thing about the American students: "The students are frustrated; they can find no place in society where alienation does not exist, where they can do meaningful work. Despair sets in, a volatile political agent . . . this is the motive power of the student movement." ("The Lessons of Berkeley," p. 39.)
18. Talcott Parsons, "Some Sociological Aspects of the Fascist Movements," p. 125.
19. *Ibid.*, p. 128. "It has been to an extraordinary extent a period of the 'dubunking' of

Students, of course, vary in the degree to which they can adjust to rapid changes in values. Many surveys of the religious views of North American students made in the last few years indicate that there has been a rather decided movement away from religious beliefs on the part of the students. If the philosophies and rituals of religious institutions do not suit modern needs, students may be deprived of the moral support that a firm belief in religion gave their fathers and grandfathers. They may continue to pay lip service to religion, and perform the religious rituals in order to avoid conflict with their parents, as a number of the Indian students interviewed for this study continued to do, but the inner meaning of the experience may no longer be important. To some students this decline in the importance of the religious experience may not be drastic, for gradually they may be able to absorb other values, and become members of other supporting groups; but for many other students a loss of belief may be a very upsetting experience and leave them with the feeling of *anomie*.

However, probably a greater problem for most students is that of the changing sex mores. This problem begins at an earlier age for young people living in the more highly industrialized countries, for it has been shown that in these countries boys and girls mature physically at an earlier age, and must therefore adjust to the emotional demands of new sex drives before they are socially or psychologically prepared to meet them.[20] This adjustment is demanded at a time when there is greater freedom between the sexes than ever before, and yet no patterns to govern freer sexual experimentation have emerged. Many North American students find that there are few limitations on the opportunities for sex experimentation; at the same time, there are still heavy penalties if they go "too far." Women students are in a particularly difficult position, for they may find that their "sex appeal" is regarded more highly than their intellectual ability at college, and for many the major part of their time is spent competing for dates and possible husbands. In order to achieve these goals they must indulge in behaviour which goes far beyond that which they were brought up to consider correct. For students living in the developing countries, college may be the first place in which both men and women students have the opportunity to make

20. William C. Kvaraceus, *Juvenile Delinquency a Problem for the Modern World*, p. 46. See also: Eisenstadt, p. 34.

traditional values and ideas, and one in which for previously stable culture patterns in such fields as religion, ethics, and philosophy, no comparably stable substitutes have appeared—rather a conspicuously unstable factionalism and tendency to faddistic fluctuation."

even tentative gestures towards friendship and dating. And, as they are pioneering in this new realm, they have to contend with their own shyness, and lack of knowledge and of confidence in their new roles, as well as with the problem of family and public acceptance. Their main difficulty may be lack of freedom to experiment in order to find their way in this carefully guarded area of behaviour.[21]

With these universal changes in mind, we can now return to assess the importance of the reasons given by students for their demonstrations; namely, political crises, economic problems, moral protests, educational reforms, and emotional release.

It has been the contention of this writer that the stated reasons for student action may be merely additional factors in motivating students, who have already been upset by the changing conditions of their environment, to go into collective action. One such additional factor which influences the student is the political climate of a country. This will certainly affect student participation in political demonstrations, particularly if the political crisis is of such a nature that it impinges on the student's life. Scott thinks that many students are drawn into political struggles at college "almost in spite of themselves."[22] However, we know that the restlessness of students does not always result in political action for, in both the highly industrialized countries and in the developing areas, many students do not show a strong interest in politics. This is especially true in recent years because students tend to come from more diversified backgrounds, and so do not necessarily have the same motivations, goals, or values.[23] Undergraduate students, however,

21. Joseph Fischer, "The University Student in South and Southeast Asia," p. 49. Fischer speaks of a study of over 1,500 students from four southeast Asian universities, of whom over 80 per cent said that their most serious personal problems had been related to sex.

22. Robert E. Scott, "Student Political Activism in Latin America," p. 71. See also: *Report of the University Grants Commission*, p. 16. "The political and economic tensions that many of the countries in Asia and Africa are experiencing are apt to be reflected in the behaviour of the young in these countries. Further, the tension consequent in the rivalry and ideologies and/or power politics at the international level has its repercussions on young men and women generally, and particularly on university students."

23. Matza, p. 207. Matza believes that the stresses, turmoil, and deviance among young people have been exaggerated. He thinks that literary essayists and positivist sociologists have overemphasized the problems of our day. He feels that they have been influenced too much by "unwarranted intellectual gloom connected with the negative assessment of modernity."

Bakke, "Students on the March," p. 205. Bakke makes the point that not all the 65,000 students of the University of Mexico City nor the 6,000 students at the National University of Bogota take part in demonstrations.

"Campus '65," p. 54. Only a minority of the American students of this sample had taken part in protest demonstrations. A much larger proportion of students said that they would sign a petition, contribute money, boycott a store, or join a picket line than had actually taken part in any of these affairs.

constitute a captive audience *par excellence* for political manipulators because they have not yet assumed their major responsibilities of work and family, and so are freer to respond to suggestion. In addition to this, they are in a milieu where rumours and excitement can spread rapidly, and at an age which responds to this stimulation.

In India, because of the small variety of extracurricular activities, the college student has few opportunities for gaining recognition; but participation in demonstrations is one way that it can be obtained. Indiscipline can bring notoriety. By leading demonstrations the student can get recognition at college, his name may appear in the newspapers, and he will have the attention of the public. His actions may be brought to the notice of politicians who could further his career. Leadership in political demonstrations can thus be an important step up the political ladder.

A country's economic problems may motivate the students to protest. One of the universal changes that occur in all countries as agriculture gives way to industry is in the system of stratification. Former caste, or social class adjustments are upset as new opportunities to gain economic or political eminence arise. This may mean that the groups who were previously in high positions are threatened by those who formerly held lower positions in the economic and social hierarchy. Opportunities for advancement may thus be opening up for some young people and closing for others. There will be strain in either case, for those moving up may have to face the stiff competition of achieving higher status without the support of their own group, whom they may outdistance; and those whose advancements are blocked may be dissatisfied. Strain may be greater if legal action has been taken to give practical aid in education and jobs to some groups and not to others, as has occurred in the case of the designation of "Forward" and "Backward" castes in the state of Mysore. Under these circumstances, the greater opportunities for advancement become apparent to those formerly deprived, and consequently a greater proportion of the population acquires ambitions to gain education, or to give education to their children, which they see as the gateway to advancement in the occupational hierarchy. This may mean that intense pressure is put on young people to acquire the prized goals.

In the sample of Indian students studied, this pressure did not seem to lead to activism, but rather to a greater effort to study and gain degrees. But it is evident that this strain is an important one to consider in studying reasons for student restlessness, particularly when there has been a lag on the part of the economic institutions in catching up with the number of students turned out by the educational system. The anxieties of Indian students are heightened considerably by the awareness of the existence of large numbers of "educated unemployeds."[24]

One of the most puzzling things about the widespread student activism is that it is occurring in the countries with the highest standard of livings as well as those with the lowest. A common feature in either case resides in the problems of many students in finding satisfactory careers. For in both affluent and non-affluent countries industrialization opens up such a variety of occupational choices that parents may no longer be able to guide their children, and there may be no agencies through which the students can learn the necessary steps that will lead them to interesting jobs. However, in the affluent countries, the demand for highly trained and professional workers is so great that most students have little worry about their future careers, except in the matter of choice. In such countries, too, the process of industrialization will normally have advanced to such an extent that family, religious, and ethnic nepotism will be partially eliminated. These countries will be in need of the best brains in order to run their economies efficiently.

Another similarity between affluent and non-affluent countries is that many of the students seem to suffer from boredom. In the affluent countries students either have more pocket money to spend, or can get jobs with salaries that will enable them to spend money on entertainment. However, increase in the variety of commercial entertainment and organized recreation has not been satisfying for boredom still exists as a cause of misbehaviour among teenagers and students; this fact has been noted by many observers.[25]

Many of the Indian students of this sample claimed that they found life in general, and their studies in particular, so dull and unrelated to their own existence that they joined in demonstrations to relieve their boredom. They have difficulty in filling in their leisure time because they have very little pocket money, and very few can get jobs that will augment the little they have.

24. Victor S. d'Souza, "Social Development, Education and Unemployment in India," pp. 377-92. For an early study of student unrest in India, see: Margaret Cormack, *She Who Rides a Peacock.*

25. Fyvel, p. 23. See also: Kvaraceus, p. 47; and Pat Pearce, "So Little for the Mind," *Star Weekly*, Montreal, April 3, p. 15. Matza, pp. 197, 198.

Another stated reason causing student unrest is moral protest. It is fairly easy for students to believe that they have rejected many of their early religious and moral beliefs, as long as the values lying behind these beliefs are not challenged by reality. College may be the first place in which this occurs, and they find themselves confronted by the real problems of their society and/or the world. This may mean that they have to face the emotional shock of realizing how privileged their positions are in comparison with the lives of poverty and destitution of those around them. Their sense of guilt may drive them into action.

> "Discovery" of the subjection of Negroes in democratic, enlightened America gave rise to the radical student movement. . . . It was intensified by the discovery of grinding poverty in the world's wealthiest nation, and by the thought of the world's greatest power being engaged in a war of attrition in a tiny, underdeveloped country.[26]

Thus, when rapidly changing conditions prevent a society's ideologies from keeping up with events, students often become disillusioned, and their only solution is to destroy as much of the system they live under as possible.[27] Hence the attraction of the idea of "the revolution" for many left wing activists.

It is impossible to estimate just how many students are moved by guilt to protest, and even if they are, whether this feeling is the main motivating factor in moving them into action. Peterson estimates that, in the United States, only a very small proportion of students, about 2 per cent, have a "powerful sense of outrage" about the inadequacies of their society, and that the great majority of American students are politically apathetic, "caught up in their vocational, academic, or hedonistic pursuits."[28] In India, students seem to be far too concerned with their own problems to have protested often over purely "moral" issues.

To what degree has educational reforms caused student demonstra-

26. Richard E. Peterson, "The Student Left in American Higher Education," p. 312.
27. Frank A. Pinner, "Student Trade-Unionism in France, Belgium, and Holland," p. 197. "The individual feels an acute need for an explanation of his discomfort or uneasiness. One of his possible responses may be the espousal of an ideology which presumes to demonstrate the moral or historical wrongness of existing conditions. He does not envisage playing a social role at all unless society is totally transformed in accordance with principles of justice or historical necessity.

"There have always existed, in all universities, groups unified by a strong central dogma and often closely related to political and social movements outside the university. Such groups tend to attract those prevented from identifying with their primary milieu, their social class or vocational group by social or psychological conditions."
28. Peterson, p. 312.

tions? As a larger proportion of young people are attending colleges and universities than ever before, they will necessarily come from very different backgrounds, even within one country, and arrive at the college with different degrees of preparedness for the college experience. In other words, each student goes to college pre-disposed by his previous socialization to become an activist or not. When he arrives, the particular college he chooses will influence his behaviour in many ways. The mere factor of size, for example, will be important in determining his relations with staff and students. It has been said that the transition from high school to the university has become more difficult, as the latter has grown in size and become more impersonal. The location of the college, the courses the students take, the "climate of freedom" that prevails, the extent to which they are given the opportunity to release their energies in extracurricular activities will all be important factors influencing student behaviour.[29]

The quality and leadership of the staff differ markedly from college to college, and from country to country. Lipset thinks that when the quality is high, students will be under greater pressure, for the expectations of their work will be correspondingly high, and this higher standard demanded of them may make them resent the university. He believes, too, that student demonstrations are influenced by faculty discontent, which again reflects faculty "quality."[30] In this study it was found that the staff of the Indian colleges tended to contribute to student restlessness, but for other reasons. At any rate, as many more students now depend on scholarships or freeships to finance their education, they must maintain high grades. Nor do such students usually have the time, or perhaps the money, to be able to release their tension in "fun."

The admission of an increasing number of students from the lower socio-economic stratas has had another effect on the colleges, for students coming from these classes (or, in the case of Indian students, from the lower castes, or villages) have no clear conception of the meaning of higher education, or an "Oxford-Cambridge" ideal of college life. They are usually not as well read or as carefully prepared for the college

29. Ferdynand Zweig, *The Student in the Age of Anxiety*, p. 23. In Oxford there are about two hundred intercollegiate clubs and societies, as well as a great many more in the single colleges. However, even though extracurricular activities are provided, students may not take part in them, and therefore may not have the opportunity of releasing their tensions through these media. In India and other developing countries, there has not been the opportunity of providing these types of activities.
30. Seymour Martin Lipset, "Students and Politics in Comparative Perspective," p. 15.

experience as are the more privileged students. They cannot, therefore, because of their "pecuniary as well as cultural poverty," contribute to college life in the same way as the majority of students did in former times.[31] For many students, college life is no longer comparable with that pictured in movies and musical comedies, where students are portrayed as spending their time in a carefree way, without serious worries or responsibilities. Instead of college representing the happiest days of their lives, it can often be a "most unhappy time of life" because of the insecurities of and pressures on the students.[32] Some of the symptoms of their underlying anxieties are shown in irrational behaviour of different sorts, such as an excessive use of pep pills, tranquillizers, sleeping pills, LSD, and narcotics. Suicide, too, may be the result of their anxiety.[33]

It is probable that students who find their education related to their needs, and feel that it equips them for a career, will consider their college training satisfactory. This is possibly one reason why graduate students do not tend to demonstrate as much as undergraduates. Barring excessive pressure on such students to work hard to retain their positions in the university, or to obtain a good job after graduation, it seems reasonable to expect that they will not tend to participate in demonstrations, for they will have a purpose, and will have no time in which to get bored, or to join their friends in rebellious action. Emotional strain will be less for those students who enter college with a clear occupational goal, a realistic image of the work world, and a reasonable belief that they can achieve their ends.[34]

The major problem facing women students is the relatively new and confusing choice between marriage and a career. In countries like the United States, where women students have been attending college for a number of generations, and in which the economy has welcomed them at least in lower professional and business positions, women students still face the necessity, while at college, of "proving" their femininity by trying to attract masculine attention. On the other hand, the

31. Seymour Martin Lipset, "University Students and Politics in Underdeveloped Countries," p. 47.

32. Ben Rose, "New Spectre on the Campus: Student Crackups," p. 9.

33. Suicide is not an unusual way out, either for Indian students, or for the population in general. A number of student suicides were mentioned in the Indian press and by informants during the period of this study. They generally occurred after a student had failed to pass his examinations. In the United States, student suicides, as well as those of adolescents, have increased in recent years.

34. Matza, pp. 207, 208.

rapid way in which they have achieved independence of action, and the growing insecurity of the economic support of their families have made most of them desire to earn their own living for at least a period of time before marriage. But the glamorous aura of marriage, and the fact that attitudes toward the position of women are still in flux, may make them hesitate to take full advantage of a college education that would equip them for competition with men students for satisfactory careers. This dilemma poses particularly difficult problems for women in developing countries. There, the norms relating to the social segregation of the sexes do not, as yet, permit social equality in the relationships between men and women in the working world. When women take up careers, they will have to contend with severe competition from men, and to endure a certain amount of loneliness, since their new positions may tend to isolate them from the companionship of men.

It seems, therefore, that there are many factors in the educational sphere that increase a student's disposition toward frustration and anxiety which, in turn, may lead him to demonstrate against the university.

The need for emotional release, or fun, is an additional reason given by the students as a cause of unrest. It is of particular importance when we consider the tensions wrought by rapid social changes. The excitement of being part of a crowd, the participation in physical combat, and the destruction of property motivate many students to join demonstrations. They are, at this point, in their teens or early 20's—an age often called "the age of revolt." They are attracted by the idea of action, for they are "simultaneously at the height of their sexual prowess, physical energy, intellectual curiosity, and their rebellion against authority. . . . In sum, they are human dynamite."[35]

Having examined some of the stated reasons for student action, we can now compare reasons for student demonstrations in the dissimilar societies of India and North America. Although the two societies are at different stages of industrial development, and face different problems, the students in both cases are living in changing political, social, and economic situations that are affecting their values and ways of life.

---

35. Seymour Martin Lipset and Paul Seabury, "The Lessons of Berkeley," p. 17. See also: Kvaraceus, pp. 31, 49. "Several specialists have pointed out that delinquency in itself may constitute a very satisfactory form of recreation, and that it is difficult for the community to substitute an equally thrilling but more conventional form of diversion. . . . Children of the wealthy upper classes often find little meaning in life and no purposes except for their short-lived, impulsive, and often malicious pleasures."

Family upbringing has been important in setting the stage for student unrest. In North America the more permissive upbringing in the smaller family has made young people more independent of their parents and, because of this independence, they are anxious to take their educational destinies into their own hands when they arrive at college. The great majority of students, too, are brought up in the sheltered environment of relative affluence, with all the luxuries that this type of society can provide. The first time they have to face the realities and problems of the world may be when they go to college.

The Indian student, on the other hand, is still part of a somewhat authoritarian and usually a large family. He will find it easier to alleviate the frustrations he experiences in trying to attain independence by releasing them in college demonstrations rather than in challenging his family by himself. In the cases of both Indian and American students it is easier and more satisfactory to release tensions in the company of peers. Being one of a group gives anonymity, and a "student" has more liberty to rebel than has a "son" or a "daughter."

The educational process, too, though different in the two societies, helps to motivate students to rebellious behaviour if they are predisposed to engage in it. In North America many students have been brought up in progressive schools, which encourage individuality in learning and expression. If they attend a university so overcrowded with students that they must take lectures with many other students, and where they receive little attention from their professors, they may feel particularly deprived and frustrated. The "quiz kids" of the 1960's demand a great deal more individual attention than the present overworked university staff can give them. Moreover, the new perspective of the younger generation of North American students has made many of them feel that the courses they are offered are not relevant to their lives, or to the lives they want to live.[36] The main factor underlying this attitude is the changing idea of the function of a university. Most students no longer think of it as an agency to train an educated élite, but expect it to lead to meaningful careers.

The Indian student, too, is often dissatisfied with his courses. He usually is not stimulated to work on his own and so does not get a feeling of individual achievement in his studies. For most, the spectre of possible unemployment, or at the best a dull, low-paid job, haunts their futures.

36. Carl Davidson, "The New Radicals and the Multiversity," pp. 62-64.

The demonstrations of the North American students seem to be concerned more with moral protests than are those of the Indian students. Being privileged people in an affluent society, the American students are not protesting against their *own* conditions, but because they are the "advantaged."

> They are the first generation that can afford to be critical. Pressure to earn a living often served to resolve parents' problems of conscience, and made it easier for them to compromise their principles in the name of survival.
>   The competitive struggle for affluence holds no challenge for them when they have already achieved a measure of affluence without struggling for it; the customary ways of earning a living are apt to look drab to them . . . thus no practical or material concerns stand in the way of a face-to-face confrontation with the anomalies, the inconsistencies and the hypocrisies with which past generations have borne.[37]

So far the demonstrations of Indian students have been of a much more turbulent nature than those on the North American campuses. The students have destroyed public and private property, and have used physical violence to gain their ends. The police, too, have become more aggressive, and many students have been hurt in the combats, and a number killed. This violence is caused probably by the tendency of the students to follow the example set by the many other groups in India who are equally affected by the changing social structure, and whose reactions to these changes have been more vehement than those of North Americans.

Earlier student demonstrations on the North American continent seldom included either student or police conflicts but, since the Berkeley incident in 1964, they seem to have become increasingly violent. Social scientists are at present arguing over the reasons for this change in pattern.[38] The reasons are probably much the same as those in India: the increasing disruption of rapid social change, the adoption of new

37. Murray G. Ross, "Why Students Rebel," (Unpublished address to the Empire Club of Toronto, February 8, 1968.)

38. See: The *New York Times*, April 28, 1968, pp. 24, 25, 111-14. In this section a representative group of American scholars and social critics try to answer this question.
    The fact that students on the North American continent are becoming more prepared for violence is seen in the physical preparations they take when they expect to be attacked by the police. See, for example, "Civil War on Campus," (no author), *Our Generation*, Vol. 5, No. 3, November-December 1967, pp. 98, 99. This article describes how about 4,000 students and police fought with fists, rocks, sticks, and tear gas for two and one half hours on the campus of the University of Wisconsin in Madison. At one point, "The students remained in their places, heads between their knees, and arms over their necks, as the police began swinging their clubs and dragging out the bludgeoned victims."

tactics learned through hearing of demonstrations of students in other countries; and, in the United States, the example of the growing violence of Negro-white relationships.

It will be only through intensive studies of the case histories of many students in different countries that we will be able to understand more fully why societies today are producing activists and hippies on the one hand, and on the other, serious students who are finding deep satisfaction in exploring the new fields of knowledge opening up to them in this era of scientific revolution. It is evident that, whatever the causes of student unrest, activists are convincing more and more students to join student organizations, and to devote themselves enthusiastically to their causes. This trend will now be considered.

STUDENT INDISCIPLINE AS A MECHANISM OF SOCIAL CHANGE

The fact that student demonstrations in India have been described as "student indiscipline" shows that the public feels they constitute irrational, "bad" behaviour, upsetting to the lecturers and educational authorities, and detrimental to the students' own education. Even the term "student unrest" has this connotation to some extent. In speeches, editorials, and articles, the Indian students have been constantly reproached for their behaviour, and they have been urged to be "disciplined and responsible." The more positive elements in their demonstrations have been almost completely overlooked.

Student demonstrations have at least allowed the students to release their tensions and frustrations in a comparatively harmless way—harmless in the sense that they may have prevented other kinds of delinquent patterns from arising. Formally organized student indiscipline serves another purpose. It helps to solidify the student culture, which may be one of the most important halfway shelters in the movement of young people from the security of the caste and/or the family to the independence and perhaps loneliness of modern society. The student culture gives the student a new and much-needed, if temporary, identification, and a new, sustaining loyalty.[39]

Another positive function of the demonstrations is that they draw attention to inadequacy or corruption within educational systems. In

39. Edward Shils, "The Intellectual in the Political Development of the New States," p. 340. Shils thinks that this is one of the reasons why many young Indians direct their feelings of rebellion against some political object. The agitation of the political group gives them a feeling of protective identity, and some security which is needed after moving away from the shelter of caste and family.

a rapidly changing society it is necessary for some individuals and groups to spearhead the changes that must be made to meet new conditions. In *The Hindu* of January 26, 1962, an editorial entitled, "Who will bell the Cat?" expressed the following point of view: As employees of the universities (which in India means employees of the government) the teachers cannot complain too openly about conditions. Most of the parents are not educated enough, or even aware of what conditions at a university should be like, so they cannot assess the academic difficulties of their children. Moreover, since the universities are being controlled more and more by the government, parents feel too helpless and too inexpert, or are too indifferent to try to improve them. Thus, the only people who can agitate are the victims of the system— the students.

The data from the analysis of student demonstrations in India described in two leading newspapers (and mentioned in the Introduction) show that of the ninety-six incidents, seventy-one demonstrations were stated to be caused by some educational problem. Twenty-three of these were directed against some phase of university administration, such as the arrangement of the offices in new buildings, the system of detention, or the withdrawal of concessions. Other sources of dissatisfaction were: the demand for salary increases for graduate students in agriculture, the curtailment of opportunities for agricultural students, affiliation to another university, and the decision of the government to revoke its promises in regard to diplomas. Another complaint concerned the withdrawal of scholarships previously awarded to poor and needy students, and the decision to make these available, instead, to students from the families of rich men, or of gazetted officers.

Thirteen of the other demonstrations caused by educational problems concerned college staffs. In six of these the students either wanted a principal dismissed, or protested against the fact that one had been dismissed. Another demonstration occurred because of the embezzlement of funds; in another case students protested against the "misbehaviour" of the staff. Protest activity was directed often against the inefficiency of teachers. One example of this was cited by a graduate student who said that when he was at college the students went on strike every year at examination time. This often happened because the students did not feel properly prepared, for lecturers would not have finished the required "portions." He said that once a lecturer taught for five straight hours just before the examination, and the students became so nervous and exhausted that they could hardly understand a word of the lecture.

Finally, two demonstrations were caused by the dismissal of lecturers, and one involved the case of a lecturer who had received rough treatment from the students.

Twelve incidents concerned the rights of students. In one of these incidents a strike occurred because four students were expelled. Five strikes or demonstrations occurred on account of student deaths; in two of these cases the students demanded judicial enquiries because they believed that the individuals concerned had been neglected by their doctors, after having undergone operations. In two cases students protested because they thought that a sick student was not being looked after properly. In another case the students demanded an enquiry when a fellow student was run over by a bus.

Of the other incidents concerning student rights, one was caused by Madras students demanding that Tamil replace Hindu as a medium of instruction, two concerned a rise in university fees, six resulted from increased bus fares (in several cases students were protesting also against the rising price of text-books), and five had to do with examinations. Nine incidents were provoked by bad conditions in hostels, which included lack of drinking water; and by an unpopular warden, by poor administration, or by thieving peons. Thus nearly 75 per cent of the demonstrations mentioned in the press in one year concerned some phase of the educational process.

Four accounts of "sympathetic" strikes were published. In two of these, it was stated that "many other colleges also joined the strike." Three of the four sympathetic strikes were organized in support of the students of Allahabad University who had gone on strike to protest about the lathi charges of the police against their fellow students.

The descriptions of these demonstrations show that many of the students' protests are directed toward seeking action which will, in some way, ameliorate poor conditions in their colleges. Informants seemed to agree that having strikes is the *only* way in which students can get things done, particularly as the student unions are usually dominated by the staff, and it is very difficult for the students to use them to discuss their educational problems.[40]

India is not the only country in which the students are beginning to play a significant role in education. In France the French student trade-

40. Joseph Di Bona, "Indiscipline and Student Leadership in an Indian University," pp. 372-93. Di Bona discusses the political role that student unions have played in some Indian universities.

union movement "administers jointly with the government a large number of student welfare funds and activities [and] sits on numerous government commissions dealing with youth, sports, cultural affairs, and similar matters."[41] In other countries, such as Belgium and Holland, the student organizations play such an important role that they, too, are referred to as "student trade unions." In describing them Pinner refers to the gradual establishment of such unions in most European countries as "a movement [which] clearly constitutes a break with the patterns of student activity in the past . . . the movement is a striking phenomenon in current history."[42] In Mexico and Colombia students are assigned important roles and their demonstrations are taken seriously by the politicians.[43]

Publicity given to recent student protest in the United States with regard to the civil rights movement and to the war in Vietnam has overshadowed student influence on education. Harold Taylor, former president of Sarah Lawrence College, said recently that the students had become the "most powerful invisible force in the reform of education" in the United States.[44] The Canadian Union of Students in Canada, the co-ordinating agency for student government representatives, has been working for several years to increase student and faculty representation on the various boards of governors of the Canadian universities to ensure that each university becomes "a true community of scholars."[45]

The growing power of students in the area of educational reform is alarming to some American writers, who feel the students are "getting out of hand."[46] Their power is increased by support from recent gradu-

41. Pinner, pp. 177-98. See also: Jean-Pierre Worms, "The French Student Movement," pp. 359-66. This is an account of the French student movements. It traces the rise of regional organizations, which began with the Association des Étudiants in 1877 and continued to spread, until by 1900 there were non-political and non-religious student associations in all French university towns. All these associations were federated in 1907 in a single National Union—L'Union Nationale des Étudiants de France. This association seems to have been able to keep a sufficiently large and devoted continuous membership and leadership to enable it to enlist many more students when a new issue appears. It is a mechanism by which students can be quickly mobilized to move into action.
42. Pinner, p. 198.
43. Bakke, p. 200.
44. "Man of the Year," *Time*, January 6, 1967, pp. 18-23.
45. William C. Heine, "UWO Becomes Focus of Student Drive." London, Ontario: *London Free Press*, Saturday, April 1, 1967.
46. Lewis S. Feuer, "The Decline of Freedom at Berkeley," pp. 78-87. See also: Clark Kerr, "The Turmoil in Higher Education," pp. 17-21. Possibly one of the dangerous results of an increase in student power is that students will become more attractive targets for political manipulators. This is the reason the national student organizations have been seen in many countries as a potential threat.

ates who have grown up during the same period of "generational conflict," and so understand young people and their reasons for revolt.[47] Students have been encouraged in their social protests, too, by such religious groups as the YMCA and the Young Christian Students.[48] An additional factor that has encouraged many activists to pursue new types of confrontation on their respective campuses is that they have sensed the fears of the administration and many staff members over organized demonstrations, and the problems they have had in handling them. To many students, even to those who are merely onlookers, confrontation has become a new, exciting game, particularly since the activists are becoming more and more daring in their tactics. Perhaps the most constructive thing they have done on many North American campuses is to initiate new experiments in education, such as the free universities. To date these have not had too great a success; they have attracted only a few intellectuals and a fringe of hippies, besides the activists themselves. Even so there is no indication that the reform ardour in this direction has abated.[49]

It is apparent, then, that much of the student unrest around the world is leading toward the initiating of reforms in the educational systems of different countries.[50] In the United States these have been credited to the New Left. "Historians will credit the student leftists of the 1960's with being a major stimulus for reforms in higher education; these will mean mainly greater personal and academic freedom for students. New, highly open structural forms will have come into being to add to the total diversity of the system. Outside the university, however, the impact of the student left still largely remains to be seen."[51]

As the Indian students become more firmly organized on a national basis, and as they learn the skills and tactics of leadership through experience, they, too, will probably play an even more vital part in helping to transform the educational system into one which more adequately fills their needs. At the present time their frustrations are being channelled more through the colleges than through any other media.

47. Seymour Martin Lipset and Philip G. Altbach, "American Student Protest," p. 332.
48. Ibid., p.330.
49. Peterson, pp. 312, 313.
50. Ibid., p. 294. "During the academic year 1964-65, there were more demonstrations about dormitory and other living-group regulations and campus food service than about United States actions in Vietnam. Moreover, larger numbers of students, most likely representing wider cross-sections of student bodies, were generally involved in protesting internal campus issues."
51. Ibid., p.314.

When students are able to release their tensions through other outlets, such as better sports facilities and more organized entertainments, when the family becomes less authoritarian, and when a more liberal attitude arises toward the mixing of the sexes, then the colleges may not bear the whole brunt of the frustrations arising from social change. However, as far as the Indian educational system is concerned,[52] it is likely that for some time students will constitute the main protest group. It may take many years to remove disrupting political influences in the colleges and universities, and lecturers may take a long time to become a truly professional group, organizing programmes for their own benefit. It is also likely that, as student protest becomes better organized, as the students begin to gain a more powerful and respected position, and as the educational system changes to meet more of the students' needs, the number of spontaneous outbursts and the instances of violence will gradually diminish.

52. Robert E. Scott, p. 97. Like the students in Latin America, "Unless [there are] changes in the educational system . . . [the methods of the extreme Left] will be repeated over and over again until its causes are recognized and remedied."

The mass media, particularly the TV, and an increasing number of articles in New Left publications help to train activists in the most up-to-date tactics. See, for example, Sam Friedman, and Mike Goldfield, "Battling the Fog: A Report on the SDS Convention." (Our Generation, Vol. 5, No. 2, pp. 106-109.) Some of the results of the convention were: the planning of a grand strategy for campus action in the coming year which was to culminate in a student strike in the spring; the establishment of a Radical Education Centre to serve the needs of campaign organizers; and studies of past campus actions, analyzing their tactics. "SDS has developed some of the most imaginative, sophisticated tactics for university campuses of any left-wing group in the world."

Appendixes

APPENDIX I
Method and Sample

The main data for this study were obtained through interviews with a sample of two hundred and fifty men and women fourth-year students attending fourteen colleges in Bangalore, the capital of Mysore State. The collecting of material was greatly facilitated by the fact that I returned in 1961 to the same Indian city in which I had done research in 1954, and so was familiar with much of the college and family life of the city. I was also fortunate in having the help of two of the same research assistants who had worked with me in the previous period. Six additional research assistants were trained in interviewing techniques as the study proceeded. As they were all recent college graduates, they were able to communicate more effectively with the students. They were also able to speak several Indian languages, as well as the regional language, Kannada. Some of the most fruitful insights came from the weekly seminars at which the interviews were thoroughly discussed.

The interviewing schedule for the study was based on the findings of my former research in Bangalore, on various articles on the subject, and on studies that had been made of youthful malaise in other countries. Twenty-one colleges in Bangalore and other parts of India were visited during the period of the research, some of them many times. Staying at staff hostels in several women's colleges gave me an insight into the residential side of college life, and addressing a number of student audiences gave me some appreciation of their response to lectures. My many discussions with student leaders, lecturers, principals, and the vice-chancellors of two universities helped me toward a better understanding of the Indian educational system.

The data obtained through the interview schedule were so varied, and the sample of students studied was so small that it was impossible to give a quantitative account of the findings, or to verify their significance mathematically. Thus, the figures given in the various tables in the text are used merely to summarize the data and to give some indication of trends, or of possible trends.

In order to differentiate the various people who gave information for the study, those interviewed by the team are called "interviewees" or "respondents," whereas the additional people who were interviewed because of their general knowledge of education and student life are called "informants."

269

Of the two hundred and fifty college students of the sample, one hundred and fifty-nine were men, and the remainder women. Fourth-year students were chosen because they had had the longest experience of college life. They were also at the stage at which they would soon be moving into the world, and so their possible apprehensions about the future might be more pronounced. The students were purposely chosen from four different communities. Brahmans and Christians were selected to see whether the "disadvantages" of belonging to a "Forward caste" affected the students' attitudes to their careers. As a contrast, students from two "Backward" castes, Lingayats and Vokkaligas, were also interviewed. Due to the difference in the number of students from these four communities who were at college, it was not possible to get an equal number from each group. In fact, only a very few Vokkaliga women were at college. The number of students interviewed was roughly in proportion to the number of each community at college (Table A).

TABLE A

COMMUNITY BACKGROUND OF SAMPLE

	Men	Women	Total
Brahman	60	46	106
Christian	31	21	52
Lingayat	31	12	43
Vokkaliga	37	12	49
TOTAL	159	91	250

The Brahman men students came from eight sub-castes, and the Brahman women students from ten. The Christian students came from two religious groups—Protestants and Roman Catholics. Of the Lingayat students, seven of the men came from five sub-castes; the remainder did not belong to a sub-caste. Only one Lingayat women student said she belonged to a sub-caste; the rest claimed that they did not belong to any. Ten of the Vokkaliga men students said they had no sub-caste; the rest belonged to seven. Four of the Vokkaliga women students said they had no sub-caste; the others belonged to three.

It was thought that in addition to caste membership, certain other background characteristics might have a bearing on the students' attitude to and behaviour at college. These were economic position, mother tongue, the size of the community in which they had lived and grown up, the amount of pocket money they received, and their place of residence while at college.

Table B shows that on the average, the income of the families of the four different castes varied considerably.

TABLE B

MONTHLY INCOMES OF FATHERS OF STUDENTS

MONTHLY INCOME OF FATHER	BRAHMAN		CHRISTIAN		LINGAYAT		VOKKALIGA		TOTALS		TOTAL
	Men	Women	Men	Women	Men	Women	Men	Women	Men	Women	
Less than Rs.100	6	8	–	3	2	1	2	1	10	13	23
Rs.100—Rs.249	20	8	5	5	7	4	14	–	46	17	63
Rs.250—Rs.499	22	11	12	5	8	1	5	3	47	20	67
Rs.500—Rs.1,000	3	11	6	5	8	1	11	5	28	22	50
Above Rs.1,000	2	5	5	3	4	–	2	2	13	10	23
No Information	7	3	3	–	2	5	3	1	15	9	24
TOTAL	60	46	31	21	31	12	37	12	159	91	250

The monthly income of the fathers of a large number of the students, and, in a few cases in which the fathers were dead, of the mothers, was under Rs.500. The families of the women students were, on the whole, better off than those of the men. Altogether, a rather large number—thirteen out of the seventy-two students who reported income—fell into the "less than Rs.100" bracket. Of the four communities, more Brahman students tended to come from families in lower income brackets than did Christians. This is probably due to the fact that a larger number of Brahman students attend college. The Lingayat students had the evenest distribution of incomes, and the Vokkaliga students were concentrated in two income brackets. The fourteen whose income was from Rs.100 to Rs.249 were all from villages. Eight of the sixteen students whose income was from Rs.500 to Rs.1,000 also came from villages, but were the sons of wealthy landlords.

In spite of the fact that the women students tended to come from wealthier families than did the men, a much larger proportion had very little pocket money, or none at all. The Brahman and Christian students, both men and women, had small amounts of pocket money. The Lingayat students had slightly more, and the largest number of students receiving Rs.50 per month, or more, came from Vokkaliga families. More women than men students received no pocket money at all (Table C).

The mother tongue of one hundred and forty-two of the students—ninety-four men and forty-eight women, was Kannada. Fifty-five others—twenty-eight men and twenty-seven women—were Tamil-speaking. Twenty-one other students—nineteen men and two women—acknowledged Telugu as their mother tongue, and of the thirty-two remaining students, eighteen men and fourteen women came from English, Marathi, Konkani, or Malayalam linguistic groups.

TABLE C

POCKET MONEY OF MEN AND WOMEN STUDENTS PER MONTH

POCKET MONEY	BRAHMAN		CHRISTIAN		LINGAYAT		VOKKALIGA		TOTALS		TOTAL
	Men	*Women*	*Men*	*Women*	*Men*	*Women*	*Men*	*Women*	*Men*	*Women*	
Rs.0—Rs.10	15	22	9	12	2	4	3	3	29	41	70
Rs.11—Rs.20	18	6	14	2	6	2	5	3	43	13	56
Rs.21—Rs.30	13	5	3	5	11	0	7	2	34	12	46
Rs.31—Rs.50	4	1	0	0	2	0	7	1	13	2	15
Rs.50+	2	0	1	0	7	0	14	0	24	0	24
No Pocket Money	7	7	0	2	1	1	0	1	8	11	19
No Answer	1	5	4	0	2	5	1	2	8	12	20
TOTAL	60	46	31	21	31	12	37	12	159	91	250

Whereas ten Brahman and no Christian students came from villages, the families of twelve Lingayat and thirty Vokkaliga students did. Thirty-four of the remaining students of the four communities came from towns, and the remaining one hundred and sixty-four students grew up in cities.

Fifty of the women students and fifty-four of the men were taking B.A. degrees; forty-one of the women students and one hundred and five of the men were taking B.Sc. degrees. Although most of the women students attended three women's colleges, a few attended co-educational colleges. A large number of the men students interviewed attended four colleges, and the remainder were distributed among seven other colleges. The sample therefore represented students from fourteen different colleges in Bangalore.

The results of a survey of places the students lived while they were at college are shown in Table D.

TABLE D

PLACE OF RESIDENCE WHILE AT COLLEGE

	BRAHMAN		CHRISTIAN		LINGAYAT		VOKKALIGA		TOTALS		TOTAL
	Men	*Women*	*Men*	*Women*	*Men*	*Women*	*Men*	*Women*	*Men*	*Women*	
At Home	44	38	22	14	13	7	9	10	88	69	157
With Relatives	10	7	2	—	4	2	3	—	19	9	28
Hostel	3	1	4	7	8	3	19	2	34	13	47
Rented Room	—	—	—	—	2	—	5	—	7	—	7
No Answer	3	—	3	—	4	—	1	—	11	—	11
TOTAL	60	46	31	21	31	12	37	12	159	91	250

APPENDIX II

Chronological Account of the Youth Festival Strike, December 8-10, 1959*

Tuesday, December 8, 1959. Demonstrations began in Bangalore and in Mysore City. In Bangalore over 1,000 students marched to the Vidhana Soudha (House of Legislative Assembly) to ask for a ten-day holiday so that they could attend the All-India Youth Festival in Mysore. Representatives of the students met the Chief Minister, but he refused to interfere with the rights of the educational authorities to grant the holidays. The students became violent. They left the Vidhana Soudha, and on their way, stoned the police, the electric domes, and the passing vehicles in Cubbon Park. They also obstructed traffic and uprooted trees. Some of the policemen and about ten of the students were injured by stones. Twelve students were taken into custody. Later the police threw tear-gas shells to disperse the students.

In Mysore City about 2,000 students collected near the administrative building in which the Festival was being held and demanded free admission to all the shows. When told that the building was not large enough to hold them, so there was no purpose in their getting holidays to attend, they became unruly, threw stones at neon signs and street domes, and damaged flower beds. Some tried to set fire to the tents at the Youth Festival camp. Others set fire to the furniture in an Indian guest house. Damage was estimated at Rs.5,000. The mob roamed around until nine o'clock that evening, attacking cars and breaking street-light domes until the city was in darkness.

Wednesday, December 9, 1959. Fighting between the students and the police in Bangalore began early. It centred around the hostel of the Central College. The students began by pelting stones indiscriminately at passing vehicles. Several police were injured by the stones. They then chased the students into the hostel, and used their lathis freely, killing one student. About fifty students were injured, some seriously. The police later used tear-gas shells again to disperse the students.

The noise of the screams roused the women students in the adjoining Maharani College, and a number of the women students raced around their college—they were prevented from going out to join the men—shouting slogans and breaking furniture.

By this time goonda elements had joined in the demonstration, and by the end of the day they outnumbered the remaining students. Destruction continued, and many electric domes and neon lights were broken. As the

---

*The information for these accounts comes mainly from newspapers, particularly the *Deccan Herald*, Bangalore. Incidental information is derived from interviews.

situation was clearly beyond the control of the temporary student leadership, a number of demonstrators appealed to former student leaders, and they called a meeting of student representatives to form a peace committee to restore order. Their first action was to ask the students to stop rioting and remain peaceful.

In Mysore City trouble again flared up on Wednesday, when the students collected in the morning. They were soon engaged in even more violent behaviour than the day before, uprooting trees and smashing the electric street lights that had remained undamaged.

Then they marched to the women's college, and demanded that the students come out and demonstrate with them. When the girls would not join them—they dared not when they saw the mood the boys were in—the boys threw bottles and stones into the compound and through the windows. Then they tried to burn down the hostel gate with gasoline. A young warden stood up to them courageously, and they left, but roamed about until they had broken all the remaining street lights in the city. Finally the police resorted to tear gas, and when this had no effect, fired four rounds. Three people were hurt by the shots. By this time the city was in a state of panic, and all the shops had closed.

Thursday, December 10. In Bangalore violence continued, but without the students. The goonda elements and urchins continued the mischief, throwing stones at city buses and at the remaining electric domes. It was later estimated that damage to the city buses on December 9 and 10 amounted to Rs.40,000. The police gradually restored order with the use of tear gas and mild lathi charges. Fifteen people were arrested. All cinemas were closed for the day. The government was alarmed enough at this point to hold a six-hour debate in the State Assembly. The discussion centred around blaming the police, and demanding a sympathetic and rational approach to the student problem.

In Mysore City the police cordoned off the university grounds in the morning, hoping that this would prevent the students from collecting in large groups. However, about 3,000 students got together to protest against Tuesday's firing by the police. The crowd shouted slogans, and waved black flags as well as the blood-stained shirt of a wounded student. A few people continued to throw stones. Early in the morning the police began lathi charges against the students and the crowd that had gathered, and they continued to chase and beat anyone they could find. In the panic many were injured, including three women. Again all the shops remained closed, for fear that property would be destroyed.

Friday, December 11. In Bangalore the situation was under control. Only a few stray incidents of stone-throwing occurred. Public opinion, which at first was strongly against the students, began to change, particularly when news spread about the "brutal" way in which the police had opened fire and killed an innocent student.

In Mysore City more efforts were made to calm the situation. All schools and colleges were given holidays until December 20 to allow the situation to cool down, and a group of prominent lawyers tried to negotiate with the students. This failed, as the students demanded that the Chairman of the Youth Festival resign before they would come to any settlement with the authorities. Mischief by goondas continued, and there was stone-throwing in many parts of the city. All shops remained closed.

Sunday, December 13. No incidents occurred in Bangalore.

Monday, December 14. An announcement was made that all colleges would remain closed until January 12, again to allow for a cooling-off period.

Chronological Account of the 1962 Strike of Mysore Students

Monday, July 23. A meeting of students was called by the Student Action Committee. Those attending decided to go on a peaceful strike for seven days, beginning July 25, if the government did not announce a reduction in fees before that date. On the same day a meeting of students in Mysore City criticized the Minister of Education for rejecting the students' request for a review of the fee situation. The students of several colleges, which were not directly affected by the rise in fees, abstained from classes in sympathy. In the adjoining towns of Manasagangothri and Chitradurga, post-graduate students, including girl students, abstained from classes and held peaceful demonstrations.

Friday, July 27. About 20,000 students (around 90-95 per cent of all students in the city) were on strike in Bangalore, and over 6,000 were on strike in Mysore City. Demonstrations were completely peaceful, except for a commotion in front of one of the colleges when demonstrators tried to get the students to come out of their classes. Most of the girl students in the co-educational colleges gave passive support, but the girls of the Maharani College began picketing and trying to persuade the students of the Home Science Institute to join them. Other students from the Law and Medical colleges, and from the Polytechnic joined in sympathy. Leaders appealed to the public to co-operate with them, and opposition members in parliament began to protest, but the Minister of Education was still adamant on his stand.

Saturday, July 28. Two more private colleges joined the striking students in Bangalore, and 5,000 students attended a peaceful meeting at which a resolution was passed to maintain the peaceful character of the strike. Some

275

students remained in their classes, and Vijaya College reported that its classes had been working normally for the past three days. Several voluntary organizations came out in support of the students. In Bangalore 2,000 students laid siege to the colleges where students were still in class.

In Mysore City over 6,000 students abstained from their classes for three days. Processions and meetings were held, and thousands of students in the different districts were on strike. In Kolar, Hassan, and Tumkur peaceful processions were held daily. In Hassan the students issued a pamphlet assuring the public that the demonstrations would be peaceful.

Sunday, July 29. More students from the professional colleges went on a three-day sympathy strike, and the P. U. C. students at some colleges were picketed as they were still in class. Meetings were held at five different colleges. The students of Mount Carmel and St. Joseph's colleges remained in class. In Mysore the strike was complete in all the arts and science colleges, and the Student Action Committee sent student representatives to a Bangalore meeting of student leaders.

Monday, July 30. The first incidents of violence occurred at Shimoga when the Chief Minister was laying the foundation stone of a new market building. Demonstrations were staged by a youth organization, the Samyukta Yuvajana Nagarika Samiti, and by students. Three incidents of stone-throwing occurred, and the police intervened with cane-charges in which three students and three policemen were injured. The next day the student leaders in Bangalore disavowed any responsibility for these incidents, and condemned them severely. However, it was an indication to them that the students were getting out of hand, and that they might not be able to control them much longer. This was one of the reasons why they gave in and ended the strike.

Tuesday, July 31. The Chief Minister and the Education Minister appealed to the students to end the strike "unconditionally." A delegation of parents also urged the students to end the strike. The Student Action Committee declared the strike over. All the students in Chitradurga were away from their classes. In Tumkur 50 per cent of the students who had been on strike returned to class after receiving instruction from the leaders in Bangalore.

Wednesday, August 1. All the college students in Chitradurga returned to their classes.

Chronological Account of the 1963-1964 Mysore Student Strike

Wednesday, December 11, 1963. Student action began on this day. The students had been asked to pay an extra fee of Rs.50, and this raised their

276

fees to Rs.250 a year. Some of the students of the Law College took the initiative and planned to strike. They formed a Student Action Committee composed of fifteen students from local colleges. The Committee members met every day, sometimes eight or nine times a day, and the direction of the entire strike was in their hands. On December 11 they called on the students to abstain from classes and go to a meeting which would be held the next day at the Central College. A large number of students attended the meeting. They agreed to agitate until the government gave in and abolished the plan to raise the fee structure. Word gradually spread, and more and more students joined in the strike.

Friday, December 13. The Committee received letters and telegrams from students in the mofussil colleges, showing their willingness to join in the demonstrations. Some of these colleges had already organized strikes.

Saturday, December 14. A large procession of students went to the Vidhana Soudha to try to see the Minister of Education. He was in session and kept the student representatives waiting ninety minutes before seeing them. This, and his tactless handling of the students and of the situation, was one of the major factors in prolonging the demonstrations. After the representatives had reported the result of their first meeting to the 10,000 waiting students they decided to go on an indefinite strike.

Sunday, December 15. Students from the engineering colleges and from the Polytechnic joined in a mile-long student procession to show their sympathy. At the ensuing meeting the students criticized the government's decision to close the colleges for an eight-day period, ten days before the Christmas recess was to begin. This is a measure often used in situations of this sort to allow the students to "cool off." The government had also asked the principals of various colleges to close the mess in their hostels, thus encouraging the students to go home. The Action Committee asked the Chief Minister to reverse the order, and request the college authorities to open the messes. Meanwhile the Chief Minister had advised the students, through the press, to call off the strike. He assured them that the government was in sympathy with their aims, but refused to meet student representatives, and referred to the strike as an "unfortunate, sad situation."

Tuesday, December 17. The Student Action Committee asked the Merchant's Association and other organized commercial associations to observe a hartal on December 20 in sympathy with the students' demands. This was to coincide with a mammoth procession through Bangalore, and jathas of students from the mofussil colleges were to join the procession. On the following days there were large processions which made their way to Mysore Bank Square. Anti-government slogans were shouted, and some students wrote their demands in chalk on passing automobiles. Processions ended in public meetings at which the different student leaders addressed the students. They announced news of the strike, told of future meetings and processions, and kept the enthusiasm of the students at a high pitch. However, admonitions against violence were always made, and the leaders appealed to the students to keep the agitations peaceful. By this time some of the private colleges had closed to avoid trouble and possible destruction of property.

Friday, December 20. Jathas of exhausted students poured into Bangalore from the different mofussil colleges. They were garlanded, and they then led the huge procession of some 10,000 students. Nine hundred volunteer students kept order, and the city maintained complete hartal in sympathy with students. The women students, who had not been allowed to walk in the procession in case this caused trouble, observed the day by remaining at home. The procession was followed by a public meeting in the evening, which was attended by about 30,000 students, and by members of the public. Student representatives from the outlying colleges addressed the meeting. A Mysore State Student Action Committee was formed.

Sunday, December 22. The State Committee met the Chief Minister after his return home. He told the Committee that the restoration of fees to the 1960-61 level would be considered at a Cabinet meeting on 26 December. The students continued their peaceful demonstrations until that date. After the meeting the Chief Minister announced that the Cabinet had decided that the fees could not be reduced to their former level. Immediately after this announcement two members of the Action Committee, and two other students began hunger strikes on the lawn of the Vidhana Soudha. The same day, at a mass meeting, thousands of students expressed their willingness to go on hunger strikes, and the Action Committee received telegrams from many mofussil colleges, saying that students would be fasting.

In the meantime the members of the opposition party, as well as members of other political parties, had shown a great deal of dissatisfaction over the government's stand. The entire Opposition walked out of the State Legislature twice (December 21 and 28), as a protest against the government's failure to settle the agitation. Three members of the Legislature had themselves gone on hunger strikes in front of the Vidhana Soudha in sympathy with the students. They were later joined by two other members. The members of the Action Committee, however, disassociated themselves from these efforts, as they did not want any political interference. They declared that the student agitation was "entirely and exclusively that of the students."

Thursday, January 2, 1964. The government announced that it would make concessions to the students by liberalizing the freeship concessions. Under this new scheme, 17,241 students would get freeships, and 6,263 would have scholarships. One thousand more students would get loan-scholarships from the government. Thus, more than half the total number

278

of students—45,000—would get either free tuition, or else assistance with their tuition fees.

In spite of this warning, when the colleges re-opened no one attended either the Central College, the government Arts and Science College, or the National, Vijaya, or Maharani Colleges. Only the Home Science Institute and Mount Carmel were said to be functioning normally. Some post-graduate students attended the morning session at Central College, but the attendance fell off in the afternoon. The private colleges had a small attendance in a few of their classes. Police were posted at the compound gates, but did not interfere with the students who entered to try and persuade any remaining laggards to leave class.

The government further notified the students in a press dispatch that the examinations were "not likely to be postponed." They thus warned the students that the latter would not be prepared for the examinations if they continued to abstain from class. The authorities also appealed to parents and guardians to persuade their wards to attend class.

Monday, January 6. The colleges re-opened. (Two extra days had been given because of the usual holidays for the cricket matches). The Chief Minister had warned that any students who abstained from class on the opening day would be liable to be disqualified from freeships and scholarships.

Thursday, January 9. The government ordered the Law College to be closed indefinitely and warned that the other government colleges would be closed indefinitely if the strike situation did not improve before the weekend.

A few days after the men students had gone on hunger strikes, the women students began a minor revolution by insisting that they would join their brother-students. The first girls began to fast at Shimoga, and the pattern soon spread to Bangalore and to other centres. This aroused a great deal of public sympathy for the students. At first, all the batches of students went on 48-hour hunger strikes, for after that period of time the police had the legal right to feed them forcibly. Three of the women students who first went on hunger strikes fasted in front of the Magarini College, and two others fasted in front of the Vidhana Soudha. They were replaced by other girls after forty-eight hours.

Friday, January 10. Many political parties, labour associations, and voluntary associations had been sending notices of their sympathy to the students, but the Student Action Committee had declined any of their offers of help. However, on January 10 a group of influential citizens formed a Citizen's Committee, headed by the Mayor. The students consented to allow the Committee to negotiate between the students themselves and the government, in a bid to end the fee-raise impasse. The Committee represented leaders of all political parties, as well as educationists and parents. At a large meeting, members of the Student Action Committee explained their demands and described the events leading up to the agitation.

Sunday, January 12. The Student Action Committee had talks that continued all day at the residence of the Chief Minister, and which also included Cabinet members. The Chief Minister did not give the Action Committee any definite assurances, but made a "heartful appeal" and "personal request to the future citizens" to end the strike. He assured the Citizen's Committee that he would call an emergency meeting of the Cabinet on January 15, to consider the situation. He requested the student leaders to call off the strike, and to have faith in him, but the leaders declined, saying that the peaceful strike would be continued until a favourable decision was reached.

The student leaders had decided to postpone their indefinite hunger strike from January 10 to 14, as a goodwill gesture to the Chief Minister who was on tour outside the state. However, after their meeting with him on January 12, they announced that, rather than call off the hunger strike, they would intensify the agitation.

Tuesday, January 14. The student leaders announced that students would go on an indefinite hunger strike, as their gesture of goodwill had failed to produce any results.They also stated that they "viewed with grave concern the vindictive and coercive measures adopted by some of the college authorities, especially of the Maharani and Renukacharya Colleges, towards the students." They appealed to the students to remain firm, and to ignore the coercive measures, announced further meetings, and welcomed the fraternal feelings expressed by the students of the Agriculture College.

Some students began an indefinite fast in Bangalore. The total number on 48-hour hunger strikes at that time was one hundred and six, fifteen of whom were women. Four students had begun an indefinite hunger strike. All these students were carefully screened by the Student's Action Committee, both for endurance, and for loyalty. The Committee was afraid that some of the students would be induced by the government to join the hunger strike and then discredit the whole movement by not maintaining their fast. At one time ninety-one students were on hunger strikes in front of the Vidhana Soudha (January 13).

On the same day, in a public meeting at Mysore, the students decided to go ahead with an intensive village-to-village "no-tax" campaign if the government failed to announce the fee reduction before January 16. On that day the Chief Minister gave a valedictory speech to teachers at a conference at Tumkur. In it he cautioned politicians against using the students to advance their own selfish interests, said that the students' behaviour lacked an understanding of the situation, and emphasized that their indiscipline was shameful. To all accusations, the student leaders replied through the press.

Thursday, January 16. After a prolonged special session of the Cabinet, the Chief Minister announced that the government had decided to concede in full to the students' demands. Immediately after the Cabinet meeting he spoke to the students who were on hunger strike, and appealed to them to break their fast. He said that a three-member Committee would be set up to go into the whole matter of the fee structure of the University. It would report in April. (Its report, when it appeared, confirmed the students' demands.) He estimated that conceding to the request for a return to the 1960-61 level of fees would mean a loss of Rs.50 lakhs to the State Exchequer. The decision of the Cabinet was sent by telegram to the student leaders in the mofussil colleges. Some of them went in a taxi to Mysore to ask the students, who were still on hunger-strike, to end their strike, as the condition of their health was precarious. The Mysore State Student Action Committee called off the strike and all other agitations. In a press note they conveyed their heartfelt thanks to the government for its decision, and to the students, the police, members of the press and the public for their sympathetic support. They asked the students to return to class. During the strike, sympathy for the students was expressed tangibly by those students in professional and other colleges not affected by the strike, through fasting, token strikes, monetary support, and prayers.

Friday, January 17. The Bangalore students returned to class. Groups of students danced in the streets until late that night to celebrate their victory. A mammoth gathering celebrated "Victory Day," and a large number of girls attended this meeting.

However, students in some of the mofussil colleges did not respond to the request of the Central Student Committee, and they continued their strike for several days. Even representatives sent from Bangalore were not allowed to speak at their meetings.

Bibliography

ABRAMS, RICHARD. "The Student Rebellion at Berkeley: An Interpretation." In *The Berkeley Student Revolt*, edited by Seymour Martin Lipset and Sheldon S. Wollin. New York: Anchor Books, Doubleday & Co., Inc., 1965.

A.L.P. "A Season of Discontent." *California Monthly*, February 1965.

ALTBACH, PHILIP G. "Students and Politics." *Comparative Education Review*, Vol. 10, June 1966.

———. "Student Politics and Higher Education in India." *Daedalus*, Vol. 97, Winter 1968.

ANGELL, ROBERT C. *A Study in Undergraduate Adjustment*. Chicago: University of Chicago Press, 1930.

BAKKE, E. WIGHT. "Students on the March: The Cases of Mexico and Colombia." *Sociology of Education*, Vol. 37, Spring 1964.

———. "Roots and Soil of Student Activism." *Comparative Education Review*, Vol. 10, June 1966.

BARNABAS, A. P. D. "Patterns of the Rural Family." *Bulletin of the Christian Institute for the Study of Society*, Vol. 4, September 1957.

BECKER, HOWARD. *Education, Economy and Society: A Reader in the Sociology of Education*. Edited by A. H. Halsey, Jean Floud and C. Arnold Anderson. New York: The Free Press of Glencoe, Inc., 1961.

BELL, OSWALD. "The Future of Scouting in Europe." Unpublished speech presented to The Third European Conference, Finland, September 1964. Ottawa: The Boy Scouts World Bureau, 1964. (Mimeographed.)

BEREDAY, GEORGE Z. F. "Student Unrest on Four Continents: Montreal, Ibadan, Warsaw, and Rangoon." *Comparative Education Review*, Vol. 10, June 1966.

BLUMER, HERBERT. "Collective Behaviour." In *Principles of Sociology*, edited by A. M. Lee. New York: Barnes & Noble, Inc., 1951.

BROOM, LEONARD AND GLENN, NORVAL D. *Transformation of the Negro American*. New York: Harper & Row, 1965.

BYROM, MICHAEL. "Good and Bad in the Beatniks." *The Aryan Path*, Vol. 32, September 1961.

"CAMPUS '65: The College Generation Looks at Itself and the World Around It." *Newsweek*, March 22, 1965.

CHISHTI, ANEES. "Role of Language in Students in Turmoil." *Seminar*, December 1966.

CHITRA, M. N. "Case Studies in Students in Turmoil." *Seminar*, New Delhi, December 1966.

COLEMAN, JAMES S. *The Adolescent Society*. New York: The Free Press of Glencoe, 1961.

CORMACK, MARGARET. *She Who Rides a Peacock*. Bombay: Asia Publishing House, 1961.

CORNELL, RICHARD. "Students and Politics in the Communist Countries of Eastern Europe." *Daedalus*, Vol. 97, Winter 1968.

DAVIDSON, CARL. "The New Radicals and the Multiversity." *Our Generation*, Vol. 5, November-December 1967.

DAVIS, KINGSLEY. "Adolescence and the Social Structure." *Annals of the American Academy of Political and Social Science, 1944.*

DAWSON, C. A. and GETTYS, W. *An Introduction to Sociology*. New York: The Ronald Press Co., 1948.

DESHMUKH, C. D. "The Present State of University Education in India." *Opinion*, Special Number 1961.

DI BONA, JOSEPH. "Indiscipline and Student Leadership in an Indian University." *Comparative Education Review*, Vol. 10, June 1966.

DRUCKER, PETER F. "The Educational Revolution." *Education, Economy and Society: A Reader in the Sociology of Education*. Edited by A. H. Halsey, Jean Floud and C. Arnold Anderson. New York: The Fress Press of Glencoe, 1961.

D'SOUZA, VICTOR S. "Social Development, Education and Unemployment in India." *Towards a Sociology of Culture in India*. Edited by T. K. N. Unnithan, Indra Deva and Yogendra Singh. New Delhi: Prentice-Hall of India (Private) Ltd., 1965.

EISENSTADT, S. N. "Archetypal Patterns of Youth." *Youth Change and Challenge*. Edited by Eric K. Erikson. New York: Basic Books, Inc., 1963.

ERICKSON, DICK. "Editorial." *California Monthly*, February 1965.

FEIBELMAN, J. K. "The Well-Rounded Graduate." *Journal of Education and Sociology*, Vol. 34, May 1961.

FEUER, LEWIS S. "The Decline of Freedom at Berkeley." *Atlantic*, Vol. 218, September 1966.

FISCHER, JOSEPH. "The University Student in South and Southeast Asia." *Minerva*, Vol. 2, Autumn 1963.

———. "Indonesia." *Education and Political Development*. Edited by James S. Coleman. Princeton: Princeton University Press, 1965.

FYVEL, T. R. *The Insecure Offenders*. London: Chatto & Windus, 1961.

GADGIL, D. R. "Some Fundamental Defects of our Present Situation." *Opinion*, Vol. 2, January 1962.

GALVAN, ENRIQUE TIERNO. "Unrest in Spain's Universities." *New Society*, No. 199, 1966.

GIBBENS, T. C. N. "Teenage Riots Round the World." *New Society*, August 1964.

GLAZER, NATHAN and SELZNICK, PHILIP. "What Happened at Berkeley." *Commentary*, February 1965.

GOLDSEN, ROSE K., ROSENBERG, MORRIS, WILLIAMS, ROBIN M. JR., and SUCHMAN, EDWARD A. *What College Students Think*. Princeton: D. Van Nostrand Co., Inc., 1960.

GONZALEZ, ARTURO F. The Moppet Market." *Reporter*, June 1964.

GOODE, WILLIAM J. *World Revolution and Family Patterns*. London: The Free Press of Glencoe, 1963.

GORE, M. S. "The Crisis in University Education." *Towards a Sociology of Culture in India*. Edited by T. K. N. Unnithan, Indra Deva, and Yogendra Singh. New Delhi: Prentice-Hall of India (Private) Ltd., 1965.

GOTTLIEB, DAVID. "Youth Subculture: Variations on a General Theme." *Problems of Youth*. Edited by Muzafer Sherif and Carolyn W. Sherif. Chicago: Aldine Publishing Co., 1965.

GOTTLIEB, DAVID and RAMSEY, CHARLES E. *The American Adolescent*. Homewood: The Dorsey Press, 1964.

GREELEY, ANDREW M. "The Age of Innocents." *Reporter*, September 8, 1966.

GUINDON, HUBERT. "Social Unrest, Social Class and Quebec Bureaucratic Revolution." *Queen's Quarterly*, July 1964.

GZOWSKI, PETER. "The New Left." *Maclean's*, November 15, 1965.

HABER, BARBARA AND HABER, AL. "Getting By With A Little Help From Our Friends." *Our Generation*, Vol. 5, September 1967.

HALSEY, A. H., FLOUD, JEAN, and C. ARNOLD ANDERSON. *Education, Economy and Society: A Reader in the Sociology of Education.* New York: The Free Press of Glencoe, 1961.

HALSEY, A. H. and MARKS, STEPHEN. "British Student Politics." *Daedalus*, Vol. 97, Winter 1968.

Handbook of Indian Universities. Compiled by the United States Educational Foundation in India. New Delhi: Allied Publishers, 1963.

HANNA, WILLIAM J. *Education and Political Development.* Edited by James S. Coleman. Princeton: Princeton University Press, 1965.

———. "Students," *Political Parties and National Integration in Tropical Africa.* Edited by James S. Coleman and Carl G. Roseberg Jr. Berkeley: University of California Press, 1964.

HARRISON, SELIG S. *The Most Dangerous Decades.* Madras: Oxford University Press, 1960.

HEATON, KENNETH L. and WEEDON, VIVIAN. *The Failing Student.* Chicago: University of Chicago Press, 1939.

HEIRICH, MAX and KAPLAN, SAM. "Yesterday's Discord." *California Monthly*, February 1965.

HESS, FRED. Quoted in Seymour Martin Lipset and Paul Seabury, "The Lessons of Berkeley." *Reporter*, January 1965.

HOLLAND, JACK. "Students,—A Survey." *College and University Journal*, Vol. 4, Summer 1965.

HUGHES, EVERETT C. "Race Relations and the Sociological Imagination." *American Sociological Review*, Vol. 28, December 1963.

———. "Level, Direction and Style of Effort." Unpublished manuscript.

KABIR, HUMAYUN. "Student Indiscipline." Ministry of Education, Government of India, 1955.

———. *Education in New India.* London: George Allen & Unwin Ltd., 1956.

———. "Letters on Discipline." Ministry of Education and Scientific Research, Government of India, 1958.

KANNAN, C. T. "Intercaste Marriage in Bombay." *Sociological Bulletin*, Vol. 10, September 1961.

KARVE, D. D. "The Teacher in Higher Education." *Opinion*, Vol. 2, December 1961.

KARVE, IRWATI. *Kinship Organization in India.* (Deccan College Monograph Series, Vol. 2.) Poona: Deccan College Post-Graduate and Research Institute, 1953.

KERR, CLARK. "The Uses of the University." Quoted in Seymour Martin Lipset and Paul Seabury, "The Lessons of Berkeley," *Reporter*, January 1965.

———. "A Message to Alumnae." *California Monthly*, February 1965.

———. "The Turmoil in Higher Education." *Look*, Vol. 31, April 18, 1967.

———. "The Exaggerated Generation." *New York Times*, June 4, 1967.

KEYFITZ, NATHAN. Unpublished Document, Summer 1961.

KVARACEUS, WILLIAM C. *Juvenile Delinquency a Problem for the Modern World.* Paris: UNESCO, 1964.

LIPSET, SEYMOUR MARTIN. "University Students and Politics in Underdeveloped Countries." Berkeley: Institute of Industrial Relations and Institute of International Studies, University of California, Reprint No. 255, 1965.

———. "Students and Politics in Comparative Persepective." *Daedalus*, Vol. 97, Winter 1968.

LIPSET, SEYMOUR MARTIN and ALTBACH, PHILIP G. "Student Politics and Higher Education in the United States." *Comparative Education Review*, Vol. 10, June 1966.

———. "American Student Protest." *New Society*, No. 205, September 1966.

LIPSET, SEYMOUR MARTIN and SEABURY, PAUL. "The Lessons of Berkeley." *Reporter*, January 1965.

LIPSET, SEYMOUR MARTIN and WOLIN, SHELDON S. eds. *The Berkeley Student Revolt.* New York: Anchor Books, Doubleday & Co., Inc., 1965.

LORD, CLIFFORD. "Hurray for Revolution." *College and University Journal*, Vol. 4, Summer 1965.

MATHER, V. S. "Nothing Wrong with Our Youth." *Journal of Education and Psychology.* Baroda, Vol. 13, April 1955.

MATZA, DAVID. "Position and Behaviour Patterns of Youth." *Handbook of Modern Sociology.* Edited by Robert E. L. Faris. Chicago: Rand, McNally & Co., 1965.

MEHTA, ASHOKA: "Group Prejudice and Political Parties." *Group Prejudices in India.* Edited by Manilal B. Nanvati and C. N. Vakil. Bombay: Vora & Co., 1951.

MICHENER, JAMES A. *The Bridge of Andau*. New York: Bantam Books, 1957.

MILLER, MICHAEL V. and GILMORE, SUSAN. *Revolution at Berkeley: The Crisis in American Education*. New York, N. Y.: Dell Publish-Co., 1965.

MUKERJI, DHURJATI PRASAD. *The Problems of Indian Youth*. Bombay: Hind Kitabs, 1946.

NANAVATI, M. B. and VAKIL, C. N., eds. *Group Prejudice in India: A Symposium*. Bombay: Vora & Co., Ltd., 1951.

NANJUNDAYYA, H. V. *Mysore Tribes and Castes*. Mysore: Mysore University, 1931.

NOSCOW, SIGMUND. "Educational Value Orientations of College Students." *Journal of Educational Research*, Vol. 3, December 1958.

NSPCI *News Features*. Issued by the National Student Press Council of India, New Delhi, Vol. 3, August 11, 1965.

PANIKKAR, K. M. *Hindu Society at the Cross Roads*. Bombay: Asia Publishing House, 1955.

PARSONS, TALCOTT. "Age and Sex in the Social Structure of the United States." Reprinted in Talcott Parsons, *Essays in Sociological Theory, Pure and Applied*. Glencoe, Ill.: The Free Press, 1949.
————. "Some Sociological Aspects of the Fascist Movements." *Essays in Sociological Theory*. New York: The Free Press, 1964.

PATEL, M. S. "Modern Trends in the Teaching of English in India." *Journal of Education and Psychology*, Baroda, Vol. 14, October 1956.

PETERSON, RICHARD E. "The Student Left in American Higher Education." *Daedalus*, Vol. 97, Winter 1968.

PINNER, FRANK A. "Student Trade-Unionism in France, Belgium and Holland." *Sociology of Education*, Vol. 37, Spring 1964.

RAO, K. BHASKARA. *Candle Against the Wind*. Bangalore: Samyukta Karnatak Press, 1963.

RAPSON, E. J. Ancient India. The Cambridge History of India, Vol. I. New York: Macmillan Co., 1922.

Report on the Problem of Student Indiscipline. New Delhi: Government of India. (No date.)

Report of the Study Group of Educated Unemployment. New Delhi: Government of India, Planning Commission, January 1956.

Report on a Survey of the Attitudes, Opinions and Personality Traits of Sample of 1706 Students of the University of Bombay. Bombay: Orient Longmans (Private) Ltd., 1960.

Report of a Survey of Living Conditions of University Students. Ministry of Education, Government of India, 1961.

Report of the University Grants Commission. Delhi: Hindi Union Press, March 1959 and March 1960.

ROSE, BEN. "New Spectre on the Campus: Student Crackups." *Maclean's,* December 15, 1965.

ROSS, AILEEN D. *The Hindu Family in Its Urban Setting.* Toronto: University of Toronto Press, 1961.

———. "Some Social Implications of Multilingualism," *Towards a Sociology of Culture in India.* Edited by T. K. N. Unnithan, Indra Deva, and Yogendra Singh. New Delhi: Prentice-Hall of India (Private) Ltd., 1965.

ROSS, MURRAY G. "Why Students Rebel." Unpublished address to the Empire Club of Toronto, Toronto, February 8, 1968.

SARKAR, CHANCHAL. *The Unquiet Campus.* New Delhi: The Statesman Job Press, April 1960.

SARMA, JYOTIRMOYEE. "Three Generations in My Calcutta Family." *Women in the New Asia.* (No date.)

SARNOFF, DAVID. Quoted in "Position and Behaviour Patterns of Youth." *Handbook of Modern Sociology.* Edited by Robert E. L. Faris. Chicago: Rand, McNally & Co., 1965.

SCHELSKY, H. "Family and School in Modern Society." *Education, Economy and Society:* A Reader in the Sociology of Education. Edited by A. H. Halsey, Jean Floud and C. Arnold Anderson. New York: The Free Press of Glencoe, Inc., 1961.

SCHERMERHORN, R. A. "Where Christians are a Minority." *Antioch Review,* Winter 1961-62.

SCOTT, ROBERT E. "Student Political Activism in Latin America." *Dædalus,* Vol. 97, Winter 1968.

SEIDMAN, JEROME M. *"The Adolescent—A Book of Readings.* New York: Holt, Rinehart & Winston, Inc., 1963.

SELZNICK, PHILIP. "Berkeley." *Commentary,* March 1965.

SEN, INDRA. "Education of the Youth." *Journal of Education and Psychology.* Baroda, Vol. 10, October 1952.

SHILS, EDWARD. "The Intellectual in the Political Development of the New States." *World Politics,* Vol. 12, April 1960.

SHILS, EDWARD. "Indian Students." *Opinion,* Vol. 2, September 1961.

SHIMBORI, MICHIYA. "Zengakuren: A Japanese Case Study of a Student Political Movement." *Sociology of Education,* Vol. 37, Spring 1964.

SIDHATA, N. K. "The Problem of Discipline in Indian Universities and Selection and Training of Personnel for Public Services." The Maharaja Sayajirao III Golden Jubilee Memorial Lectures, 1955-56.

SMELSER, NEIL J. *Theory of Collective Behaviour.* London: Routledge & Kegan Paul, 1962.

SRINIVAS, M. N. *Report of the Seminar on Casteism and Removal of Untouchability.* Quoted in *Politics and Society in India.* Edited by C. H. Philips. New York: Frederick A. Praeger, 1962.

"Students in Turmoil." Seminar, New Delhi, December, 1966.

"Students—A Survey." *College and University Journal,* Vol. 4, No. 3, 1965.

THEODORSON, GEORGE A. "Romanticism and Motivation to Marry in the United States, Singapore, Burma and India," *Social Forces,* Vol. 44, September 1965.

THYAGARAJA, AIYAR, V. R. *Mysore Census, 1911,* Vol. 21, Part II. Bangalore: Government Press, 1912.

TOWNSEND, AGATHA. *College Freshmen Speak Out.* New York: Harper & Brothers, 1956.

VAIZEY, JOHN and DEBAUVAIS, MICHAEL. "Economic Aspects of Educational Development." *Education, Economy and Society: A Reader in the Sociology of Education.* Edited by A. H. Halsey, Jean Floud and C. Arnold Anderson. New York: The Free Press of Glencoe, Inc., 1961.

WALKER, KENNETH N. "A Comparison of University Reform Movements in Argentina and Columbia." *Comparative Education Review,* Vol. 10, June 1966.

WOLFENDEN, JEREMY. "Political Rebirth on the Campus." *Daily Telegraph* and *Morning Post,* June 4, 1965.

WORMS, JEAN-PIERRE. "The French Student Movement." *Comparative Education Review,* Vol. 10, June 1966.

WOODLEY, RICHARD. "It Will Be a Hot Summer in Mississippi." *Reporter,* May 21, 1964.

ZWEIG, FERDYNAND. *The Student in the Age of Anxiety.* London: Heinemann, 1963.

Index of Authors

Index of Subjects

Activists, 7, 243n, 244, 255, 263, 267
Adolescents, 218
Alienation, 251, 252
Ambitions: of Christians, 176, 177, 180; of Brahmans, 173-76, 180; definition of, 169; of Lingayats, 178, 180; of men students, 159-80, 193, 194; of parents, 169-94; strain and, 255; of Vokkaligas, 178-80; of women students, 180-94
Anglo-Indians, 122, 123
"Angry young men," 217, 218, 219
Anomie, 252, 253
Anxiety: of men students, 237; of women students, 260. *See also* Frustration; Strain
Authority, 141-44, 251
Berkeley, 1, 2, 6, 11, 12, 16, 16n
Boredom, 88, 256; and indiscipline, 18, 107, 113, 114, 238
Brahmans: abbreviation for, 118; ambitions of, 173-76, 180; anti-Brahman movement, 119; and educational system, 120, 121n; and jobs, 119, 121, 167-69; number of, at college, 120n; political power of, 118, 119, 119n; religious beliefs of, 151; security of, 118-20; Brahman students, 118, 125

Careers, 159-94, 256; and marriage, 192, 259, 260; of men students, 160-80; of women students, 187, 188, 192, 259, 260
Caste, 117-25; and ambitions, 157, 158; Backward, 117, 118, 120, 125, 147, 158, 193, 255; and change, 158, 222, 231, 255; and the educational system, 118; Forward, 117, 118, 120, 123, 158, 193, 255; and marriage, 224; nepotism, 120, 193; and relation to indiscipline, 22, 125, 157, 158, 234; security of, 117-20; urbanization and, 157, 158
Change: in affluent countries, 2, 3; in attitude to lecturers, 83, 94-96, 264; in attitude to women working, 187-93; and caste, 158, 222, 231, 255; disruption of, 253, 260, 263; in the educational system, 84-93, 250, 257-59; in the family, 144, 150, 158, 222, 223; and indiscipline, 263-68; and industrialization, 206, 249, 255, 256; in marriage patterns, 128, 222, 223, 232; and moral protests, 257; and parents, 137, 250; and politics, 260; and religion,